ABORTION AT WORK

A *bortion* *at* Work

IDEOLOGY AND
PRACTICE IN A
FEMINIST CLINIC

Wendy Simonds

RUTGERS UNIVERSITY PRESS
New Brunswick, New Jersey

Library of Congress Cataloging-in-Publication Data

Simonds, Wendy, 1962–
    Abortion at work : ideology and practice in a feminist clinic / by
Wendy Simonds.
    p.   cm.
    Includes bibliographical references (p.   ) and index.
    ISBN 0-8135-2244-7 (cloth : alk. paper). —
ISBN 0-8135-2245-5 (pbk : alk. paper)
    1. Abortion—Social aspects—United States—Case studies.
    2. Abortion services—United States—Employees—Case studies.
    3. Feminism—United States—Case studies. I. Title.
HQ767.5.U5S54   1996
363.4'6'0973—dc20   95-19055
                                                    CIP

British Cataloging-in-Publication information available

Published by Rutgers University Press, New Brunswick, New Jersey
Manufactured in the United States of America

I dedicate this book, with love,
to those with whom I have been most intimately connected
in the procreative sense:
my mother, Bobbie Simonds;
my father, Gordon Simonds;
my sister, Lauren Simonds;
my true love, Randy Malamud;
and our child, Jacob Alon Simonds-Malamud.

CONTENTS

CONTENTS

ACKNOWLEDGMENTS

I want to thank K. T. Slaughter, who was my original connection with the women whose work and words are the basis of this book. I wish I could thank the women by name here. You know who you are! It was truly a privilege to be let into your lives, and I shall always be grateful.

Joan Acker, Myra Marx Ferree, Jo Freeman, Jenny Kronenfeld, Pat Martin, and Rose Weitz read and responded to various drafts of articles that preceded the book; their comments were helpful in shaping pieces that eventually grew into chapters (especially Chapter Three). Pat and Myra's conference on feminist organizations was an invaluable opportunity to meet comrades in research. (Parts of Chapters Three and Four appear as an article in their book *Feminist Organizations: Harvest of the New Women's Movement* [Simonds 1995].) Ivan Karp, Amy Lang, Kate Nickerson, and other faculty members and students at the Institute of Liberal Arts at Emory University offered useful comments on a presented version of Chapter Two. I thank Alex Hicks, Rick Rubinson, Tina Brownley, and Ivan Karp for keeping me gainfully employed at Emory since 1990. My editors, Marlie Wasserman and Martha Heller, facilitated the writing process; and Steve Maikowski was particularly reassuring when Marlie left. It has been wonderful working with Martha Heller, who seemed to understand from the start what I meant to do and who was extremely helpful in suggesting ways to express my arguments clearly. Once again, it has been a pleasure to publish with Rutgers University Press.

Randy Malamud and Barbara Katz Rothman were wonderful readers and creative editors. Their reactions to a messy draft were instrumental in both the reorganization and completion of the book. I thank them for discussing this project with me since its inception.

The child-care work of Laura Crawley, Kim Springer, and George Williams enabled this book. Thank you, thank you, and thank you! Stephanie

ACKNOWLEDGMENTS

Funk, Kate Ellis, Pat Mikos, Diana Jones, Tammy Gilmore, and Laura Crawley served as my teaching assistants; their labor contributed to my ability to do research and is very much appreciated.

As always, my family sustained my work by taking an interest in it and by making me feel worthy of it. Thanks to Bobbie Simonds, Gordon Simonds, Lauren Simonds, Danny Malamud, and Judie Malamud. Randy Malamud and Jacob Simonds-Malamud inspire me on a daily basis, each in his own way; together they make my life happy, which makes writing possible. Dweeb Simonds, once again, deserves praise for consistently warming and refraining from eating the pages.

Abortion Work and Feminist Ideology

When *Roe v Wade* made abortion legal in this country, I was ten years old. I have no memory of the event. And though I have never had an abortion myself, abortion is part of my personal history. I think this statement is true for all women. We are all somehow enmeshed in a story about sexuality, about omissions, about clandestine pleasure, about bodily integrity and denial, and about exposure to feminist and anti-feminist ideologies. Maybe it sounds like a cliché after all these years, but the feminist slogan from the 1970s, "the personal is political," continues to ring true.

I don't think each woman's story is particularly unusual, but we rarely tell our stories, so they come to seem peculiar, private, and, very often, embarrassing. This book tells a story about abortion workers who negotiate for themselves a feminist sensibility that justifies what they do and that enables them to envision a better world. My experiences talking with them and watching them on the job have led me to conclude that everyone ought to take a holistic approach to procreative issues; we need to look into our pasts (both our individual and our collective histories) and to pull all the strands of the "story" together in order to imagine productive developments for the future.

Of Sexuality and Silences

Not long after I learned to read, my mother gave me a book called *How Babies Are Made*. I think I must have been about five or six years old. She said I should read the book in my room and then we would discuss it. My mother looked serious; this was clearly not an ordinary book. It told the tale of

1

procreation gently, moving from flowers to chickens, then to humping dogs, and, finally, to humans—he "inserting" his penis into her vagina to create the tiny baby. As I remember them, the illustrations looked like photographs of figures made with cut-out snippets of paper, very pristine and neat. The book said nothing about pleasure, nothing about nonheterosexual sexuality, nothing about unwanted pregnancy, because the goal of sexual union—whether of daisies or people—was clearly procreation. I was rather disgusted by the book, especially the human section. I remember feeling disappointed and reluctant to go back into my mother's room.

"Did you understand the book? Do you have questions about it?"

"Do *you* do that?" I asked her.

My mother said yes, she did do it with Daddy, and she explained it was something "two people who loved each other very much" did with each other. I put it out of my mind.

Some years later, when I was in the fifth grade, the boys and girls split up to see films. Ours was about growing breasts, pubic and armpit hair, and about menstruation. A cartoon girl started out flat-chested and hairless, and gradually, her breasts inflated and hair began to grow from her crevices: these changes were called "secondary sex characteristics." I had seen breasted and pubic-haired women in my father's *Playboy* magazines. None of these representations felt as though they had anything to do with me. I can't remember how menstruation was depicted in the film. I already knew all about puberty from my mother, who always told me well in advance about what might happen to my body. When we reconvened, everyone was all giggly and red-faced; we didn't tell the boys what was in our film, and they didn't tell us about theirs.

As far as I was concerned, the onset of secondary sex characteristics proved a miserable nuisance. In sixth grade, boys grabbed the girls' breasts, yelling, "Tits!" They assaulted us on the playground and in the classroom, when teachers weren't looking. Their actions were meant to humiliate us and to demonstrate their ability to be our humiliators; this motive seems clear to me now in a way it didn't then. Then, we felt embarrassed, annoyed. "Stop it!" we would shout, but they didn't. We didn't tell the teachers, and we didn't tell our parents.

I cried when my mother took me to J. C. Penney's to buy my first bra. My six-year-old sister, wanting to make me feel better, said, "Wendy, I wish *I* could have one!" "Shut up," I said. To me, breasts were simply a regrettable burden, something my body was doing to me against my will. I slumped, not consciously trying to hide my breasts, but, in retrospect, they seem the obvious reason for an adolescenthood of bad posture. The same year my breasts sprouted, I became convinced I would get my period. My mother had gotten hers early, at nine, and I was almost eleven. I was worried that menstruation would happen without my knowledge, that suddenly I would be oozing blood all over the place, and everyone would know. I wore minipads in my underwear for about a month, just in case, but nothing happened. Gradually my obsession faded.

In seventh grade, sex education was a part of science, a "module." (Parents had to sign a permission slip in order for their children to take this module; if they did not, their kids were given library assignments.) It was held in the school auditorium, and we were assigned every other seat. Talking was a crime: the teachers reprimanded us not by name but by the numbers on our seats and gave us demerits that translated into points deducted from our grades. They created this militaristic model, no doubt, to minimize our losing control because of the excitement that might accompany knowledge of the world of heterosexual sex. It wasn't funny; it was serious stuff, scientific. We did learn about orgasms in that class, but they sounded very unappealing: blood engorgement, muscle spasms, fluid emissions—all involuntary and clinical.

Mostly we learned about disease. Sexual activity led to disease, and then, along with painful sores, it led to humiliation—and a bad reputation for girls—when you had to tell your partners they might have the disease too. We watched many films about disease; poor actors experienced burning sensations, broke out in rashes and hideous sores, and, ultimately, felt regretful and ashamed because they had to 'fess up.

We also saw film versions of sperm and egg uniting, like underwater sea creatures. We made carefully labeled drawings of the reproductive organs of men and women: vulva, urethra, fallopian tubes, vas deferens (which I remembered by thinking of Dick Van Dyke). The goal of the course was clearly what the primary aim of most sex-education programs continues to be: to keep kids from "doing it." What happened when we "did it" was not addressed except with the moral tale of venereal diseases, with their various vile and pus-swollen manifestations, some of which, if we were lucky, could be treated with antibiotics.

Probably there were people "doing it" then, or so my mother seemed to think. None of the girls I knew did it, but I remember a friend telling me that if she was dared to "go all the way" in a game of Truth or Dare, she would pretend she had, so the other game players wouldn't think she was a prude. This friend and I had, together with two boys, played Truth or Dare to the point where the boys put their hands under our shirts and into our pants. I remember feeling frightened, like I was waiting for some sort of revelatory experience, and then, when none presented itself, I felt disappointed and bored. I would have been ashamed for anyone to find out about it. Despite all the supposed openness of my "sex education," these surreptitious experimental forays felt unpleasantly dirty, made me nervous. I did not like the boys, and I did not like them touching me, but I let them do it anyway.

The summer after seventh grade, I began to menstruate. I was the last in the group of my four closest friends. My mother bought chocolate ice cream, and we celebrated (a pleasant contrast to one of my friend's experiences: her mother had actually slapped her across the face). I asked my mother not to tell my grandparents, but she did anyway. They said that they were proud of me and that I was growing into a fine young woman. Their pride was contagious; I called my father to tell him. I could tell he didn't know what to say, but he congratulated me.

I was relieved when my friend from the Truth or Dare game moved on to giving hand jobs and blow jobs to high school boys, leaving me behind; I was uncoercible here and didn't understand what was in it for her. She did it because they wanted her to and because she wasn't supposed to, and also because she wanted them to be interested in her. It seemed to me as repellent as the copulation of humans had seemed years earlier in *How Babies Are Made*, but now it was not the physical act that disgusted me so much as the obvious use of my friend by these older boys as a masturbatory tool. I vividly remember my mother confronting me about my friend's misadventures after overhearing us talking. "What do you think about what she's doing?" my mother asked me. I didn't want to talk about it; it embarrassed me. My biggest concern was that my mother would tell my friend's mother what my friend had been doing.

The common threads that run through my sex story so far include: a dread of bodily embarrassments, a lack of control, a number of hidden deeds. There was some openness and a little ice cream, but these goodies were overshadowed by misgivings about and silence on the subject of sexuality. Perhaps it seems that none of this story relates to abortion. But it does: the secrecy and lack of agency in our personal sexual lives converged most dramatically in our dread of pregnancy. And for many years in my life and the lives of my friends, all our possible or actual pregnancies were unwanted, fearful prospects. Getting pregnant meant getting caught. Getting caught seemed awful enough on its own; getting pregnant had unique consequences.

I don't remember much talk about abortion. I am certain that we didn't learn about it in seventh-grade sex ed—although it would have been legal by then. My blow-job-giving friend had conscientiously arranged her sexual activities to avoid the possibility of pregnancy, as far as I knew. In high school, my impression was that the girls who "did it" were careful. During my senior year and before I ever had intercourse, I was fitted for a diaphragm; my mother encouraged this when my sexual activity seemed imminent. (Our earlier nervous honesty over the *How Babies Are Made* incident had by now grown into a much easier trust.) None of my friends in high school discussed abortion. Possibly they may have been careful or fortunate in not getting pregnant, but I doubt this was true for everyone.

Not until I was in college in the early 1980s did I meet women who talked openly about abortion. I became involved in feminist groups, which seemed to foster intimate friendships that broke down some of the walls that had been built so sturdily during earlier years. My boyfriends and I didn't talk about abortion explicitly as far as I remember, but I knew that if I got pregnant, I would certainly have an abortion. My period was erratic, so I had pregnancy tests relatively often. I can remember standing in a phone booth in the dead of summer, drenched in sweat, waiting on hold for the results of my first test. "Negative," the woman said. Stunned, I said nothing. Negative, negative. I felt lightheaded, nauseated. Negative, negative. I couldn't think. "That means you're *not* pregnant!" she said. My relief was palpable. When I hung up the phone my hand was shaking. After the first couple of tests, I stopped feeling so anxious, and eventually I would not even worry when my period took two months to come.

During my last year of college, I took a course called Psychology of Women, in which I remember an older woman discussing her past abortions with regret. She thought about how old her aborted "children" might be had she continued her pregnancies. And now that she had children of her own, she couldn't imagine having an abortion ever again. I was surprised by her guilt and said so. I saw abortion as the unavoidable consequence of pregnancy at that point in my life: I did what I could not to get pregnant, but I felt that only the pain would worry me if I ever had to have an abortion. I didn't understand why she considered abortion to be morally reprehensible. She didn't think it was morally wrong, she said, just felt some guilt, wished she hadn't *had* to do it. She didn't wish she hadn't *done* it though, I remember thinking; but I also knew that for her there was only a shade of difference between one kind of regret and another.

One winter night that same year, my roommate tested her urine with a home pregnancy test and got a positive result. She had had one abortion "already" and was angry with herself for getting pregnant again. I was supposed to go out of town the night she did the test but delayed my trip because she seemed so upset. I contrived fun activities to distract her. We smoked a joint and painted our faces like clowns, acted silly, and succeeded in taking her mind off the pregnancy. She, too, like the woman in my class, felt guilty;

the pain of the abortion was secondary to feeling as though she'd failed, and failing twice, aborting twice was wrong. It turned out she wasn't pregnant; the home test was wrong.

Abortion Work

During my first year of graduate school, I went to work part-time at a nonprofit abortion clinic in New York as a "social services counselor." I had found my way to a Ph.D. program in sociology through feminism and hoped, ultimately, to be able to combine activism and scholarship. The isolation I felt spending most of my time reading made me long for an immediate way to express my feminism in activism. I began at the clinic by learning how to do "contraceptive counseling" and then advanced to abortion counseling. My prescribed goal was to describe the abortion to each client; to make sure she was certain she wanted to have an abortion; to take her blood pressure, temperature, and pulse; and to guide her through the signing of various informed-consent forms—preferably in under twenty minutes. On a busy day, I would talk to nine or ten women about the abortions they were about to have.

I would hear the clients' stories—both because it was my job to elicit them and because most women seemed to expect that they would be called upon to explain themselves. It was not unusual to discover that I was the first person to be told about these pregnancies and the only person to hear why these women decided they wanted to abort. Sexual activity was shameful in the younger women's lives; and unwanted pregnancies served as a confirmation of their guilt. "My parents would throw me out of the house if they knew." "My boyfriend would want me to have it if he knew." I learned in brief about screwed-up relationships galore through my conversations with these women, who were ashamed or afraid to tell their parents and boyfriends but brave enough to subvert their relationships in order to claim an often unsatisfying, yet precious, sliver of liberation. A bigger problem than screwed-up relationships was poverty: countless times women told me they "couldn't afford" a child. These women were resolute, even if regretful, by the time they got to me.

I saw only a few women cry during my two years as an abortion counselor and met only one woman who had clearly not made up her mind. I saw an uncountable number of teenagers who didn't enjoy the sex they were having but seemed powerless to stop it and powerless to get their boyfriends to wear condoms. "He won't wear it—says it's uncomfortable." "He won't wear it—says he can't feel anything." "He won't wear it—says he's too big." (I would stretch the condom over my hand, down the length of my arm: "Bigger than this?") I worried about these young women, sleeping with self-absorbed young men who sounded as though they could care less about their girl-friends' sexual pleasure or about preventing pregnancy. To demand sexual relations on different terms did not seem possible to these young women. What other terms? Where would these terms come from?

As I'd learned about sex, it wasn't up to us to call the shots: we gave in—or not. The arena in which we experienced heterosexual encounters was often a combat zone; almost every source of information to which we had access proclaimed that boys' desires and concerns differed radically from girls', and at least implicitly condoned furtiveness and shame. I can't say exactly how I learned that an alternative was possible, only that inklings of feminism some-how got through and that my mother's influence enabled me to think differ-ently about sex from the way most young women or men I knew thought. I did not consider my thinking feminist until much later, in retrospect. Grow-ing up, my peers and I lacked a consistent ideological framework that sug-gested that active and pleasurable sexual experience was a possibility—much less our right—or that sexual practice (as we knew it) could be analyzed so-ciologically, linked to other aspects of lived experience, denounced, or dras-tically reformulated.

Working at the clinic, I considered abortion to be a powerful move on the part of the young women I counseled; but they, like my college roommate, often experienced it only as a failure. Sex remained furtive, whether it was carefully undertaken or not. They often talked as though they had done something wrong, and abortion was simply the price they would pay: two hundred dollars, bad cramps, and, in many cases, a big secret to keep from everyone in their lives who mattered.

At the clinic where I worked, abortion counselors were discouraged by the management from engaging in long sessions with clients or staying with them during their abortions. If we took our time or left our offices, the clinic slowed down, and the average waiting time could creep to two hours or more. The work was draining; I often felt overwhelmed by the intensity of clients' apprehensions and unhappiness. Most of the counselors didn't like dealing with women who had had several abortions; they saw them as irresponsible at best or, at worst, stupid. But I liked "repeat aborters" because they already knew what to expect and weren't afraid of the abortion. They offered less emotion for me to soak up; they were easy to process in ten minutes.

I quit my job at the clinic to write my dissertation but also because I'd had enough of the clinic. I didn't consider it to be a feminist place. While the clients got adequate medical care and the counselors were solicitous, I felt the staff, in general, was overly directive, paternalistic, and even callous at times. I was tired of feeling like an apologist for the organization's routines and practices. I was burned out. I focused on my research (which was not related to abortion) and teaching. I did not miss the clinic, though I felt a sense of loss because I gave up on it.

During the summer of 1989, I marched on Washington in a pro-choice demonstration, surrounded by the largest crowd I had ever seen. It felt wonderful even though I believed it was a useless gesture. Maybe the size of the crowd meant people would really join together to fight the fallout of *Webster v Reproductive Health Services*, whatever it would be.

In *Webster*, the Supreme Court reversed a decision of the United States Court of Appeals for the Eighth Circuit; the Appeals Court had ruled unconstitutional a Missouri law (signed by the governor in 1986) requiring "that all Missouri laws be interpreted to provide unborn children with the same rights enjoyed by other persons. . . . Among its provisions, the Act requires that, prior to performing an abortion on any woman whom a physician has reason to believe is 20 or more weeks pregnant, the physician ascertain whether the fetus is viable" (Muldoon 1991: 192). The law also prohibited abortion counseling or the provision of abortions (except in cases where women's lives were endangered by their pregnancies) by public employees and the use of public facilities for abortions. Thus, the Supreme Court, in overturning the Appeals Court decision and endorsing this Missouri law, stopped short of nixing *Roe* altogether by allowing individual states this level of regulatory power. Anti-abortion activists promptly began working to put restrictions—like parental consent and waiting periods—into effect and to draft further legislation that would limit women's access to abortions. The 1989 march looked, in retrospect, like a feminist delusion of agency.

By the time I finished graduate school in 1990, the political landscape seemed far bleaker than I could have imagined in the years I worked as an abortion counselor. Worrying about whether women received respectful treatment or actively participated in their abortion experiences—as I had worried when I worked at the clinic—now seemed a frivolous luxury. (The federal government had already slashed funding for Medicaid patients' abortions in all but a few states with the 1977 Hyde Amendment; New York was one of the few states that continued Medicaid funding.) Women's access to abortion was increasingly imperiled over the course of the 1980s, both de facto and de jure.

Anti-abortion groups with particularly aggressive tactics were spreading across the country, blocking women's entry to abortion clinics, swearing to God they would close down the "baby killers." The frequency of arson and bombings at abortion clinics increased during the 1980s with a total of 153 reported incidents between 1980 and 1992. (This statistic does not include attempted bombings, bomb threats, invasion, vandalism, assault, death threats, kidnapping, hate mail and harassing phone calls, burglary, and picketing. The total number of all these incidents of violence and disruption was 1,187 between 1977 and 1991 [Blanchard 1994: 55–57].) Anti-abortionists stepped up their harassment of doctors, other clinic workers, and their families in the 1980s (though they did not begin shooting people until 1993). Advertising on billboards and on television also became part of the game plan of several anti-abortionist organizations. Fewer and fewer medical students were trained to do abortions; fewer and fewer doctors were willing to become abortionists. The number of abortion facilities declined as hospitals got out of the abortion business, and few new clinics were established to take up the slack. Between 1982 and 1992, the total number of abortion-providing facilities (including hospitals, clinics, and private physicians' offices) dropped 18 percent; by 1992, 84 percent of U.S. counties had no providers (Lewin 1994). Pressure from anti-abortion groups led private corporate support for abortion to drop precipitously.[1] The Reagan-Bush regime set in motion a plethora of restrictions on abortion that created the possibility of an all-out gutting of *Roe v Wade*. They contributed to a climate in which violence against abortion-providing facilities was tolerated. This climate fueled the growth of an extremist group within the anti-abortion movement that would take up arms to murder and wound abortion doctors, escorts, clinic staff members and clients in the 1990s.

Doing Feminist Research

After graduate school, I decided to get back into abortion work but this time as a researcher. So much was changing so fast: all of a sudden the legal right to abortion seemed so precarious that it reminded those old enough to remember of the time before *Roe*. I wondered what other feminists were thinking. I wanted to find out what people working "on the front lines"—in the words of one woman I interviewed—were thinking about abortion, in terms of how they evaluated their day-to-day work experiences and how they looked at the issue on a broad political and ideological level. I hoped my research would enable me to combine my political and academic concerns fruitfully.

The Womancare Center (a fictitious name), a private, nonprofit clinic in a southeastern U.S. city I will call Anyville, had seen its share of protesters intermittently since its founding in 1976. In 1988, hundreds of Operation Rescue demonstrators converged from all over the country and besieged Anyville's abortion providers for several months. Because the Womancare Center (or the Center, for short) was avowedly feminist, Operation Rescue made it a special target. In 1990, when I started my research, Operation

Rescue's demonstrations had diminished; a group of faithful locals (ranging from half a dozen to about thirty in number) picketed the Center and harassed its clients one or two days a week.

A student of mine put me in touch with Hallie, a friend of hers who worked at the Center. (All the names used here are fictitious.) Through Hallie, I met Tanya, who was in charge of community outreach and education at the Center. Tanya arranged for me to attend a meeting at the Center, where I told of my research ideas and began to recruit participants.

I set out to interview the staff about its relationship with protesters. Originally, I envisioned a straightforward interviewing project that would focus on the effects of Operation Rescue on Center workers. More broadly, I wanted to find out what it was like to work at a feminist job in a time that workers perceived as profoundly anti-feminist and conservative, a time of seemingly endless Republican backlash against women. Abortion workers continually worry about restrictive legislation, potential dismantling of procreative-rights legislation for women, and the attitudes that foster these threats. I wanted to investigate the personal emotional toll and ideological consequences of doing abortion work in a hostile sociocultural environment.

Often, when sociologists enter into communities and begin to get to know them, we become increasingly enmeshed in our research environments. We learn how little we knew to start with. Straightforward projects grow larger, messier, difficult to imagine finishing. This happened to me. As I talked to these women and began to work as a clinic escort on Saturday mornings, I found that my interest in the Center grew; I became fascinated by the complexities of the organization and curious about the work it was doing. Along with all the grander political implications of the work, more mundane daily issues arose in the interviews: complaints about too much hard work, not enough staff, high turnover—all in all, complaints about an administrative practice that some workers saw as decidedly nonfeminist, not in keeping with the Center's mission as they thought and had been taught it should be carried out. They also spoke of the difficulties involved in doing abortion work in language I found intriguing, language that transgressed the usual pro-choice "line," where fetuses, if spoken of at all, are known as "pregnancy tissue." Here was explicitly graphic and gory talk coming from very pro-choice women. Was there a conflict here between some women's ideological positions as pro-choice feminists and what they called their "gut reactions" to abortion? What was the relationship between their gut reactions and the cultural climate surrounding abortion? How did this talk threaten various silences (among people in general, among feminists in particular) about sexuality and abortion?

I wanted to go inside, to see what I had been hearing about. I wanted to learn how these women's ideas about what it meant to be feminist translated (or not) into action on the job. Investigating the Womancare Center would allow me to think at once about the development of the women's health movement, abortion politics, and internal struggles among feminists in the late 1980s and early 1990s.

Informed by feminist critiques of conventional methodology, I worried about being intrusive, about using people for my own gain. I hoped that my encounters with "subjects" would not be a one-way street; I like to think that participants can also gain from research, as many feminist researchers have claimed (see, for example, Oakley 1981 and Reinharz 1992, 1983). But perhaps feminist ideals are antithetical to ethnographic work, as Judith Stacey suggests: "Ethnographic method exposes subjects to far greater danger and exploitation than do more positivist, abstract and 'masculinist' research methods. The greater the intimacy, the apparent mutuality of the researcher/ researched relationship, the greater is the danger" (1988: 24). While I believe Stacey argues persuasively about the potential hazards of any kind of social science observation, I also think that, to use Stacey's own words, "rigorously self-aware" researchers can guard against betrayals or misrepresentations, and that feminist methods (such as the desire to portray research participants' conceptions as they see them and to take pains to protect their interests) can make ethnography coherent with feminist goals. We are well served by Stacey's reminders that we must be careful and honest in our research relationships.

In February 1992, when I approached the Center's clinic administrator, Nancy, about doing ethnography, she exacerbated my anxiety about justifying ethnography. She asked me to put into writing what, exactly, I wanted to do at the Center and to explain why she and the executive director, Emma, should agree to let me do it. And so I asked myself, How could I distinguish myself from an opportunistic voyeur? How might I justify my presence given my own doubts about the potential one-sidedness of the benefits of participant-observation? I tried to be as straightforward as I could, to let Nancy and Emma know, from the outset, that I felt awkward about my position. I wrote:

> Ideally, what I would like to do is "hang out"—spend time inside the Center to see how it works, how you all work together: I'd like to get a sense of how the work gets done and also see for myself what it is like to be there. . . . As I've been talking with people, I've become increasingly interested in the Center as a feminist organization, and would like the opportunity to see *how* feminist ideals translate (and don't translate) into the daily routines of health care provision. . . .

I am also interested in learning more about your history, so that I can place it . . . within the development of the women's health care movement and of the women's movement in general. . . .

What I am asking, then, is to study the Center rather intensively. I want you to know from the outset that one of the issues that plagues my research—and *should*, in my view, plague all feminist research—is how to forge a relationship with research participants that does not make them into "objects of study"; [how to make] participants' views of their situations . . . central in the presentation of "findings"; and [how to assure that] the researcher doesn't only take what she needs, but contributes. I will do this however I can, and in whatever ways you think would be appropriate. . . . I have done work in this area, and would love to learn how work gets done by helping out in whatever ways I could. I do believe that research like this is productive in a broad perspective as well: in terms of feminist politics and the future of procreative freedom (not simply in academic terms).

Administrative response to my request took several weeks. I called Nancy regularly and felt like a pest. When she told me that she and Emma had approved my request and that I could start coming in, I was elated. For the first month or so, she and I scheduled my visits so that I could see a variety of services. After this trial period, Nancy said people seemed to be comfortable with me around and that I could come in whenever I wanted.

Between April 1992, and January 1993, I spent one-half to one day each week as a participant-observer at the Center. (I continued to visit the Center after January 1993 but less frequently.) The Center had five basic groups of employees: administrators (who ran the Center); administrative workers (who collected money, handled insurance matters, did the bookkeeping, and so forth); supervisors (who carried out the policies of the administrators and coordinated various "clinics" and "groups" at the Center); health workers (who provided services that did not require medical expertise); and medical workers.

During my fieldwork, I observed most of the scheduled activities that took place at the Center. I sat in on various staff meetings—large monthly meetings that included everyone and smaller meetings where supervisors and health workers grappled over the daily running of the Center. I observed "groups," or information sessions, in which health workers explained abortion procedures, took vital signs, and led women through extensive informed-consent forms. I watched first- and second-trimester abortions—including the initial procedures: sonography, laminaria insertions, and digoxin injections. Laminaria, sticks of compressed seaweed, expand as they absorb liquid, gradually dilating the cervix so that it will more easily (and less painfully) accommodate the larger forceps doctors use in later abortions. Digoxin is a chemical injected into the fetal heart the day prior to all twenty-one- to twenty-six-week abortions at the Center. Emma told me the chemical "stops" the heart. When explaining digoxin to clients, Center workers always used the word *stop*, but when talking to me, they often described digoxin as what "kills" the fetus. Digoxin makes fetuses more malleable and, thus, easier for the abortionist to remove. A few workers told me that digoxin also ensured that no fetus would be born alive and that the administration decided to use it for this reason as well. I observed the work that went on after abortions, in the sterile room, where health workers weighed and evaluated fetal tissue, and cleaned and sterilized instruments in an autoclave machine. In addition to abortion services, I observed donor insemination and "well woman" annual checkups. I chatted with nurses and clients in the aftercare room. I sat with workers while they took calls in the phone room, and I ate lunch with them in the kitchen.

It was fun. I came to like the women and to feel welcome and comfortable in their workplace. No doubt this comfort was facilitated by the fact that it was not *my* workplace. Though I held women's hands during some abortions and made small talk with them, and "swooped" (cleaned) an occasional room between clients, I wasn't doing work that was visible to the staff when I was at the Center. And no doubt my popularity was, in part, a function of my availability as a listener when individual workers wanted to let off some steam. Center women often did vent their frustrations openly on the job, but, as someone who did not have competing complaints of my own, I may have offered a more welcome ear than co-workers did.

As various people came to confide in me, I learned more about the "dirt" that proliferated beneath the overt goings-on of this workplace. (Such dirt exists, I presume, in all workplaces.) I suppose I went through a process of disillusionment similar to what new workers at the Center experienced as they encountered obstacles that forced them to reevaluate their idealistic expectations. They learned—as I did too—that the Center was no perfect, pristine bubble of feminist contentment. To workers, it often but not always felt different from other places they had worked. Sometimes, for some women, once they began to spot flaws, the problems seemed to build on themselves until the routine at the Center held few pleasures and meager rewards. Other women scaled back their expectations, attempted to conserve their energy, and tried to look upon work at the Center as just an ordinary job.

Outside pressures always intruded on these women's efforts to diminish the intensity of their labor because abortion work cannot be an ordinary job in a culture that casts abortion as a deeply contested moral issue. Helping to provide abortions might become ordinary, routine, and repetitive for these women, but, outside the clinic, abortion was deemed a giant dilemma, an unresolvable gray area, and a social problem. The women could not ignore the sociopolitical ramifications of doing abortion work.

Through the efforts of anti-abortionists, abortion has been epitomized as a moral dilemma. Language on both "sides" of the issue slants purposefully in opposite directions. Anti-abortion factions personify the fetus and either erase women from the picture (and from their grotesque pictures) altogether or depict aborting women as neglecting their God-given calling as mothers. The pro-choice movement declares the when-does-life-begin question unanswerable and, thus, irrelevant, and makes use of both liberalism and capitalism in crafting its language. As Barbara Katz Rothman points out, pro-choice rhetoric describes women as individual self-owners entitled to control over our bodies. If I "own" my body, it is mine, and anything within it counts as my property. Thus, abortion becomes an exercise in unarguably justifiable individualism (Rothman 1989). Meanwhile, anti-abortionists attempt to muster grass-roots support by scorning women's decision making (in favor of abortion) as misguided egotism that bespeaks the downfall of "family values," the rise of selfishness (the opposite of "natural" maternalism).

Each side refutes the other's language: anti-abortionists call themselves "pro-life" and refer to their enemies as "pro-abortion," while activists fighting for abortion rights counter the "pro-life" term with "pro-choice" and contest the validity of the "pro-life" label by referring to their opponents as "anti-choice," or more simply, in the lingo of Center workers, as "antis." Both sides conjure up images of threats to the American way of life. Pro-choicers proclaim the endangerment of liberal individualism and bodily integrity, and anti-abortionists predict the destruction of the patriarchal, heterosexual family unit by misguided women (whether we be aborters, workers in the paid labor market, lesbians, bisexuals, or sexually active and unmarried heterosexuals).

When I began this project, I sensed that anti-abortion forces and their rhetoric were winning, fueling and fueled by a backlash against feminism, building and riding high on Republican victories and the popularity and prominence of reactionary media demagogues like Pat Robertson and Jerry Falwell. I did, indeed, find that abortion workers shared my uneasiness over the growing public intolerance toward abortion and over a resurgence of regressive notions about women's potential and sexual expression. Even works by pro-choice scholars seemed to me to demonstrate that some of the relativism of the abortion-debate mentality—the notion that abortion is a moral dilemma that can be acceptably resolved either way—had begun to spill over into feminist thinking. Writers began to adopt a nonpartisan stance that worked to legitimize anti-abortionists' activities and claims.

For example, in their ethnographic work Kristin Luker (1984) and Faye Ginsburg (1989) offer vivid portraits of anti-abortion community groups and leaders and provide valuable insights into the mind-set of anti-abortion women, but I found myself troubled by their painstaking nonjudgmental and disinterested presentations. Both authors insist they are rightfully outside the fray they have entered. Luker writes, "If I have done my job well, both sides will soon conclude that I have been unduly generous with the opposition and unfairly critical of themselves. They will become annoyed and perhaps outraged as they read things that they know to be simply and completely wrong" (xiii). Ginsburg writes, "I have made every effort to respect the integrity of both positions in the abortion debate, as I understand them. . . . It is not my place or task in this book to take a partisan position" (xi). Later on, she tells how activists on both sides believed her to be one of theirs, based on their interpretations of a television documentary she produced on the Fargo conflict in 1982. To me, it seems that these writers, in their attempts to make a foreign ideology understandable, endorse the ideology *as tenable.*

A "value-free" interpretation of abortion may even slide—perhaps unwittingly—into endorsing the anti-feminist position. Celeste Condit slips over the edge, in my view; she writes:

> Even if we dismiss, at least for now, the pro-Life claim that a fetus is a person with a Right to Life, we should not dismiss the grounds they ["pro-Lifers"] offer us. . . . If, indeed, we block out their partisan overstatement and concentrate on the substance of what is left, the pro-Life rhetoric indicates with gleaming clarity that the fetus has value in its material being, its potential, and its "spirit." . . . The pro-Life argument forces us to face the real violence in abortion, and their truths are necessary to keep us morally responsible. (1990: 214–215)

Similarly, Kathleen McDonnell suggests that feminists need not support abortion. "Some feminists are beginning to perceive a dissonance between our stance on abortion and our stance in other areas. Feminism has tended to ally itself with nonviolence, . . . with nurturance and respect for life. . . . Yet abortion is in some sense an act of violence, and indisputably results in the termination of life" (1984: 25). That people who consider themselves feminist have adopted the language of the anti-abortionists demonstrates the power the backlash movement accrued during the 1980s. To me, such equivocations on the part of feminist writers call for denunciations, for renewed commitment from those of us who don't see room for compromise, those of us who see anti-abortion sentiment as lacking integrity and as antithetical to our feminist agenda.

I don't see a way out of the life versus choice impasse that structures the cultural debate over abortion. I have read various news stories about groups from both sides who sit down together, supposedly to hash out some sort of compromise position (see, for example, Lewin 1992b). Ginsburg offers convincing evidence of concerns activists on both sides share; and Luker writes that the debate is too complex simply to dismiss one side of it:

> This book was written to explore my own feelings about an enormously complicated topic. While the militants on both sides would have us believe the abortion debate is actually very simple, such simplicity is both a necessity and a luxury for them. A necessity because we must believe that the things about which we are passionate are either clearly good or clearly bad. But because the belief in simplicity reduces any possibility of dialogue or learning or coming to terms with real human dilemmas, it is a luxury that neither the society nor the debate itself can afford. (1984: xiii)

Frankly, I don't believe a happy middle ground of dialogue exists, and not because pro-choice and anti-abortion factions have painted ourselves into corners with our militance. We may share a concern with nurturance, as Ginsburg writes, but when it comes down to brass tacks, we will never agree about abortion. This conviction, however, does not mean that a stance in favor of procreative freedom precludes complexities and complications, nor need it mean latching onto a simple dogma. As Center workers showed me, doubts may coexist with conviction, yet they need not dilute conviction. Many of these women disliked certain aspects of providing abortion, and even felt that some components of their jobs challenged them to "face" abortion in new ways, but they did not feel any closer to an anti-abortion stance. They might understand the framework that shapes the other side's view of abortion and might respect anti-abortion activists' right to believe whatever they believe; but, ultimately, they did not—and I do not—believe a debate was possible.

The language of pro-choice activists is deficient because women often don't feel we actively choose: an "only choice" is no choice at all. Center women used the language of the pro-choice movement because they were part of it, but they also critiqued it for not addressing the actual deeds of abortions—choice language could cover up what abortion "really looks like." These women believed in absolute "truths" about abortion—truths that are not murky precisely because they are based in a woman-centered philosophy and practice.

Unlike Center workers, most Americans lack a cohesive philosophical framework for thinking about abortion. Poll data show that people buy the moral-dilemma approach promulgated by anti-abortionists. Polls suggest that the general public is rather wishy-washy when it comes to abortion. Support for the continued availability of abortion has hovered at around 70 percent since the late 1970s, but a majority does not support abortion in all circumstances. When abortion is diced up into various hypothetical situations, majority commitment to women's procreative freedom unravels.

People are most likely to see abortion as appropriate when a pregnant woman's life is endangered by the pregnancy, when her pregnancy resulted from rape or incest, or when the fetus is "defective." Support for legal abortion wanes (ranges from less than one-half to one-quarter of those polled) if a woman "cannot afford any more children," if she "does not want to marry the man," or if the "pregnancy would interfere with [her] work or education."[2] A 1990 *New York Times*/CBS poll showed that 48 percent of Americans surveyed agreed that "abortion is the same thing as murdering a child," and only a third of those surveyed agreed with the statement "abortion is sometimes the best course in a bad situation" (Toner 1990).

As these poll data show, the act of abortion is troubling to many Americans. Tatalovich and Daynes write that "the public never fully accepted the right of abortion on demand" (1981: 84), and they chart the public's wary view of abortion rights through the 1970s. They conclude that "the Supreme Court's decisions [in the 1970s] would appear to enjoy public support, but other data suggest that public support for Wade is soft. . . . By the late 1970s the pro-life movement was becoming more effective in articulating its position, whereas the pro-choice forces may have taken their victory for granted and not sustained their propaganda momentum" (130). Since Tatalovich and Daynes's study, the threat to women's right to legal abortion has grown.

Though qualified support for legal abortion remains consistent, support for women's decision making does not. People's willingness to conceive of abortion as the result of a woman's irresponsibility or her cavalier attitude toward pregnancy may indicate (as Tatalovich and Daynes predicted) that the rhetoric of anti-abortion activists has been successful. However, abortion has been repoliticized since the early 1990s, so the 70 percent commitment to aboration in general may now be more strongly felt. Large-scale surveys may provide a general picture of people's ideas about any subject, but they cannot tell us how people are actually thinking or what factors (including the phrasing of survey questions) influence their thoughts.

In this book, I show how women who work to provide abortion think about abortion. Thinking about abortion, in this context, means far more than making abstract decisions about whether generalized women should be able to end hypothetical pregnancies. An exploration of Center workers' thinking about abortion involved looking at how they felt about their work; how they connected with and distanced themselves from their clients; and how they crafted for themselves, through their jobs, a feminist identity that then shaped how they evaluated their work, their relationships (with clients, co-workers, family, and friends), and political issues.

My work draws on and contributes to continuing feminist sociological efforts to uncover how personal views about abortion and feminism are shaped by social forces (for example, Echols 1989, Evans 1979, Freeman 1975, Ginsburg 1989, Luker 1984, and Martin 1989). This study is also indebted to ethnography that examines service work and "dirty" workplaces (for example, Ball 1967, Detlefs 1984, Hochschild 1983, Hughes 1971, Joffe 1986, Leidner 1993, Lipsky 1980, Simonds 1991, and Walsh 1974). I show how Center staff members worked through a moral minefield of anti-abortion rhetoric to arrive at feminist "truths," both general and specific (and always in support of abortion); how they dealt with ambivalent feelings about their work, about feminism, and about feminist practice; how they cast their work as crucial to the status of women; and how their experiences "doing" feminism on the job led them to think about the future of procreative freedom. I believe an examination of the intricacies of political work (including the ideological construction work of activists) can help us move productively toward resistance and revision in the future.

This book is based on my ethnographic research and interviews with thirty-one Center workers. (See the Center Personnel Table for interview dates and demographic data on participants.) I conducted one set of (seventeen) interviews between fall 1990 and summer 1991. I conducted a second set of (sixteen) interviews in the summer and fall of 1992 (including one woman whom I interviewed twice during this period and three women interviewed during the first period whom I reinterviewed during this period). A third set of (five) interviews (three of which were second interviews) was conducted between summer 1993 and summer 1994; this last small group apprised me of changes that had occurred after my official ethnography ended in January 1993. Each interview lasted between one and three hours, and all but one were tape-recorded.[3] The interview format was casual and loose in order to facilitate participants' agency in shaping discussions. I did lead each participant in common thematic directions: I asked each worker to describe her history at the Center and as a feminist, the ups and downs of her work, her views about the workings of the organization, and her sense of the current and future politics of abortion in the United States. When I interviewed a woman a second time, we discussed her perceptions of changes at the Center along with political changes relating to abortion that had occurred since her first interview.

The interviews defy neat categorization because the macro- and micro-level circumstances under which they occurred changed continually. Interview transcripts impose an artificial sense of closure on each woman's views; public events continually transformed the conditions of each participant's work and, thus, her experience and evaluation of it. Over the course of my interviewing, anti-abortion protests diminished locally, so workers' direct experience with anti-abortion attitudes at the Center lessened. Ironically, at the same time, legislative restrictions on abortion increased both locally and nationally. A parental-notification law went into effect in the state where the Center is located.[4] The Supreme Court's *Webster* decision of July 1989 was backed by the *Casey* decision of June 1992, which upheld most proposed state restrictions on abortion as legally sound.[5] Later in 1992, though, political changes that workers viewed favorably occurred. With the growing likelihood of a Democratic presidential victory, Center workers spoke more hopefully than before about the future of abortion rights. And after Bill Clinton was elected, participants talked enthusiastically about the ground they thought might be gained, always stressing that they were guarded in their optimism.

Clinton's success fueled fanaticism within the anti-abortion movement; anti-abortionists began killing people rather than concentrating only on destroying abortion-providing facilities. Michael Griffin murdered David Gunn on March 10, 1993, in Pensacola, Florida. Rachelle Renae Shannon shot and wounded George Tiller on August 19, 1993, outside a clinic in Witchita, Kansas. (Tiller returned to work two days later [Johnson 1993: 5].) George Wayne Patterson, the doctor who replaced Gunn at the Pensacola clinic, was shot and killed on August 21, 1993 (this case has not been connected with anti-abortionists). Garson Romalis, a Canadian abortion doctor, was shot at through the window of his home in Vancouver and wounded on November 9, 1994 (at this writing, the Canadian police and FBI are investigating the case; no suspect has been named). Also in Pensacola, Paul Hill shot and killed John Bayard Britten and his escort, James H. Barrett, on July 29, 1994. Hill also wounded June Barrett (James Barrett's wife). On December 30, 1994, John Salvi 3d went on a rampage at two clinics in Brookline, Massachussetts. Salvi murdered Shannon Lowney and Leanne Nichols (both receptionists) and wounded five other people. The following day, Salvi was arrested in Norfolk, Virginia, just moments after he opened fire on another clinic (no one was hurt in his third attack). Doing abortion work has obviously become more dangerous; indeed, anyone who enters an abortion clinic is at risk.

Within the Center, changes were plentiful during the four years I studied the organization. Many staff members came and went; of the women in my first cohort of participants, only two of seventeen remained in 1995 (Elise and Hallie), and of the women who took part in the second and third set of interviews beginning in 1992, four of fourteen (Julia, Hannah, Janice, and Mimi) remained three years later.[6] Center administrators made various bureaucratic and procedural changes, including the implementation of a more precisely codified hierarchy, and renewed adherence to explicit rules governing workers' behavior, including enforcing a dress code. The administrative work moved off-site as Center operations expanded. After two years of searching, administrators hired a feminist doctor (Sarina) as staff physician in June 1991; she left in February 1993, and administrators went back to hiring doctors part-time to fill in their schedule as best they could. In 1991, the Center gradually extended the length of gestational time through which abortions were performed, from twenty-one to twenty-six weeks; and it redesigned the way in which first-trimester abortions were staffed by collapsing two jobs (the doctor's assistant and the woman's advocate) into one in order to cut costs.

The Organization of This Book

Abortion at Work is divided into two parts. Part One, "Feminists Working" (Chapters One through Three), examines the women's narratives about their work routines; situates that work historically within the context of the feminist movement and the anti-feminist countermovement; and describes the ways in which working at the Center influenced the women's thinking about themselves, abortion, and feminism more generally. Part Two, "Working Feminism" (Chapters Four and Five), focuses specifically on staff members' internal organizational interactions. Together, both parts of the book consider how Center women negotiated various definitions of feminist ideals and feminist practice in a hostile political environment.

In Chapter One, "Feminist Work: Health Care Provision and Identity," I describe the history of the Center and its place in the women's health care movement. I examine staff members' definitions of feminism and feminist care, and their descriptions of achieving a feminist identity in concert with their work at the Center.

In order to illuminate some of the ways in which feminist identity and practice are constructed on the job, Chapters Two and Three explore how Center workers built feminist methods of thought and action through their encounters with anti-feminist, anti-abortion opposition, both on and off the job. Chapter Two, "Feminist Abortion Practice: Getting Graphic," details how doing abortion work both challenges *and* affirms feminist ideology (as defined by workers)—how they learned to think about abortion by focusing on notions of choice, sexual expression, body image, privacy, wholeness, and women's agency. Many Center staff members described second-trimester abortion work as troubling or unpleasant. This chapter presents their discussions of coming to terms with late abortions and, in so doing, contending with the popularized discourse of anti-abortionists.

In Chapter Three, "Anti-Feminism Personified: Encounters with the Enemy," I describe the Center's battles with anti-abortion groups, focusing especially on its encounters with Operation Rescue, which began in 1988. I detail workers' personal histories with anti-abortion protesters and their assessments of how Operation Rescue demonstrations affected them and their work. Center women spoke of how they managed the intense emotional reactions they felt as victims of anti-abortionists' verbal assaults and as mediators of clients' experiences of anti-abortionists' attempts to dissuade them from abortion.

Part Two begins with a consideration of internal hierarchical politics. Center workers spoke repeatedly of the disparity between how they, as health care workers, aimed to treat women (respectfully) and how they, as workers, were treated by the administration (without this same respect). In Chapter Four, "Feminist Workplace?: Examining Contradictions in Institutional Ideology," I discuss workers' and administrators' assessments of the organization's ability to live up to the feminist ideals it preached. I describe changes over time in how administrators ran the Center, as they moved from a collective to a clearly delineated power structure, and I focus on several conflicts that divided staff members in the 1990s.

As African American women gained a presence among Center staff members, the organization began to consider ways in which racism manifested itself. Administrators eventually announced that the Center would take formal steps to address the problem and to build antiracist organizational values. Chapter Five, "Purging the Enemy Within: Feminists Approach Racism," examines ways in which the staff members constructed "race" and how they denied, recognized, and "worked on" racism. Some white women saw the administration's commitment to an examination of racism at the Center as insincere, a vehicle by which it avoided addressing the real issue, which these workers considered to be a class issue: the division between management and workers (discussed in Chapter Four). Black women concurred that the management/worker split exacerbated "racial" antagonisms but worried that white women simply wanted to deny the problem's existence. I analyze a workshop on "cultural diversity" (the first in a series undertaken by the Center) as emblematic of current trends in evaluating "race" and racism.

Finally, in the Conclusion, "Feminism and (F)utility: Assessing the Future of Procreative Freedom," I explore workers' views of the larger political framework that regulates abortion. Their descriptions of working at the Center reveal striking contrasts: they experienced it as exhausting and exhilarating; familial and anomic; wonderful and disgusting. They saw the organization as helpful and helpless; ideologically pure (feminist) yet sullied (racist). Most of these women engaged in internal struggles in which liberalism and radicalism collided. Their belief in "the system" (voting, writing to elected officials, and so forth) contrasted with their sense that the system simply did not have women's best interests at heart. This chapter ties together the various issues set forth in Parts One and Two by showing how the work of these women enabled them to build a feminist identity and to believe in collective feminist power, while it also instigated doubt and cynicism about whether such "goods" as these could triumph over anti-feminist powers.

RESEARCH and life outside it fuse in compelling ways. It was at the Center that I had my own wanted pregnancy confirmed. Here I was, twenty-five years after first learning "how babies are made," writing my own book about women who help other women not to make babies while I embarked on the process of making a baby.

I had done two home pregnancy tests but had difficulty crediting their accuracy (remembering my college roommate's false positive). After dancing around the issue by asking two health workers, Lee and Nell, about the reliability of home tests, I confided that I thought I might be pregnant. They said they didn't especially trust home tests because they can sit on drugstore shelves for too long and "go bad." "Do you want to be pregnant?" they asked, cautiously. I said I did. "What are we waiting for?" They hugged me when this third test displayed an almost instantaneous purple plus sign. This time in my life, positive *was* positive.

I asked Nancy whether, as my pregnancy advanced and became noticeable, I should stop observing abortions; a few of my friends had suggested it would be inappropriate. "Absolutely not," she told me. "We support all women's decisions," she said, and clients should be aware of this policy also. It was quite obvious to aborting women that some other women elected to have babies when they were pregnant, she said. It would be silly to attempt to protect Center clients from reality. She reminisced about her own and other co-workers' pregnancies; all of them had worked up until the birth of their babies. This was, I felt, ideal feminist practice: recognition and support for different paths of action in women's lives. Of course, nothing is quite so simple since the world in which we act is not ideal in this egalitarian sense: we do not all have the opportunity to choose from the same set of options. Center women knew this to be true too. Through their work they fused ideals with reality, constructing compelling feminist visions.

PART ONE

FEMINISTS WORKING

CHAPTER 1

Feminist Work

Health Care Provision and Identity

Emma and Nancy founded the Womancare Center in late 1976. The Center's history and Emma's and Nancy's personal histories are inextricable from developments in the feminist movement, specifically the politicization of abortion and of women's health care. In this chapter, I place the Center within the context of recent feminist activism, focusing particularly on the women's health care movement and the anti-abortion countermovement; I explore the ways in which staff members—both workers and administrators—conceived of feminist identity, both in their self-definitions and in their evaluations of the services they provided.

Patricia Martin writes that an organization can be considered feminist if it "(a) has feminist ideology; (b) has feminist guiding values; (c) has feminist goals; (d) produces feminist outcomes; (e) was founded during the women's movement as part of the women's movement" (1990: 185). The Womancare Center fulfills each of these requirements to varying degrees. But Martin's definition is problematic because of the word *feminist*. What, precisely, makes a value, goal, or outcome—and, thus, an organization—feminist?

In the Center's early years, staff members did not debate the meaning of feminism. Simply providing health care services in a woman-run setting that had been designed in opposition to mainstream medical practice *was* feminist. For many, health care provision was the defining feature of feminist practice. In the interviews I conducted, though, staff members articulated various working definitions of feminism and aired a wide range of opinions about whether the Center *worked* as a feminist institution (in its values, goals, and outcomes). Their narratives about establishing feminist identity and practicing feminist principles are the subject of this chapter.

In the organization's infancy, Emma and Nancy did all the work at the Center except performing the abortions. The Center was open to serve clients only one day a week. A few other women were involved on a part-time basis at first. During the first year, Nancy said, doctors performed an average of four abortions per week at the Center. As Emma and Nancy found more doctors willing to do abortions, they extended Center hours. Gradually, they expanded both staff and services.

By the time I came to do my ethnographic work at the Center in 1992, it had grown into a nonprofit organization with an annual budget of over two million dollars. The Center was now one of a handful of abortion providers in Anyville and the only one with roots in the women's health care movement. Most of the city's other abortion providers did not offer abortions through the twenty-sixth gestational week, as the Center did; and none of the others offered late abortions under local anesthesia.[1] Except for the public hospital, the Center was the only nonprofit abortion provider in town. Center doctors performed an average of seventy abortions (the majority of which were first-trimester) each week. The Center also offered routine gynecological care and ran a donor-insemination program and an AIDS hotline geared especially to women.[2] Approximately 90 percent of the Center's annual income came from abortions.

Center staff numbered forty-five. These workers included four administrators: the original founders, Emma and Nancy, held the positions of executive director and clinic administrator, respectively. Trudy, who joined the Center two years after its founding, was director of administrative services. A director of development, Cathy, joined the upper management in 1992. The staff was comprised of seven lower-level administrative workers (two of whom worked part-time); one health educator; one lab technician; six nurses (five working part-time); three doctors (two part-time); four supervisors; and nineteen "health workers" (four part-time). The staff ranged in age from the late teens to the early fifties. The Center's top four administrators were white and heterosexual; among the rest of the staff, eleven were African American (two administrative workers, six health workers, the lab technician, one supervisor, and one of the per diem physicians) and one was Latina (a health worker). (See the Center Personnel Table for the demographic characteristics of those interviewed.) Approximately one-fifth of the Center staff were openly lesbian. All of the Center's activities were nominally supervised by a board of directors; at the time of my fieldwork, the board rubber-stamped Emma's decisions about clinic protocol.[3]

The line of command ran downward from the executive director (Emma) to the other members of upper management, Nancy, Trudy, and Cathy. Trudy took care of the budget, supervised administrative workers, and did the hiring and firing. Cathy worked on public relations and fund raising. Nancy managed the day-to-day running of the Center; the four supervisors reported to her. Supervisors coordinated activities. Each day of the week featured a different clinic or set of clinics; first-trimester abortion clinics, second-trimester abortion clinics, laminaria ("lam") clinics, and well woman clinics all occurred at specific times. Health workers counseled clients in groups as part of each clinic, except for the well woman clinic, where nurse-practitioners met individually with each client. Each clinic required a particular configuration of health workers; supervisors managed the flow of the activities and ensured that the phones were always staffed. One supervisor, Hannah, made up each month's schedule. Health workers counseled women who called the Center; ran "groups" (where they explained various procedures to clients); prepared clients individually for contact with medical personnel; discussed test results or various diagnoses with clients individually; attended to clients—or "health worked"—during second-trimester abortions; aided the physician—or "assisted"—during second-trimester abortions; and both attended to clients and assisted the physician at the same time—or "advocated"—during first-trimester abortions. Health workers and supervisors rotated being on call when the Center was closed.

The Old Days

In order to bring the Center into historical perspective, I want to review the most salient elements of one and a half centuries of the history of abortion and women's health care activism in the United States. The events I describe only sketchily represent the complexity of the past. (For more in-depth views of these historical developments, see Baehr 1990, Gordon 1974, Lee 1969, Luker 1984, Messer and May 1988, Mohr 1978, Petchesky 1984, Ruzek 1978, and Staggenborg 1991.)

The law did not regulate abortion in the United States until the mid-nineteenth century, and "it was not until after the Civil War that legal restrictions on abortion became enshrouded in a morality of sexual repression" (Hole and Levine 1971: 280). The founding of the American Medical Association (AMA) in 1847 facilitated regular physicians' group efforts to professionalize and to exclude competitors (Mohr 1978: 147–170). Physicians sought to enhance their status by achieving the criminalization of abortion; they thereby gained authority over a realm that until that time was not considered either a medical domain or a moral issue. As with childbirth, physicians wanted to drive off competition and become the sole arbiters of when and how abortions would be done. By the turn of the twentieth century, legislation in most states prohibited abortion except in special cases when doctors deemed it permissible (Ginsburg 1989, Luker 1984, Mohr 1978, Petchesky 1984, and Rothman 1989). "The argument that physicians made . . . was that abortion was a crime against the fetus, the potential baby, made acceptable only when doctors thought it was necessary" (Rothman 1989: 110).

Physicians capitalized on the sexual conservatism fueled by upper- and middle-class white men's negative reactions to women's rights advocates and to "abortion's prevalence among the 'wrong' women (white middle-class Protestant married women) while immigrant and Catholic birthrates climbed" (Petchesky 1984: 2). Eventually, physicians and birth control crusaders openly endorsed measures—including forced sterilization—to limit the procreation of groups deemed undesirable, as they popularized the "science" of eugenics in the 1920s.

Eugenic notions drove Margaret Sanger's birth control movement, and, ironically, a spiffed up global version of 1920s eugenics, population control ideology, fueled the eventual *reform* of laws restricting procreative intervention. Eugenicists and population control advocates both sought to limit poor people's procreation. Doctors played a prominent role in the fight to decriminalize abortion in the twentieth century, just as they had worked to criminalize it in the nineteenth century. Midcentury, debate erupted within the medical profession over the "therapeutic exception" that made abortions permissible depending on individual doctors' interpretations of their patients' situations. "Strict constructionists" sought to spell out the specific rules applicable to abortion provision, arguing for a narrow interpretation of exceptions for health reasons, while "broad constructionists" tested the margins of the therapeutic exceptions (Luker 1984).

Despite the fact that public opinion did not support abortion rights during the sixties, by the middle of the decade, various professional groups were calling for the liberalization of restrictive abortion laws. "In 1964 the Association for the Study of Abortion was founded by doctors, theologians, social workers, and lawyers to compile data on abortion and to make it a public issue. The same year . . . Bill Baird established the Parents' Aid Society in New York to help women locate qualified (albeit illegal) abortionists" (Ruzek 1978: 20). In 1968, the American College of Obstetricians and Gynecologists recommended that therapeutic exceptions be granted quite liberally. "In determining whether or not there is a substantial risk to the woman's physical or mental health, account may be taken of the woman's total environment, actual or reasonably foreseeable" (cited in Davis 1985: 58).

Second wave feminists, whose movement grew out of the civil rights and the antiwar movements, would become the most important players in the struggle to gain, and then maintain, procreative freedom. "The abortion struggle provided the initial impetus for a broader women's health movement by creating widespread awareness of how medical and legal systems obstruct women's right to control their own fertility" (Ruzek 1978: 26). Feminist groups "provided the most visible external pressure for change in abortion laws" (Petchesky 1984: 129); second wave feminists drew on the examples set by civil rights and antiwar activists, and utilized a variety of strategies from sit-ins to speak-outs in the fight for procreative freedom. Ninia Baehr documents a radical U.S. pro-abortion movement as beginning in the early 1960s with the work of Pat Maginnis, Rowena Gurner, and Lana Clarke Phelan (the "Army of Three"), who organized and distributed referral lists of illegal abortionists and held classes on do-it-yourself abortions in California (1990: 7–20). Maginnis and Gurner founded the Association for the Repeal of Abortion Laws, which grew into the National Association for the Repeal of Abortion Laws (NARAL).

Between 1967 and 1970, twelve states reformed their original nineteenth-century abortion laws (which allowed abortion only if a woman's life was endangered), modeling their new laws on the American Law Institute's 1959 recommendation that abortion be legal when a woman's health, rather than only when her life, was at stake; when the pregnancy resulted from rape or incest; or when the fetus would be born with "grave physical or mental defects." By 1970, New York, Hawaii, and Alaska had repealed their laws but maintained a variety of restrictions such as requiring that abortions be done only by licensed physicians and only in licensed hospitals, that women be state residents, that women get their husbands' or parents' permission, and that time limits be observed (Hole and Levine 1971: 282–286).

As attempts at legal reform showed success and repeals proved hollow because of the many restrictions that were maintained, most feminist groups shifted their focus to amending rather than repudiating state regulation of abortion. NARAL changed its tactics and renamed itself the National Abortion Rights Action League when the fight for reform rather than repeal seemed to be yielding results. Other feminist activists held that repeal would be the only morally just course of action because the law ought not make women's bodies its jurisdiction—hence the slogan "keep your laws off my body." Also, these activists argued, the law could not be trusted to protect women's interests; repeal would be the only way to ensure absolute procreative freedom. (See Baehr 1990 and Staggenborg 1991 for an elaboration of this position.) Seeking repeal of abortion laws was essentially a laissez-faire strategy, according to Rosalind Petchesky. "It contains an implicit assumption that the 'right to choose,' or the relegation of abortion to the private sphere, will in itself guarantee that good, safe abortions will be provided" (1984: 131).

On January 22, 1973, the Supreme Court handed down the *Roe v Wade* and the *Doe v Bolton* decisions, which struck down all existing state laws pertaining to abortion. *Roe* successfully challenged an 1854 Texas law that made abortion illegal except when a woman's life was threatened by her pregnancy; and *Doe* successfully challenged a Georgia law that allowed abortions approved by hospital committees only when a woman's life was threatened or in cases of rape or fetal abnormality. Kristin Luker speculates that the Court agreed to hear the cases because both were "products of a nationwide social movement" spurred by national organizations dominated by professional elites (physicians) who "appeared to be . . . 'disinterested.'" She writes that because over a dozen states had liberalized their laws in conflicting ways, the Court probably wanted to take a stand before an inevitable snarl of legal challenges developed; thus the Supreme Court was not responding directly to feminist agitation (1984: 142–143). The Supreme Court ruled that, on the basis of the "right to privacy," first- and second-trimester abortions (with some caveats) were "medical decisions" in which states could not interfere. Both decisions show, as Petchesky points out, that "public policy to liberalize abortion was *nowhere framed in feminist terms*" because the law avoided "declaring access to abortion a *social right and need of all women*" (1984: 289).

The Supreme Court decisions provided a rallying point and unifying moment for anti-abortionists. "From the mid-1970s to the present, there has thus been an ongoing movement-countermovement dialectic between the contemporary women's movement and the various CM [countermovement] groups that have challenged that movement" (Buechler 1990: 187). The *Roe* decision signaled a demographic shift in and an expansion of the membership of anti-abortion groups. "Before the Roe v. Wade decision, anti-abortion activism was the province of male Catholic professionals; after the decision, these groups were overwhelmed by an influx of self-recruited housewives and a proliferation of prolife groups. The typical new participant was a married mother with a high school education who was not employed outside the home" (Buechler 1990:195).

While feminist activists felt triumphant about these legal victories, countermovement activists worked hard to gain exposure for their views. Even though, as Steven Buechler writes, anti-feminist goals—prevention of the success of the Equal Rights Amendment (ERA) and the (re)illegalization of abortion—were not shared by the general public, the new countermovement activists "brought an intensity of commitment, a tactical sophistication, and a willingness to engage in single issue politics that overcame the fact that they were not advocating popular positions" (1990: 196).

In retrospect, some scholars depict feminists of the 1970s as naive, as too secure in their success and, consequently, careless about keeping defenses up. Some writers portray feminist activism as fizzling into an introverted phase they denigrate as "cultural feminism." They characterize 1970s feminists as politicos who got sidetracked into women-run businesses like clinics and women's bookstores, an indication to these writers that feminists became apathetic about effecting broad-based political changes (see, for example, Echols 1989, Faderman 1991, and Jaggar 1983). In contrast, other feminist scholars see the shift from protest activism to health care practice as ideologically continuous rather than as a sign of complacency, helpless apathy toward large political structures, or separatist defeatism. Suzanne Staggenborg documents how grass-roots ventures developed into a mighty pro-choice movement, writing, "The staying power of the movement [into the 1990s] is due in large part to its development of formalized organizational structures and professional leadership" (1991: 148). Sheryl Ruzek, who wrote about the feminist health care movement early on, recognized its radical potential:

> The "invention" of self-help gynecology more than any other event transformed health and body issues into a separate social movement. Self-help gynecology was born on April 7, 1971, at the Everywoman's Bookstore in Los Angeles. For some time, feminists had met there to discuss health and abortion issues. After exhausting "book learning," Carol Downer, a member of the group, urged empirical observation. That evening, Downer inserted a speculum into her vagina and invited the other women present to observe her cervix. . . . Self-examination and self-help gynecology . . . were revolutionary concepts. For self-help provided women the opportunity to reclaim parts of themselves controlled by male professionals." (Ruzek 1978: 53)

Self-exam spread. "Within a year after Downer began publicizing self-examination, over 2,000 women had attended clinics and demonstrations" (Ruzek 1978: 54). Downer and her colleagues advocated the use of yogurt (rather than prescription medicine) to treat yeast infections, popularized the process of menstrual extraction, and worked to establish clinics dedicated to woman-centered care.[4] Downer's practices spread to feminist groups across the country.

The Womancare Center Then and Now

In the mid-1970s, Emma and Nancy were initiated into the women's health care movement through their participation in self-exam sessions. Both women found their experiences transformative. Nancy said, "When I went to the self-help clinics it was like somebody opened another *eye.* . . . I just became so much more aware of my body in a way that I hadn't. I was also real young. I mean, I had just graduated from college, and at this time [1973], there weren't any books on women's health. . . . There just wasn't that consciousness about our bodies as there is now."

Nancy said that she saw the potential inherent in self-help come to life when some women she knew opened a clinic in Florida. "It's not just looking at your cervix, but . . . it was the *revolution.* You know, it was women, empowerment. . . . [Self-help principles] showed how we could do it and how we'd been kept from doing it. It was such a concrete thing." She worked as a volunteer in her friends' Florida clinic. When she moved to Anyville a couple of years later, she met Emma through the fledgling women's health care community.

Together, they began running self-help clinics out of their apartments. Nancy said, "After doing the self-help clinics for a while, it just became really frustrating to tell women how health care *could be* and not have anyplace to refer them." They drove to visit the clinic in Florida. On the way back to Anyville, Nancy said, "We decided we were going to open our own clinic." They each spent a month training informally at other clinics. Emma said, "I got two hundred dollars from my mother, and she got two hundred dollars from her mother, and that was our resources for starting the Center!" Nancy kept her job working in a lawyer's office in order to support their new endeavor; Emma, who had been working as a counselor in another local (but not, in her view, feminist) abortion clinic, quit, and worked full-time to set up the Center. Two other women who had been part of their self-help group became peripheral participants in the Center.

All the original Center women were in their early twenties. All were heady with the newfound promise of the women's health care movement, and they were enthusiastic about putting feminist ideals into practice. Emma said:

> We started out as a collective, and we started out with all women who shared the same philosophy: that we, first, were absolute in our conviction that abortion was a right of women; that we were all committed to the principles of self-help and sharing health information. And we also had other political convictions of similarity, of knowing that, besides the importance of women having control of our body, that we needed to

have broader control of our life; we needed to have more say-so in the political process, and really to have more democracy.

As a collective, Center women provided health-care services and engaged in political work together. They shared the labor equally within the Center and reaped the same meager financial benefits, as Trudy described:

At that time, really everyone who worked here did everything, from doing the abortion counseling to balancing the books, to cleaning the bathrooms, to just everything. Also we were involved in, you know, what we considered a political movement, so we . . . would also attend a lot of community meetings, and go to national conferences. . . . We were all working about . . . sixty hours a week, sometimes more. . . . There were usually about maybe five what we called full-time regular staff. . . . We also would take percent salaries depending on the financial situation of the Center in any particular week. So we would meet every single week, Monday morning, and evaluate how much money we had and then we would figure out how to divvy it up, and what bills needed to be paid, and what bills could wait.

The women all made decisions together by consensus; the minimal organizational structure consisted of rotation into various teams that addressed specific tasks. As it grew, the Center's structure became increasingly hierarchical; in Trudy's words:

I think as times changed and kind of got more conservative over the years—through the eighties—we did find the need . . . for people to have more specialized jobs and also [to move] into a more hierarchical structure. And I think that was for a number of reasons. I mean, one is that some of us who were in the collective at the time were starting to have children. . . . It became more difficult for us to work that many hours. . . . I think there also was a recognition that not everyone had the ability . . . or the willingness to work in that particular way and that, in order to survive as an organization, we needed to create a structure where we could accommodate a wider variety of—I guess a greater disparity in—commitment levels and levels of responsibility. . . . We found, . . . even in the collective structure like that, that different people did have different talents and skills. . . . The other thing that influenced our situation was, you know, the increasing government regulation of businesses in general and abortion facilities in particular. . . . It seemed that there was a certain structure that you needed to have to deal with those regulations. . . . We really needed to have, say, one person in a position of clinic administrator that really had that as their responsibility. It was too much . . . rotating different people through that position. And I think different people showed different levels of leadership too. . . . When we did go to the more hierarchical structure, for example, . . . it was pretty obvious who should be the executive director. I don't think that it was ever really a big discussion. You know, it was obvious that Emma was the person that had that level of leadership. I think other people sort of fell into place.

Trudy saw the shift toward a more regimented and complex bureaucracy as a logical development, as did the other Center women who moved into upper management. They believed initiating a hierarchy would enable the organization's survival and that it would also benefit them personally. Nancy said that before they stratified duties, they all worked sixty-hour weeks and spent about a third of that time in meetings. When she and Trudy each got married and wanted to start having children in the early 1980s, a sixty-hour week was no longer feasible. "So there was, from Trudy's and my perspective, kind of a need to pull back. . . . Emma and I had always kind of been a team with sort of shared responsibilities, but there was . . . always a part of me that kind of recognized that she also had the time and the inclination [to take charge]; she didn't have other things going on in her life. . . . And so it was recognizing her leadership, and honoring it, in that sense."

Gradually, over the course of the 1980s as the Center continued to grow, the hierarchy became more multitiered and solidified. By the time I began interviewing in 1990, the only women who had worked at the Center when it was a pure collective and still remained were Emma, Nancy, Trudy, and Meryl (who ran the donor insemination program). A few of the women I interviewed reminisced about greater fluidity in the structure of the Center in the mid-1980s; even so, most were accustomed to thinking about the Center's collective days as institutional lore from a bygone era.

Most of the supervisors and workers (both administrative workers and health workers) were young women in their twenties, with a few exceptions. These new young feminists came to the Center idealistically naive, in the eyes of the clinic "old guard." The younger women's idealism and excitement about feminism echoed Nancy's and Emma's original enthusiasm and sense of possibility when they founded the Center. Unlike Emma and Nancy, the younger women grew up during a time when abortion was legally available and, yet, during a period of reactionary backlash against the gains made by the feminist movement. They saw 1970s feminists like Emma and Nancy as admirable role models in some ways but were also cynical about how professional they had become. The younger Center women seemed nostalgic for the past, perhaps because they saw little chance for involvement in the sort of all-consuming activism that characterized the Center's early days.

In the 1990s, as compared with the 1970s, feminist ideology has become—both within and outside the clinic—more diffuse in some ways; in other ways it seems less evident. For instance, women's labor force participation rates have increased since the 1970s, as has the level of women's support for liberal feminist principles. At the same time, anti-feminist rhetoric has gained general widespread legitimacy (see, for example, Faludi 1991). Specifically, anti-abortion groups have been successful at a national legal level with the *Webster* and *Casey* decisions. Feminism has changed, and feminists have changed; sometimes they eye each other warily across generations. At the same time, white feminist groups have made attempts to address their own exclusionism. Most of the women involved in the early days of the women's health care movement were white and middle-class. In 1992, the Center's staff members were multi-"racial" and came from various class backgrounds. Some women had been exposed to feminist thinking, as they defined it, for as long as they could remember; others began work at the Center with little sense of a personal feminist connection.

Becoming Feminist Health Care Providers

When I asked Risa, a health worker, what she thought it meant to provide feminist health care, she responded:

> To give woman-centered, woman-controlled care. . . . It's important that a woman is well informed. You give her options; you don't just tell her: "This is what you have to do." . . . And you encourage her to make her own decisions based on the information that she's received. And you also encourage women to know that it's important that they know that if they don't control their health care, then . . . they're not going to get adequate health care. . . . [Clients] need to ask questions and not just let people feed [them] stuff. That's the kind of attitude we encourage at a feminist clinic.

Risa's comments nicely summarize the institutional culture at the Center. The Center routinely taught new staff members that providing feminist care meant treating women nonjudgmentally and honestly. Center workers saw themselves as educators who provided women with information and support, helped women gain access to their own bodily realities, and enabled clients to feel actively involved in their own health care. They believed that feminist health care differed substantially from traditional medical treatment, which tended to deny women autonomy and power. Health workers encouraged clients to challenge medical authority, or, as Risa said, "You need to ask questions and not just let people feed you stuff." With this metaphor, Risa portrayed the medical model as infantalizing women (infants are "fed") and entrapping us (prisoners are sometimes force-fed).

Health workers believed clients armed with formerly withheld information would become active health care consumers rather than simply the bearers of bodies acted upon by medical professionals. In this sense, their approach holistically eschewed the medicalization of women's bodies inherent in the pathology-seeking model. Mira, a supervisor, elaborated:

> The medical field has been so mystified that doctors . . . think M.D. stands for medical deity. . . . This place is different. . . . We try to give [women] as much control over that situation as possible. Every woman here has an advocate. . . . Anything that happens here is discussed with her. . . . We counsel our medical workers: "They are not patients; they are *clients*. We are providing a service. They are not sick; they're pregnant, you know, or they have a vaginal infection."

Health workers usually introduced physicians to clients using both their first and last names and dropping the title (yet ensuring that the client would know the doctor was a doctor, saying, for instance, "This is the doctor who will do your abortion, Sarina Jenning"). Some black staff members read this gesture toward the demystification of medical authority as demeaning when black physicians were introduced casually; and they were less likely than their white co-workers to drop the "Dr." Rae said, for example, "I see the disrespect that they [white health workers] give Dr. Alton: 'This is Roger.' *No:* 'This is *Dr. Alton.*" When you're [doing] . . . an abortion, . . . you don't want to be introduced to your patient as 'Roger.' 'I'm Dr. Alton. Period.' He's said that to me himself." Rae believed that white co-workers were so committed to an anti-medical position that they refused to recognize that demystification and loss of authority carried different consequences for white and black physicians.

For the most part, Center staff members agreed that conventional medical practice entailed telling women what to do or, at least, approving or disapproving of our decisions. In contrast, Center health workers and medical staff usually did not question a client's decision to abort her pregnancy unless she took the initiative to speak of her ambivalence. Health workers saw this *lack* of interrogation as feminist; they believed that conventional abortion-clinic practice forced women to justify their decisions and placed clinic staff in the role of judgmental, and potentially condescending, authorities. Carole Joffe (1986) and I (Simonds 1991) confirm that, in conventional clinics, counselors routinely ask clients to explain how they reached their decisions to abort; to talk about who else knows about the abortion; to discuss whether they have considered "alternatives to abortion"; and inadvertently to put clients on the defensive (if they are not already defensive). As Mira said, "We don't *counsel* women like a lot of other places. . . . We assume if a woman says, 'I'm here to have an abortion,' that she's thought about that." In many clinics, a major goal of abortion counseling is to get clients to use contraceptives immediately thereafter. At the Center, though, staff members said they did not "push pills" or other methods of contraception on clients having abortions; they trusted clients to decide whether—and when—to use contraceptives.

Several health workers pointed out that they occasionally dealt with ambivalent clients, even though Center methods were predicated on not probing women for doubts. Greta, a health worker, said, "There are some women who are like, 'I don't *know* what I want to do,' and the system . . . is we assume women are totally clear in their decision the minute they walk in the door. If they're not, we have to back up. . . . And that's challenging from a . . . workflow point of view." She said there was "no set system" for counseling ambivalent women; she tailored her approach to fit her impression of what individual clients needed. She made sure to speak to ambivalent clients apart from any accompanying friends, lovers, or relatives "because I want them totally away from the influence." Clients who expressed ambivalence in group sessions talked with health workers individually. Clients also had private conversations with health workers while waiting in exam rooms for the physician.

Ilene, another health worker, said that institutional practices had loosened up over the course of her employment; staff members had grown less stringent about avoiding talk that might be perceived as invasive, in her view. Though she said she regretted the fact that training had become less strict, she liked the openness this laxity permitted her in talking with clients. Many health workers talked about bringing their own experiences to bear in talking with clients; they consciously broke the medical taboo against personal involvement. They wanted to counteract the professional distancing that commonly characterized caregiver-client interactions because they believed connections foster rather than inhibit beneficial health-care experiences. Ilene said she often related her own abortion experiences to clients who seemed to be going through similar experiences:

Sometimes when I do a woman who's had several abortions, we'll sit and just talk. . . . And for me that's good. I mean, you know, it's kind of selfish on my part because I feel better. Here's somebody who's the same place I am; they keep getting pregnant no matter what they do. You know, and so I feel better, and then I know she feels better because . . . how many people in the world can you sit and talk to about how many abortions you've had? . . . Some women [health workers] don't go into any of that. But we all sort of have this respect of the women [clients]. . . . [We] at least try to . . . not make her feel bad. And if she's feeling bad, [we ask], "What can we do about it?"

Caregiver-client conversation, as Ilene described it, could become an exchange in which both participants engaged as empirical experts and from which both participants emerged feeling validated.

Center women deliberately did not comment on clients' behavior or decision making except in an affirmative manner. They did, however, make overt political remarks because they wanted to proselytize their views about how health care should occur and to urge clients to fight for women's procreative freedom. In their view, health care interactions should be based on reciprocity, as Ilene described. They believed that freely shared information would correct power imbalances. Open communication among women, they believed, could produce only a positive outcome. In the same way that the 1970s health care activists heightened self-awareness and sparked community among feminists, workers educated in the principles of the self-help movement continued to promote progressive politics at the Center in the 1990s.

Ellen, a nurse-practitioner, described the work she did to make each woman more than simply a body she examined. She tried to take each client's life into account and treated her kindly and affectively; she provided her with information that demystified medical power. "If I show a woman how to view her cervix, that takes away my power of putting in the speculum," she explained. Ellen didn't want that kind of power; she considered it "male." Female power, to Ellen, was nurturant power, maternalistic power:

This is so pat. You know, I hate to say this, but if the world was run by women, we wouldn't have . . . the wars that we have. We just wouldn't because women are mothers. What I'm talking about as feminist is that approach where . . . it's not a power approach. It's an approach to consider all the people involved. That's what women do. . . . It doesn't always work out that way [that everyone is satisfied], but to me, there's at least a genuine effort to figure that out.

Ellen offered this definition of ideal feminist practice in regard to both client-staff relations and institutional policy. (I discuss institutional policy in

Chapter Four.) As many feminist scholars have done, Ellen pointed to differences between male and female ways of thinking and behaving (see, for example, Belenky et al. 1986, Gilligan 1982, Ruddick 1989, and Tannen 1990). Ellen said that it did not matter to her whether there were biological bases for the differences she perceived; all people should be urged to adopt the characteristics she described. Pervasive at the Center was the notion that the world would be a better place if men were more like women in the idealized terms Ellen elucidated: more nurturant, better listeners, more attuned to the needs of others, and less caught up in status and power distinctions. Center women recognized that not all women were socialized exactly the same ways, that not all women fit this model; most believed that feminists should try to reclaim these stereotypical feminine traits because they were the sorts of qualities that made people "good."

Christine Webb reiterates Center workers' concerns in her edited volume, *Feminist Practice in Women's Health Care* (1986), writing that the achievement of egalitarian relationships with clients ought to be the goal of feminist health care providers. "True sharing and demystification of technical jargon are only possible in an equal relationship in which neither partner has more rights or privileges than the other. This kind of sharing and equality allow open discussion and mutual questioning and challenging of opinions. Through these processes people develop confidence in their ability to understand and take charge of their own health" (1986: 183–184). Many nonmedical staff members resented the Center's reliance on medical personnel (especially doctors) because only medical staff can perform crucial practices (such as abortion and gynecological examinations). Egalitarianism in health care practice cannot be achieved as long as specialized expertise remains a province of medical workers. No one expected this situation to change; the lay staff hoped that hiring feminist medical staff would at least help. Health workers and administrators often bemoaned the dearth of feminist doctors; nurses and nurse-practitioners were more likely to share Center visions about health care practice because their training was less "masculine" than that provided in medical school.

In her work on client/health care professional interactions, Sue Fisher suggests that nurse-practitioners may demonstrate an alternative to the medical model, but she also holds that doctors need not be seen as monolithically immersed in conventional professionalism. Fisher positions herself between Eliot Mishler's (1984) condemnation of physicians as inattentive to clients' lives apart from and as part of their bodies (physicians tend to ignore what he calls the "voice of the lifeworld") and D. Silverman's (1987) postmodernist conceptualization of provider-patient conversations as a "plurality of voices, each interrupting and interpenetrating the other" (in Fisher 1993: 91). Fisher sees hope in nurse-practitioners' legitimization of the social experiences of clients but holds that "neither the medical model nor the asymmetry usually associated with the provider-patient relationship has disappeared" (107). Her comparison of two consultations (doctor/patient and nurse-practitioner/patient) suggests that a complete leveling of power dynamics is impossible; no one can be "a neutral objective provider of medical care" (110). Fisher endorses the nurse-practitioner's less directive style over the doctor's authoritarianism.

I do not think that Center workers' assertions that they were anti-medical meant that they believed they could achieve neutrality; rather, they provided access to bodily knowledge, showed clients their abiding respect, and allowed expression that would typically be stifled or even silenced in medical interactions. They did not tell clients what to do, but they did offer advice. When they drew upon their own experiences in talking with clients, they abandoned pretenses of neutrality, but their demeanor encouraged clients to see their input as noncoercive and anecdotal.

Women who had worked at the Center since the mid-1980s or longer tended to ground their discussion of feminist health care in self-help and self-exam. Newer employees were exposed to self-exam as part of their training, but because the Center no longer included self-exam groups as part of its services, as it did in the late 1970s and early 1980s, newer staff members were more likely to describe feminist health care with reference to the provision of abortion.

For the staff members who came to the Center during its days as a collective, self-exam was an electrifying political experience. The ideals behind the self-help movement—that bodily and sexual knowledge were both empowering and political, that this knowledge had been denied women and ought to be claimed—were new to them, yet these assertions resonated with their experiences. In contrast, employees who began working during the late 1980s or early 1990s might have never heard of self-exam or the self-help movement, though they had certainly been exposed to the rhetoric of consumer-clienthood that the movement popularized.

Several younger health workers recounted their surprise at encountering self-exam as part of the initial health worker orientation sessions. As Rae said when I interviewed her in 1992, "I wasn't familiar with it at all. And I was very hesitant. But I felt that within time I could get unhesitant, you know. I mean, I was like a typical female who had those hang-ups about body, and body odors. . . . I had to be pretty much eased into it." Similarly, Diana told me in an interview in 1994 that she was stunned not only at the idea of self-exam but at the unabashed attitude of the supervisor leading the session:

She had an open conversation about herpes. She was getting a lesion on her cervix. And that for me—hoo! I mean, first off, I'd never seen a cervix before. Second off, I'd never been around a group of women that spoke so openly about their bodies and sex, and you know, herpes! [She whispers]: "Shh, I don't want anybody to know I got herpes!" You know, that's the environment I came from: "Oh, she got herpes—she nasty!" . . . That for me was overwhelming.

Indoctrination for Diana was complete; she and her co-workers all came to wholeheartedly promote the ideals they saw embodied in self-exam. Many credited this sort of learning experience at the Center with improving their self-images and helping them to become stronger women. Diana said, "I think through that comfort of my body I've grown a lot. . . . I think my personal growth has been so *profound.*"

Over the course of my fieldwork, I had the opportunity to participate in one self-exam training session. I sensed that we all felt awkward at first, but the tension dissipated as we became involved in what we were doing. Looking up our own and each other's vaginas became interesting, rather than odd or embarrassing. Everyone's was different, and some of the differences, the supervisor who led the session explained, provided evidence of where we were in our menstrual cycles (or, in my case, pregnancy). I think we all were glad that we overcame whatever reservations we might have felt before we deprivatized our crotches and that we enjoyed the connection that came out of a shared sense of embodiment as women. But I wrote in my field notes, "I didn't experience this amazing sense of new identity or empowerment that I associate with self-help groups of the seventies." Self-exam no longer initiates women into a new movement; like a sit-in or a candlelight vigil, it feels like a ritual performance undertaken to revive a tradition, a way of connecting with the not-so-distant feminist past.

Many of the staff members at the Center practiced self-exam regularly on their own; occasionally they would do self-exam in small groups like the one in which I participated. Self-exam was offered as a framework for understanding how health care should be for women, even though clients no longer participated in self-exam groups. Nurse-practitioners were supposed to offer clients the opportunity to do self-exam individually. However, the nurses I observed did not offer to teach self-exam but, instead, invited clients to look at their cervices in a mirror. Ellen said, "We're not given time to do that. You can't teach someone to put a speculum in and look at their cervix in five minutes. . . . I rarely do it. I always ask the woman if she wants to do it, and usually they say no. . . . I always try to show them their cervix. . . . Most women will want to see this." Though organizational practice has, in this way, strayed far from its origins, most workers still considered the Center to be antimedical and preferable to most of the health care options available to women.

Emotional Labor

Many staff members contrasted the care they were providing with treatment they had received in the past, often recalling abortions they had had years earlier. Anne, a supervisor, said:

> [The] people [at the clinic] really didn't care about your emotional setting. They didn't care what happened a week after that. You know, you read the forms, you have your abortion, you leave. And I mean, there was no personal—there was no time to emotionally release any stress or anyone to just talk to. . . . Even if I wanted to express myself, . . . there was no one there to listen to me. . . . There was no support before, during, or after the procedure. I thought I was having a possible complication about three days later; there was no one to call. The office was closed. You know, and then me trying to keep it away from certain family members, and then not being able to do that because I thought I was having a medical emergency. I mean, there was no one to tell me, "This is nothing to worry about. This is normal. This is what you need to do." . . .
>
> It's an alone feeling. Being a woman, and having to make that decision at that particular point in my life, it was already making me feel alone. And then to get to the place where I needed support or where I could possibly talk about it—because you can't really talk about abortion too many places and be accepted—the place that I went to, there was nothing. You couldn't talk about it there either.

Several women reported experiences similar to Anne's and said they felt they had missed something that they could not even identify until they happened to receive feminist care or came to work at the Center. Lois, a health worker who had a second-trimester saline abortion at Pavillion, the only other clinic in Anyville that provided late-term abortions, was not told that she would actually go into labor. "It was like, 'We're going to give you an injection, and then you'll wait around for a while.'"

Before coming to work at the Center, Risa lost a job at Pavillion. She said, "I know it was because I was very vocal about how I felt about the way they treated the women. . . . They were real quick to make people feel stupid, and real quick to talk . . . down to them, and just really disrespectful. Just like, 'I got something you need, therefore you need to kiss my butt to get it.'" Center staff members regretted that most women remained unaware that an alternative to standard treatment exists; they believed experiences at the Center often impelled clients to reconceptualize their past medical treatment as inferior to feminist care.

Several staff members cited positive health-care experiences as motivating them to seek employment at the Center. Janice, for example, had had two abortions. She described the first one as "really bad," but her second abortion, at the Center, was such a positive experience she called it "life changing." So when she applied for a job at the Center, she knew she would enjoy the work environment but was anxious that providing abortions might reopen old wounds. "I was just so amazed after I came away from that place [the Center]. . . . I just couldn't believe it. . . . I knew from that experience that that was the kind of place I wanted to be, but still there were other things that I had to consider . . . feelings that I might have to deal with that would come back about being there, having an abortion." Janice had felt extremely guilty about her pregnancies and about her first abortion, a response she attributes to her "real conservative background." The second time she decided to have an abortion, she said, "In a way I almost felt like, well if I got pregnant, then I *deserve* a bad experience." But at the Center "they gave me attention, but they didn't dote on you and feel sorry for you or anything like that, so it was just totally empowering by the end of it. . . . I realized it was an empowering experience to have this abortion and be treated with respect." Center staff members assuaged Janice's guilt by making her feel cared for and thus worthy of care.

The word *support* recurred throughout workers' narratives: they believed they provided a kind of nurturance that medically oriented providers rarely offered. Bad abortion experiences like Lois's or Anne's or the mistreatment of clients observed by Risa fueled workers' conviction that an alternative should exist and made them proud of their efforts to make certain clients would not feel degraded, ignored, or powerless at the Center. To achieve this end, they explicitly detailed each step of every procedure in information sessions for clients, and then, when they performed exams, health-worked, or advocated, they told each client what was happening to her as it occurred. They connected with clients empathetically, spoke soothingly to women in pain, did their best to ensure that clients would not feel alone during their abortions. Staff members experienced a vicarious pleasure in each client's "empowering" experience (as Janice christened it) at the Center.

The intensity of their work also presented drawbacks; the costs of providing sincere care were high. Much of their contact with clients resulted in their soaking up these women's emotional energy. As they eliminated the distance that practitioners usually maintain, they made themselves vulnerable to burn-out. Possibly, *any* stance caregivers take in their relationships with clients can lead to destructive outcomes—to all the signs of burn-out or high stress, from exhaustion and frequent physical illness to compulsive activities like smoking, which was quite common among Center staff—or to self-protective tactics—such as attempts to achieve distance from clients, like feigning sincerity. A high level of engagement with clients may cause caregivers to attempt to reduce the intensity of contact.

Medical students learn early on to establish boundaries between themselves and their clients. Even though they eventually might find they need to disengage from clients, Center women believed this aspect of medical socialization was indicative of what was wrong with the medical profession: physicians do not value nurturance. The first "patients" medical students encounter are, after all, *dead*. All patients may be seen in the light of these first encounters and, thus, may become potential cadavers. Medical educators categorically disregard or deny the emotional potency cadavers might have for the living and teach students to do the same. Indeed, Frederic Hafferty writes that "introspection and reflection are terminal diseases in medical school" (1991: 191). Both Hafferty and Peter Finkelstein (1986) write about the classroom culture in anatomy labs, which encourages various distancing strategies such as rough language, rough behavior, cadaver stories, and jokes. Students give cadavers silly or odd names that "always emphasized the cadaver's origin somewhere else, geographically, socially, or ethnically," Finkelstein writes (33). The medical language students learn reinforces the notion that "one dissects anatomic material; one does not look backward to the person once invested in this body" (Finkelstein 1986: 29). For medical students, then, the humanity embodied in the human body becomes a secondary, if not a dangerous, concern. Finkelstein writes, "If the body is stripped of the rights and considerations given to the living, it is lowered both in status and in its capacity to arouse emotion" (31).

Hafferty writes that the women medical students he studied were "more reflexive about their own reactions to lab as well as more aware of the reactions of others," more "supportive and empathetic," and "more comfortable with a language of emotions" than the men medical students (1991: 197). Center women repeatedly expressed the notion that women care better—and recognize the importance of caring more—than men do. They saw women doctors as preferable to men simply because they hoped that gendered training might persist in the face of medical training. They knew that the medical model holds that doctors ideally should learn to make their jobs easier by not allowing themselves to become too involved with their patients. Hafferty writes, "To imply that one can care too much, however, does raise the possibility that one can care 'too little.' The threat of becoming too insensitive represents a vital issue for some students" (190).

In any caring context like the Womancare Center, those who resist disconnection may end up disconnected anyway. Literature on burn-out describes behavior brought about by emotional intensity or stressful time demands as similar to that brought about by resisting involvement: in short, the outcome is caregivers who do not or cannot care anymore. (Bailey 1985, Cherniss 1980, and Freudenberger 1975, write about burn-out as an occupational hazard in service work. Lorber 1984, Marshall et al. 1991, Melosh 1982, and Reverby 1987 write specifically about stresses women encounter as health care providers.)

Arlie Russell Hochschild (1983) studied workers who resorted to "deep acting" strategies, which often led to identity crises as they became unable to separate themselves from the acting demanded of them on the job (and Hafferty draws on this work in his ethnography of medical students). Several Center women mentioned this sort of anxiety-related strain and described their attempts to pull back. Anyone who interacts with people as part of her job is "working on people," routinizing the behavior of service recipients so that institutional goals are met (Leidner 1993). Center workers learned to see the management of clients' emotional responses to abortion as part of their job; at the same time, extremely emotional clients were quite upsetting. They also created a snag in the flow of the work, disrupting the routine for everyone.

Health workers assuaged the emotions of others with their own emotional labor. Though it wore them down, they believed this practice had to be central to the provision of feminist health care, and they would have liked to see all caregivers adopt their mode of interactive practice. Ironically, their emotion-work shielded physicians at the Center from involvement with clients. The doctor entered the examining room to perform an abortion after the client had undressed and climbed onto the examining table. The health worker introduced the doctor to the client and then described the doctor's actions as they occurred (saying, for example, "Now you'll feel her insert two gloved fingers. . . . Now you'll feel the speculum. . . . Now you might feel a stinging sensation; that's the local anesthesia," and so forth.) If the client remained calm and kept still, the abortion proceeded smoothly, and the doctor rarely spoke to the client again until just before leaving the room. If the client had difficulty remaining composed, the health worker tried to help her relax, coaxing her to close her eyes and to concentrate on slowing her breathing down. If the client took a while to calm down, the doctor might interject instructions, usually in a more authoritative tone than that of the health worker (saying, for example, "I need you to keep your hips on the table and your knees relaxed; I really can't continue unless you stop moving"). These interactions, in which the health worker acted as mediator in order to accomplish feminist goals, also reinforced typical doctor–lay staff relations, in which doctors are excused from emotional involvement. Doctors might, in fact, get impatient while health workers engaged in this labor, seeing it as delaying their own work.

As many of their narratives attest, health workers took pride in their nurturing style and were disappointed in themselves when they exhausted their capacity to muster empathy and give of themselves. Risa said, for instance:

> It gets to a point where I just get sick of smiling and being nice to people, and I get sympathy burn-out where it's like [I'm thinking], "I don't care if your thirteen-year-old daughter is pregnant and she's twenty-six weeks! I'm sorry, I don't care." You know, and then I feel bad. And when I start feeling like that I have enough sense to go and get someone else to see that woman. Because she doesn't deserve that behavior, you know. So I like phones because, like, I can *end* the contact by hanging up the phone. I don't have to see them out. I don't have to be there to see them cry.

Routines may offer workers protection from the stress of emotional expenditures. Robin Leidner discusses how the McDonald's staff members she studied used company-prescribed routines to enable them to go on automatic pilot. "For those who preferred to expend as little emotional energy as possible, the formulaic routines had real benefits," she writes (1993: 136). Certain Center routines likewise offered a respite from intense interaction. Hannah talked of enjoying sterile-room work (evaluating and packaging fetal tissue) because "you had your own pace and you didn't have the client contact"; she found this work to be a welcome regular relief. Center workers, as Risa and Hannah described, took refuge in whichever tasks they found least emotionally demanding and used these times as recuperative so that they were able to return to high-intensity emotional labor.[5]

Center workers did not portray emotion-work as an institutional demand but rather as a mark of feminist integrity *and* a burden feminist women, especially, were likely to shoulder. Risa said, "It's hard to say, well, you leave your work [at work] . . . when you do the kind of work that we do. Because you're a woman, you know. Your work is part of you if you work in an abortion clinic or do any kind of health care." Women are socialized not to disassociate ourselves from others; feminism, as most Center workers talked about it, meant that women ought to especially value our connections with other women. Center workers saw faking sincerity as preferable to showing that one did not care. But faking indicated that one was burned out and ought to take restorative measures—or even leave the Center.

Several staff members said clients' hypocritical attitudes toward abortion contributed to their burn-out. Health workers might also become disappointed in clients who did not eagerly embrace the opportunity to become active participants in their own health care and who behaved as though the Center were an ordinary medical facility. Hallie said, for example, that she was annoyed by clients who "don't understand why we're so nice to them after going to Pavillion or wherever—people who come in feeling guilty, feel they deserve to be treated like shit, and so they treat *us* like shit." Their mission to provoke feminist awareness could not always be easily achieved. Yvette said:

> It used to be that just more and more of the clients at the Center were feminist, and now you get a few, but you really don't get that many. You get more women who either are so uneducated . . . [they] have never heard of it [feminism], and it's nothing to them . . . [or] the people who come in and say, "I think abortion is bad, but I'm a student" or "I'm a housewife" or "I'm a butcher, baker, candlestick maker," . . . women who have been raised with this mentality of "my job is to love and nurture children, and women who don't do that are feminist bitches." And I think at least those women get a little confused when they see how we treat them. If nothing else, they see that we're good to them.

Center women found the notion that feminism was antithetical to nurturance insulting because their feminist praxis centered on a valuation of caring.

Most clients, health workers agreed, did see a difference between typical medical treatment and the feminist care they received at the Center. Indeed, many clients were stunned by the quality of care at the Center (as Janice described her own experience earlier, for instance), and most were appreciative. On the whole, I found that Center workers were far less likely to disparage their clients than women I knew when I worked at another clinic (see Simonds 1991); even when they experienced client-related burn-out, they rarely took it out on clients or made fun of clients behind their backs. (They also talked about burn-out as linked to their lack of structural control; I return to this subject in Chapter Four.)

Health workers tended to see uncooperative clients as caught up in their own personal morass of problems. Lee talked about clients who were reluctant to give her their phone numbers, despite her assurances that the Center would protect their confidentiality. "While I can appreciate that the woman may be threatened by someone else finding out about the abortion, . . . it's frustrating to have that turned back against me like *I'm* the enemy." She gave several other examples of instances where clients behaved offensively and said, "I wonder whether it's that this whole situation doesn't have any other outlet at all—and certainly no positive outlet—and here I am willing to talk . . . about the abortion, so I get all the negative shit that, you know, has its source elsewhere." Increasingly, anti-abortionists (whom Center workers called "antis") have put women who have abortions on the defensive, Center workers said, and these women may feel as though they deserve invasive questioning or callous treatment.

Many workers spoke of dealing with clients who felt conflicted about abortion rights or who even declared that they were against abortion (on the phone, in group sessions, or while waiting in the exam rooms). Yvette said, "I've had a lot of people [clients] tell me lately, 'I used to be pro-choice, but now I'm not.' And that one really bothers me." Health workers sometimes confronted clients by asking them how they could have an abortion if they were anti-choice, as Janice described: "I get mad, but I . . . just present the opposite side view. 'Well, you know, if you are anti-abortion, then maybe this isn't the decision that you want to make,' you know, and just try to present it in a way that, well, that it's not really compatible to be anti-abortion and to have an abortion. 'Well, my situation's different.' 'Okay, right!'" Janice laughed, using sarcasm to dismiss a client's claim to a unique route to abortion.

Clients would attempt to justify their own abortions as necessary compared with the frivolous abortions of other women. Many health workers said, as Janice did, that they often assured such clients that their situations were not unusual. This recurring conversation frustrated staff members, who often found it easiest to simply ignore clients' anti-abortion remarks. Carrie, a health worker, said, for instance, that she rarely felt she had the energy or desire to argue with clients and that she worried she might not argue politely. She believed that what she would like to say expressed too much anger to maintain the nurturing stance she had been taught. "It makes me really angry—it really frustrates me—that you're coming in here to have an abortion and telling me that you don't believe in it! That you would deny other women the choice, the option that you have now to come in here and do this!"

Because they knew their work would not necessarily result in pro-choice clients, workers sometimes felt angry with clients or at least ambivalent about all the effort they expended in their attempts to ease clients through the abortion experience and to protect them from the antis. As Celia, a supervisor, said, "You do this whole job of, like, protecting the clients—but who's protecting you?" Some staff members wondered whether their style was too solicitous: maybe if feminists were less protective of women, there would be more of a public outcry against anti-feminist activities and dogma.

The Search for a Feminist Community

Many workers talked about how they had been motivated by general feminist political leanings in seeking employment at the Center. Some, like Carrie, had first-hand experience with nonfeminist workplaces. "I quit a job I really hated working for a law firm, and I knew that I wanted to do something [that] . . . especially helped women, . . . something that agreed with . . . my political beliefs, such as being a feminist, having a fairly liberal outlook." Others, like Mira, simply knew they wanted to find a job that was outside the mainstream. "When I graduated [from college], I wasn't sure what I wanted to do but knew I wanted to do something in the feminist arena, something political. . . . The ad said . . . "advocating for women during their abortions, doing support counseling," and things like that, and I thought, well, there's my foot in the door to, you know, some kind of feminist workplace or . . . the feminist community here." Like most of the others, Carrie and Mira started working at the Center without any comparable experience but armed with a pro-feminist sensibility that predisposed them to feel personally gratified by their jobs.

Staff members who had prior experience with abortion or women's health care work were not accustomed to the full range of activities in which they were expected to engage at the Center. In most abortion clinics, the division of labor is much more rigid. For instance, when she worked at Pavillion, Risa mainly answered the phone. Deva, a health worker, had experience in a clinic (in another state) where her entire job consisted of sterile-room work.

The fluidity of their work at the Center facilitated health workers' contact with each other and made on-the-job training easy. Each worker began by taking phone calls and progressed through the various tasks involved in health care provision at the Center. These tasks were ordered in terms of complexity and culminated with assisting the physician during second-trimester abortions. The training period lasted until a health worker had been certified to do every job from phones to assisting, which could take as long as a year. All health workers described their training process at the Center as "intensive," and most felt that the training system—learning on the job and being judged by more advanced co-workers as they demonstrated their ability to perform each successive task—worked effectively.

Many Center women credited their work with inspiring them to take actions that intensified their feminism. Greta said, "I stopped going to school when I first started working there because I went home every night with stacks of literature to read, and I bought anatomy books. I bought women's studies books, modern literature written by women. I did an amazing amount of studying." Thus, politicization on the job could motivate workers to study on their own, and then this reading could further enhance their feminist development. For many staff members, work at the Center was the impetus for beginning or resuming formal education in health care fields with the explicit aim of becoming feminist practitioners. For example, during the few months after my fieldwork ended, Tanya, the health educator, completed her B.A. in nursing; Greta left the Center to begin a physician's assistant program; Lucy (a nurse I did not interview) went back to nursing school to get certified as a nurse-practitioner; and, after being fired in 1993, Lee began a prenursing program.[6] These women talked of how their interest in women's health care and their feminist identity were consolidated at the Center and spurred their decisions to seek formal training to become medical workers.

The women's ideas about feminist health care practice were enmeshed in broad idealistic visions of the eradication of the oppression of women or of all oppressive relationships. Everyone, when asked to articulate her own definition of feminism, first responded with astonishment at the magnitude of my question. But most did have answers, though they often prefaced them with caveats, insisting they were inadequate generalizations. Emma and Deborah, a health worker, offered fairly concise descriptions of what it meant to be a feminist that are consistent with the views of many staff members:

> EMMA: I really view feminism as a world-view where the society cares about women and children in the way that nurtures that and views it as a real treasure.

> DEBORAH: To me it means that I recognize the oppression of women, and for me, personally, it means that I put that in a . . . world context [in which] oppression means different things for women of different nations, for white women, for women of color, . . . and changing that is . . . a critical part of what it means to fight for a more humane society. And any society that isn't fighting that isn't going to get there.

Feminists, as Emma defined them, are people who value women and "nurture" the valuation of women and children (or women's realm); she did not elaborate about what would have to change for this shift in the collective consciousness to occur. Deborah saw the oppression of women as linked to and distinguished from other kinds of oppression; various women's experiences of oppression might have common elements but were not necessarily equivalent. Ideally, in Deborah's view, all forms of oppression must be attacked at the same time, and feminists were people who waged this attack.

Staff members often drew on or reacted against each other's ideas or behavior in describing how they formulated their individual views of feminism. Center women worked closely with each other, often socialized with each other outside of work, and sometimes lived together as roommates or lovers. (During my ethnographic work, Toby, a health worker, and Carrie were roommates, and so were Risa and Julia. There was one romance between a nurse and a health worker, neither of whom participated in my study.) Strong bonds formed, and so did occasional antipathies. Center women often cited each other; they also talked about internal rifts. Each woman evaluated her colleagues according to her own developing feminist moral sensibility, often finding women to admire, to learn from, to emulate—and, less often, to hold up as bad examples of sisterhood.

When I first interviewed her, Rae hesitated when I asked whether she saw herself as a feminist. Because of what she was learning about feminism from her co-workers' talk and actions, she was uncertain about whether she wanted to join them in feminism:

> If I went by the dictionary or . . . what some of my co-workers consider to be feminist, I probably would fall short. . . . I think a feminist is a woman who truly believes that she is equal, who truly believes she is good. She truly believes that she needs to do what she needs to do for herself, and that there is no one else that can give her certain things for herself. . . . I believe that a feminist is a woman who doesn't feel like she needs a man to do anything. So, one reason why I say I think I differ from . . . some of my co-workers . . . and I don't know if it's—I don't want to say it's—a black-white thing, but I find it more common in more of my black co-workers than within my white co-workers. . . . If a man could take on that responsibility of being the head of the household financially and . . . quote-unquote taking care of me, I wouldn't necessarily be completely opposed to that. . . . Some women would feel that that doesn't make you a feminist, but I don't agree with that.

Rae described some of her white colleagues as too dogmatic because they were ready to dismiss certain behaviors (relying on a man financially, for example) as evidence that a woman was not feminist. These white women universalized their own experience, which, in Rae's view, meant they ignored the realities of many black women's lives (in her case, struggling as a single mother to eke out an income, living in a situation where financial dependence looked like a luxury, not bondage).

My concern as a . . . black feminist woman and, say, Janice's concerns as a white feminist woman are total *opposites*. My first concern is how can I take care of myself because . . . my family doesn't have money. . . . I can say that my biggest worry is not, you know, who's killing the planet; I'm worried about who's going to kill my son. Do you know what I'm saying? . . . Now I have some of the same concerns: poor women, the right for poor women to have abortions. . . . But I also feel that just because they are white and I am black that sisterhood . . . is not a complete link for that simple fact of the color barrier.

Her experiences with white co-workers who, in her view, arrogantly insisted on an exclusive definition of what it meant to be feminist made Rae wary of embracing the label for herself. She did not want to ally herself with feminism if it incorporated racism, if it were defined by white women for black women.

But by the time of her second interview a year later (September 1993), Rae had decided on another course: she would not allow what she saw as the misguided views of others to exclude her from feminism. She had resolved to accept uncertainty and variety as part of the definition. "I guess I can understand now what that word feminist . . . means to me and what [it means] to the next woman; it's not going to be necessarily the same. And I'm okay with that." Rae would not consider anyone who proclaimed herself to be feminist as a feminist; she reserved judgment until she could determine whether a person was "for women" and "supports women" in ways she would credit as valid. Some women, she had learned from working at the Center, "think that they have to be these mean people because they're trying to be as manlike as possible. It's kind of like they don't get it. . . . How can you be for women if you're constantly knocking them down?" Rae believed feminists should treat others with respect, while also maintaining their own dignity and not letting others—men or women—mistreat them. Through her encounters at the Center (both positive and negative) Rae felt she had gained confidence in herself: this self-confidence, to her, was central to her feminist identity.

Carrie said that she could not define feminism without contradicting herself. She believed feminists ought to eschew exclusivity, so if she were to say what makes someone feminist or not she would engage in antifeminist practice. At the same time, she strongly felt that she could tell who was feminist and who was not. In her discussion of what it means to be feminist, she both asserted and questioned liberal notions of selfhood:

It's hard to define feminist without using the word *not* a lot because what comes to mind to me is: A feminist is someone who doesn't do this or doesn't do that. And that's counter to what I believe a feminist is anyway. Because I could say a feminist is someone who doesn't discriminate against women, . . . who doesn't give in to other people's ideas about how she should be, how she should look, . . . what limits she should have on her life, things like that. . . . But a feminist is also someone who doesn't define herself as being antithetical to something else. Because to define yourself as being not a part of the male hierarchy, not a part of male ideas, or of a male structured society . . . is to define yourself in terms of something other than yourself. And I think that to be truly feminist is something that might not even exist in our society. It's more than equal rights, and it's more than equal opportunity.

If "male" ideology constrains women's lives by usurping our agency to define ourselves, feminist ideology that merely contradicts masculinist ideology still operates on its terms, Carrie felt. We cannot entirely remove ourselves from what we did not create or re-create ourselves wholly in opposition to what surrounds us, Carrie recognized. Even in social structures that oppress us, she believed, it does not serve women well to portray ourselves as voiceless. She wanted to move beyond liberal feminist notions ("It's more than equal rights, and it's more than equal opportunity") of achieving social change, but she did not know where to go. Carrie's notion of feminist practice was constrained by a society rife with postmodern contradiction: she would have liked to believe a feminist ideal alternative could exist but knew alternatives must be grounded in present circumstances, which she viewed as ideologically poisoned and poisonous.

One might expect a more definite, ripened feminist vision from women who had a longer experience with feminism in their lives. Indeed, the two oldest health workers at the Center, Deborah (forty-eight) and Elise (fifty-two), described long personal histories of feminist identification. Deborah came to feminism via the antiwar movement of the late 1960s, and Elise, more atypically, saw her feminism as grounded in her association with the Catholic Church. Both women developed a feminist identity through women-centered communities.

> DEBORAH: By the time that I joined the antiwar movement, which was in 1968, . . . there really was a women's movement. And they were, at that point, even, on reasonably good terms. . . . I joined a women's consciousness group. Part of what I went through at the time . . . was somewhat parallel to coming out as a lesbian, but it wasn't the same thing . . . I think the one facilitated the other. . . . I think the women's consciousness raising facilitated my coming out

as a lesbian in the sense that . . . [I realized] I felt closest to women. I liked to work with women the best. I liked to theorize with women the best. I liked to do actions with women. . . . The only thing I wasn't doing with women was sleeping with them, you know. And then that made me like really try and search myself around that question, and I realized actually I'd always been attracted to women sexually. It's just I'd never really allowed that to be a possibility. . . . In terms of calling myself a feminist, it was completely part of developing myself as a *political* person.

ELISE: Tanya said to me one day, . . . "You know, women don't think of themselves as a group." And I thought, "Oh shit, you know, that's the truth!" And I *always* have, you know, because . . . I was in the convent all those years. . . . I think one of the things that was confusing for me—and, as time went by, I began to feel more comfortable with it—[was that] the Catholic Church was just too small. And . . . I really liked a whole lot of things about other places, like world-views and things like that. . . . Actually, I probably didn't do much different there [in the convent] than I'm doing here. You know, it's passing on right information, helping people to be able to manage their lives.

Both Deborah and Elise described their work at the Center as continuous with the commitments they developed earlier in their lives—to political action (in Deborah's case) or to education (in Elise's) that would help others, especially women. Elise outgrew the Church's narrow margins, but Deborah—like the Center administrators who came of age in the same climate—expressed nostalgia for the activism of the late sixties and early seventies. "It was a really exciting time because . . . you could really believe that the revolution was at hand." In the 1990s, the same issues that first aroused her activist spirit remain unresolved, as feminism had, in many circles, become a dirty word. Deborah, like many other staff members, experienced the Center as a refuge from conservatism and a means of participating in the battle against reactionary politics and policy. Deborah said, "That's part of why I love being here, because here it's, like, okay to be a feminist. . . . In most places where I do work or do things, it isn't."

Many Center women, like Elise and Deborah, said that woman-identification or specific mentorships (or both) brought them to the Center in the first place. Several younger health workers said their mothers served as feminist role models for them and thus played an active part in their decisions to do abortion work. Julia's mother had been a feminist activist for all of Julia's life;

she had been active in the ERA fight and remained a prominent figure in the politicization of health care issues for African American women. Julia graduated from college with a business degree. After college, she cleaned houses while she searched for a job in business. Coincidentally, Emma (who knew Julia's mother) hired Julia to clean her house. When the Center was hiring, Julia applied. "My first orientation brought back a lot of memories of things I did in the past," Julia said. And though she had deliberately tried to differentiate herself from her mother by majoring in business and had "never really thought about what it means to be a feminist," she felt immediately that the work at the Center suited her. Feminist activism was in the air she breathed growing up; coming to the Center taught her that her mother's legacy might indeed be her calling.

Nell, who began working at the Center while enrolled in college part-time, said that her mother's feminism consciously motivated her. She said that her mother's influence, along with the politicizing of abortion around the time of the *Webster* decision, were the factors that led her to apply for a job at the Center: "I wanted to get more involved, so I called [the local chapter of NARAL] and started doing work with them, and started escorting [clients]. . . . I was trying to find a job that would put me more in what I wanted to do, working with women."

Anne's great-grandmother, grandmother, and mother were rural direct-entry midwives, who helped women give birth and illegally abort unwanted pregnancies:

As a child, I never knew what my grandmother was doing. . . . But, yes, my grandmother was performing abortions up to about fourteen, fifteen weeks for many, many years. . . . She taught my mother how to be a midwife. . . . It was just taught down family history. . . . Women were coming up pregnant out in the fields, and . . . they did what they had to do to take care of themselves in those days. . . . They had their own underground network system. . . . Everyone in the community knew what she did, but it really wasn't spoken of.

When she got older, Anne's grandmother and mother talked openly to her about their skills; they taught her to see birth and abortion as part of the same continuum of procreative freedom. Anne said her mother took pride in the work Anne had chosen at the Center, and Anne saw this work as the extension of a family tradition.

Even given their predisposition to feminist politics and their interest in women's health care, many health workers spoke of their training period as especially transformative because of the co-workers with whom they forged

close ties. Lee said that when she began at the Center, she was "pretty ignorant about abortion." She said, "I've always identified myself as pro-choice,
but, in the past, I've said things like 'Well, abortion should be legal, but *I*
could never have one.'" Being mentored by more experienced workers enabled her "to get past a lot of clichés" like that one and helped her to combat
her "ignorance" about abortion. Lee described how a co-worker's remark
taught her to rethink her initial objection to the use of "abortion as birth
control." She said, "I remember hearing somebody . . . say, 'Well, abortion *is*
birth control. Birth control is where you don't have a baby, and that's what
abortion is about, and it's on the same continuum as using the pill, using the
diaphragm. It's a way you can avoid having an unwanted pregnancy.'"

The mentorship of more experienced health workers often contributed to
newer staff members' growing feminist belief systems, but mentor status was
not necessarily based on length of tenure at the Center. Women came to
respect certain co-workers because they saw them as particularly insightful.
Risa, for instance, described how African American lesbian co-workers had
challenged her prejudices against lesbians:

> Through my working at the clinic . . . I've really had to work on my
> homophobia. . . . Just talking about it, you know, saying somebody was
> "an ol' dyke." . . . [My coworker said,] "*I'm* a dyke." Like, "Oh! I didn't
> mean that about *you*, see. You're not *like* them." You know, and they were
> like, "That's what they [whites] say about black people. You need to
> check yourself on it." I was *horrified*. . . . And then one of my friends says,
> "Risa, you're so homophobic. Has anyone *ever* approached you?" I was
> like, "No." "So get over it!" That's embarrassing, you know. . . . That
> helped.

Risa described learning from being immersed in a community that unmasked
the hypocrisy of social environments where an anti-gay attitude was accepted.
Risa responded to their challenge by modifying her stance because she liked
and respected these women and because their argument was convincing. She
was embarrassed that she had insulted them and "worked on" changing her
thinking to eliminate what she had now been taught to see as discriminatory
stereotyping analogous to racism.

Mentorship might emerge out of worker camaraderie, a nonhierarchical
exchange based on mutual respect (as in Risa's case), or it might develop in a
more conventional way. For Mira, reflecting on her four years at the Center
as she prepared to leave to go to graduate school full-time, mentorship meant
modeling herself on others whom she admired as more knowledgeable than
she:

I've learned to think much more as a feminist. . . . Whenever I'm in a situation and I'm unsure of how to answer or what position I should take on this new issue that I've just heard about, I think to myself, "How would Meryl, Nancy, or Emma answer this question? What would their view of the situation be?" And then I know that that is the feminist view. . . . I trust that much that I've been in a feminist place, that if I think like they do, I will think like a feminist.

Mira stated explicitly that she had found ideal feminists to model; over the course of her employment at the Center, she consciously appropriated what she admired in them to shape her own feminist identity.

Not everyone saw the Center as a benevolent system of sisterly mentorship however. Rae described the potential for abuse in the training system. When she started work, she said, "I used to wake up in the morning and say, 'God, I don't want to go in that place!' And some days, I still feel like that. . . . They treated me so bad. They stripped from me all my self-esteem, as far as my . . . ability, what I do at work. Those women can be really cruel at that clinic." Rae considered white co-workers' denigration of her abilities to be evidence of their racism. Risa, too, complained about the training process, describing some white co-workers as impatient and annoyed with having to teach less advanced health workers:

It was hard being new because other people already knew stuff, and sometimes people would forget that they were an incoming health worker at one point, you know, also. They wouldn't be very nice all the time. But I learned quickly to get people off my back. . . . I would just tell them I didn't know. "You either need to tell me or I'm just going to assume that I need to do something this way. It'll be messed up and you're going to end up having to do it over again." . . . People will be just really mean about the information that they had and you didn't, you know, just totally invalidating the fact that you're new and you're learning.

Notably, white women who started at approximately the same time as Rae and Risa and who were trained by the same people did not call the process demeaning or the trainers abusive. Other black staff members confirmed Rae's and Risa's view that some white staff members tacitly assumed that black women were less competent workers than white women. Rae and Risa completed their training feeling self-assured because they learned to disregard condescension on the part of more senior white co-workers and because they bonded with each other and with other women, especially other women of color, who began working at the Center when they did. This route to self-assurance required more effort for Rae than for Risa, as their narratives suggest, because Risa already felt more comfortable challenging unfair treatment. Rae learned from Risa and other friends not only to shield herself from the cruelty of others and to resist internalizing their negativity but also to openly question it.[7]

Sarina, the staff physician, came to the Center hoping it would be a feminist haven that would offer an alternative to her experiences in mainstream medicine. Medical school and beginning a residency in surgery had facilitated Sarina's feminist awakening:

> I grew up in the South. I was raised in a family where women were supposed to be very attractive and quiet and shy. . . . I was kept very sheltered. . . . [In medical school] they [faculty] let you know that they don't think that you're as capable as men, that you're inferior. And I'm *not* less intelligent. . . . And that you can't do the same work. And I *did*. I started to get angry. . . . When I went into the hospital setting . . . I was sexually harassed. . . . That's when the alarm started to go off: there's something wrong with this system! What is this? I don't know how to deal with this! . . . I started to pay attention to what some of these women [colleagues] said, and I started to read [feminist literature]. . . . My husband had *no concept* of what feminism was. He was scared to death of it. He resented every female friend that I had. . . . The marriage just fell apart in a very short period of time. . . . I changed enormously.

Her experience in medicine and her exposure to feminist ideas changed Sarina's thinking; her growing identification whith women changed the course of her career and her personal life. She quit her residency in surgery to go into preventive medicine and got a master's degree in public health. She divorced her husband. She resisted the stripping away of compassion and caring that she saw as inherent in medical training. She became resolute in her stance that "to be a feminist means to treat women with dignity and respect."

Sarina's first job as an abortionist was with Planned Parenthood. She had not learned to perform abortions in medical school, so she learned how to do first-trimester abortions on the job. The environment at the Planned Parenthood clinic was not much better than her prior experiences. "It was a rude awakening for me to go into a job where I was the only female physician . . . and to basically be discriminated against. . . . I got disillusioned very quickly with the place."

The Center seemed ideal at first. Sarina immediately felt very much a part of a feminist community with the health workers and supervisors. She said, however, that she always felt excluded by Center administrators from any important decision making. Once again, she felt forced to contend with feminist disillusionment on the job:

> I have learned over the past year that, working in this clinic, traditionally physicians have been viewed as . . . the bad people. . . . They were traditionally people who came in one day a week or a half day a week on their day off, who really didn't have that much commitment to this. They had a private practice on the side, so they were not involved . . . in the decision making . . . [or] in the actual running of the clinic. And, for me, it was very difficult because I wasn't like that. . . . I grew to love the staff very much, . . . but I was still excluded from all upper management meetings, from any decision making that was done. . . . I had viewed myself as part of a team that comprises this clinic, but I have not been treated that way. . . . I'm tired of feeling like I don't fit in anywhere.

The feminist community she thought she had found finally failed, in her view; the management did not uphold her definition of feminism because it did not treat her with "dignity and respect." Sarina ultimately concluded that the Center was not a truly feminist community. Indeed, many staff members held that a prime goal of feminist praxis ought to be a mutual respect among women in spite of differences among us and that this respect should serve as the foundation for any higher level of collective consciousness, or community. Many health workers believed, with Sarina, that Center administrators had gradually given up their commitment to maintaining the Center as a feminist community.[8]

As their stories show, workers' experiences at the Center may have molded them into feminists, may have made them better feminists, and may have enabled them to formulate specifically feminist critiques of the world around them—including critiques of feminism itself and of their own work environment. The Center was more than simply a backdrop to the development of definitions of feminist practice; it both contributed to and hindered this development. Even when their experiences on the job angered or alienated them, the women working there expressed an enduring faith in feminism as they had come to define it and a fondness for the aspects of their work lives at the Center that fostered their feminist sensibilities.

CHAPTER 2

Feminist Abortion Practice

Getting Graphic

Center women spoke about abortion as a political issue, and they also talked about what it literally and practically means to do abortions. They believed that ideally these two ways of discussing abortion ought not be separated. Staff members framed abortion with talk of women's sexual expression, body image, privacy, wholeness, and agency. Yet they also evaluated these terms for framing abortion as inadequate given their observations at work. Their talk about doing abortion work turned to the emotional intensity of caring for aborting women and their "gut reactions" to assisting the abortionist during second-trimester abortions or processing fetal tissue when they did sterile-room work.

Center workers commonly said their thinking about the meaning of abortion changed on the job. Before coming to work at the Center, many of the women had accompanied friends during abortions or had had abortions themselves, but they described this level of personal contact with abortion as quite different from the intimacy with abortion they gained as Center employees. In short, doing abortion work entails rethinking rhetoric. Many staff members described moving beyond pro-choice language in their thinking and working to combat the rhetoric of anti-abortionists. In their quest to integrate disparate emotions about late abortions, they attempted to decode the rhetorical gulfs between the rights/requirements, woman/mother, and fetus/baby dichotomies on which the opposing languages of anti-abortionists and pro-choice activists rely. They sought a woman-centered philosophical standpoint—one that would rebut what they saw as the denial of "truths" in anti-abortion rhetoric and that would also challenge the glossing over of abortion that pro-choice language promotes.

In this chapter, I describe how Center women did their work and examine the ways in which they constructed an empirically based feminist epistemological framework for thinking about abortion. I draw on Center women's descriptions of abortion work and on how the practices at the Center compared with abortion work I had observed prior to my fieldwork as a counselor in a much more mainstream clinic in the mid-1980s. The two clinics, I discovered, were worlds apart.

Over the course of my fieldwork at the Center, I observed approximately thirty abortions. Staff members at first asked clients whether it was all right if I came in during their abortions, usually explaining that I was a sociologist studying the Center. Most clients quickly assented to my presence. As time passed, staff members tended to announce my inclusion rather than asking clients whether it was all right with them. The first time Rae did this, I insisted that she ask the next client. She told me, "Come on—it's like you work here!" and went on to inform the next client, "Wendy works here too. She's observing." Over the course of my fieldwork, I watched abortions from all angles, but I most often stood next to the clients. Positioned there, I could assist health workers a little bit by holding clients' hands or talking to them when health workers became involved in other tasks.

During 1991, the Center gradually increased the length of gestation during which its doctors would perform abortions from twenty-one to twenty-six weeks. Gestational measurements, as is standard medical practice, were taken from the beginning of a client's most recent menstrual cycle, not from the point of fertilization that truly marks the beginning of pregnancy. (In medical lingo, a pregnancy of twenty-one weeks' gestation is referred to as "twenty-one weeks LMP" [last menstrual period].) These measurements were verified by sonogram for all clients having second-trimester abortions. For more advanced pregnancies, staff members determined the length of gestation by measuring the biparetal diameter (BPD), the width of the fetal head, and did not rely on a client's report of her last period or the date of conception. (The BPD increases by two to three points, or tenths of a centimeter, per week of pregnancy after the first trimester.)

By the time I began my fieldwork in March 1992, abortions up to twenty-six weeks had been performed at the Center for several months. I had heard quite a lot about these late abortions from the staff members I interviewed, and I was eager to observe this work and to meet Roger Alton, the physician who performed all the abortions after twenty-one weeks. Staff members were generally pleased with the way administrators had instituted the change. They cited the raising of the gestational limit as an example of feminist, though not participatory, institutional decision making. Staff members viewed the extension of abortion services as a conscious decision administrators made to benefit clients rather than an attempt to increase revenues. They also praised administrators for their gradual method of implementation, which they saw as evidence that the administrators were attuned to workers' concerns about staffing later abortions.

> TOBY: We felt like we had a lot more input. . . . Ultimately, I think we felt it was for the good of women. . . . There wasn't any other motive. [We felt] that doing this, although it would be hard for us, would be really good for women. And that's why I think people adjusted to it a lot better.

> MIRA: We took that increase in gestation very slowly. . . . Roger was ready to go. . . . The management wanted to, too, because . . . we were so excited that women who were twenty-six weeks could get an abortion at our clinic and not have to go to Pavillion and do a saline induction. . . . But we were also extremely sensitive to what that increase in gestation was going to do to us as human beings. . . . We're just not hardened to the fact that abortion is hard. The women . . . are going to be in more pain. . . . The abortions are going to be longer. The assistant is going to have to watch a much, you know, a further abortion. And the sterile-room woman has to handle that tissue. And there's a marked difference between twenty-six weeks and twenty-one weeks in terms of fetal development. . . . They would go up one BPD point a week, which is nothing [a very small change in fetal size]. . . . We had [meetings] where we talked about our feelings. . . . We talked about the ambivalence about wanting to provide this service and being really excited about it and being really nervous about handling that tissue.

> HANNAH: I think he [Roger] does, you know, a great job. So I felt like the women were getting a good procedure. And then I also feel . . . thank God that we're doing this! Because it's either us or Pavillion. So I'm glad we're doing it. I think it's put a lot of stress on everybody because clinics are longer. . . . More complications,

you know, can happen. The woman's bleeding longer. The woman might be having a little bit more pain. . . . That's hard too.

In Toby's evaluation, administrators acted altruistically. All three women described the staff as altruistic as well, saying in so many words, We may not always like what we have to do, but we will do it anyway because we believe in the larger good these abortions will bring to the women we serve. Hannah and Mira detailed the drawbacks of the more invasive abortion procedure, while emphasizing the quality of care women would enjoy at the Center. Hannah even characterized these later abortions at the Center as a godsend to clients. (Lois was the only worker who criticized the administration for not accommodating those who had difficulty staffing late abortions. "It's pretty much said that if you are uncomfortable about it, tough shit," she said. Lois did not suggest another course of action the administrators might take.)

Like Mira and Hannah, many staff members declared their pleasure that women could have late second-trimester abortions at the Center instead of at Pavillion. Pavillion performed induction abortions, which entail actual labor for the aborting woman; it also used general anesthesia, which made its procedures riskier. Staff members called Pavillion a "mill" that was far more dedicated to profits than clients.

Workers said they enjoyed the opportunity the two-day procedure provided them to forge closer bonds with clients. Ilene said:

I like that we go up to twenty-six weeks. For a while it kind of gave me some things to learn. . . . Plus it gives a whole new dimension to working with those women who come for later abortions. It's, like, great because they almost can't have an abortion. They're almost about to have a baby, and they don't want to. And they're real appreciative. And they, more than anybody, appreciate how we try and make it better for them and how we try and be with them, and the comfort we try and give them. . . . That feels good. . . . It's nice to be with them for two days.

As Ilene described, many clients felt rescued at the last minute from pregnancies they did not want to continue; they considered Center women their benefactors. Workers thrived on clients' gratitude. They also admired clients for the effort they put into arranging second-trimester abortions and the fortitude they demonstrated during their abortions. Ilene expressed her awe at how brave some clients were. "The courage that these women show is amazing. I couldn't be that courageous, even with somebody standing there helping me."

Staff members often told me that until they came to work at the Center, they thought about abortion primarily in terms of women's need to end unwanted pregnancies. Then, as they worked as assistants or did sterile-room work, they came to see abortion as it happened from the point of view of practitioners, whose concerns also involved the substances evacuated from the womb—fetal tissue, amniotic fluid, blood. Health workers often described second-trimester abortions or sterile-room work as troubling or unpleasant and, in some cases, as disgusting or abhorrent. But as their narratives show, all health workers tried to keep women central, even as they attended to abortion's other angles. They replaced the pro-choice everywoman whose right to choose justifies abortion with real women whose life situations often made other "choices" look unimaginable. They fashioned a feminist philosophy on abortion that they found more meaningful than the pro-choice rhetoric they knew before.

Abortion Routines

The Center offered a broad range of services to clients (including routine care, treatment of sexually transmitted diseases, AIDS testing, and donor insemination) yet staff members devoted most of their energy and labor to abortion work—including preliminaries, such as giving the results of pregnancy tests to clients and taking phone calls, where they described abortion procedures, discussed prices, and scheduled abortions. For women with annual incomes under $50,000 or without insurance, first-trimester abortions (between six and twelve weeks LMP) cost $315 at the Center during the week and $340 on Saturday. The cost rose with each subsequent week after the first trimester. At sixteen weeks, an abortion cost $550; at twenty weeks, $900; and it cost $2,350 for a twenty-six-week abortion. According to Center policy, prices were determined by a sliding scale; women who earned over $50,000 a year or whose insurance covered abortion were charged the "real fees," which, according to administrators, reflected the actual cost of performing abortions.[1] The Center offered discounts to clients with Medicaid (which did not cover abortion in the state where the Center is located); these clients paid $265 for a first-trimester abortion, $500 for a sixteen-week abortion, $800 for a twenty-week abortion, and $2,150 for a twenty-six-week abortion. Several abortions each month were subsidized by a local (not Center-based) WIN (Women in Need) fund. Occasionally, health workers negotiated reduced rates for individual women with the Center's administrators and doctors. Since I did my fieldwork, this practice has been essentially eliminated.[2]

Sarina, the staff physician, performed all the first-trimester abortions and many of the second-trimester abortions through sixteen weeks LMP; the

Center paid several other doctors per procedure to perform the rest of the second-trimester abortions. Roger did all the abortions that required two days (the first for laminaria insertion and digoxin injection; the second for the abortion).

At the clinic where I had worked in the mid-1980s, we counseled each client individually; each counselor recited the same litany anywhere from four to a dozen times each day. In contrast, at the Center, as Mira said, "We don't counsel women here"; private consultations were the exception rather than the norm. Center health workers considered themselves educators rather than counselors—they gave information about abortion and instructions about what to expect afterward. Clients met in groups with one health worker before their abortions.[3]

During the course of my fieldwork, I observed about a dozen groups led by several different health workers. They each covered the same material in roughly the same order, working from the same script, which supervisors designed to ensure that everyone offered the same information. During first-trimester abortion clinics, health workers ran groups for women having abortions for the first time and abridged groups for women who had had abortions before. During second-trimester clinics, a health worker ran a group on laminaria insertion ("lam") and digoxin injection, both of which occurred the day prior to the abortion, and then another group in which she (or another health worker) focused specifically on the abortion. In all groups clients and health worker sat in a circle. All the health workers I observed as group leaders encouraged clients to ask questions and solicited their responses to the information presented.

During group meetings, health workers displayed a small three-dimensional pelvic model, along with various instruments that the nurses or physician would use. They showed laminaria that the nurses used to dilate clients' cervices (in second-trimester-abortion groups); they showed the stabilizer, dilators, forceps (forceps are only used during second-trimester procedures), and cannulae (plastic tubes) that doctors used. They did not show the needles used to inject the cervical anesthetic or, in the case of second-trimester abortions, especially large dilators or forceps or the needles used to inject digoxin into women's uteri.

After describing the abortion procedure clients would have (vacuum aspiration in the case of first-trimester abortions or dilation and evacuation [D & E] for second-trimester abortions), health workers listed the sedatives available during abortions. Almost every client chose a sedative, perhaps in part because health workers presented these options so matter of factly. Next, health workers read through the risks on the authorization-and-informed-consent form they passed out to the group.[4] They advised clients about how to take care of themselves after their abortions and emphasized that fever, excessive bleeding, and strong cramping were signs that something could be wrong (an incomplete abortion or infection); they told clients how to use the twenty-four-hour hotline. While clients read through and initialed the consent form item by item, the health worker circled the room (sometimes assisted by another health worker, if someone was available), checking each woman's blood pressure and pulse and giving her a thermometer to take her own temperature.

During abortion clinics, two health workers staffed separate exam rooms. Each health worker (whether she was advocating during first-trimester abortions or health-working during second-trimester abortions) accompanied clients individually from the room where the group session was conducted into the exam room where the abortion would be performed. She instructed each client to undress from the waist down and gave her a paper drape. While the client undressed and climbed onto the examination table, the health worker looked over her chart and began talking casually with her in an effort to put her at ease.

In the New York clinic where I worked, I had accompanied roughly a dozen clients during their first-trimester abortions. Unlike the situation at the Center, nonmedical staff at that clinic were discouraged from attending abortions. (Nor were clients allowed to bring anyone with them; at the Center, a woman could bring one person with her to a first-trimester abortion and, in special circumstances, to a later abortion.[5]) At the New York clinic, counselors who wanted to—and most did not—could accompany clients who were especially nervous or afraid about their abortions, but most counselors referred clients whom they felt were very apprehensive or anxious to other clinics where first-trimester abortions were available under general anesthesia (see Simonds 1991). Also at that clinic, no staff members had a role equivalent to that of the health workers at the Center. Instead, the doctor's assistant, positioned next to the doctor at the woman's crotch, gave instructions to a client throughout her abortion. She told the client what to do, giving directions like "put your feet in the stirrups," "slide down on the table," but she did not attend to the client's emotional needs, did not hold her hand, and did not tell her what the doctor was doing, as Center health workers did.

In all the abortions I observed at the New York clinic, the clients appeared to experience a great deal of pain. At the Center, all the women I observed during first-trimester abortion procedures seemed to experience only mild discomfort. After observing a first-trimester abortion at the Center for the first time, I wrote in my field notes: "I don't know if it's the whole style of the experience, the fact that they give sedatives to clients who want them, or what, but this abortion seemed like no big deal at all. The woman was quite calm the whole time, and never appeared to be uptight or suffering." Many clients at the New York clinic told me that their abortions were worse than they had expected; I never heard a client speak this way at the Center.

In a typical first-trimester abortion, Sarina first performed a pelvic exam in order to estimate the length of gestation and to feel the position of the uterus. If she could not judge the length of gestation precisely enough, a health worker performed a sonogram. Sarina might need to confirm the length of gestation with a sonogram when a client was under six weeks pregnant or when she was uncertain about whether a pregnancy was at the end of the first or beginning of the second trimester. Staff did sonograms on all clients having second-trimester abortions in order to facilitate precise measurement of the BPD (on which the details of the abortion procedure and the fee scale relied).

After the pelvic exam (and, if necessary, the sonogram), Sarina swabbed the cervix with an antiseptic (Betadine) and injected an anesthetic (Xylocaine) into the cervix. Next she attached a stabilizer to keep the cervix immobile and began to widen the opening of the cervix, the os, with metal dilators. She then inserted a cannula and signaled the health worker to step on a pedal that turned on the aspirator. While the machine was on, Sarina swept the cannula gently through the uterus, switching to a narrower cannula in order to navigate more easily as the uterus began to contract. Throughout, the health worker described Sarina's actions and reminded the client to take long, slow, deep breaths. When Sarina finished, the health worker turned the machine off with the foot pedal. Sarina took the covered jar containing the fetal tissue and the cannulae to the sterile room so that the health worker assigned to sterile-room duty could evaluate the tissue before the client left the Center. (Occasionally, health workers discovered too little fetal tissue; in such cases, Sarina reaspirated.) The health worker helped the client down from the table, gave her a maxi-pad, waited while she dressed, and brought her into the aftercare room, where she rested until her bleeding and cramping had lessened. (First-trimester-abortion clients could leave after as little as fifteen minutes.)

Clients all received literature reiterating postabortion care instructions, including information about what to do in case of an emergency. All clients were given antibiotics to take after their abortions, along with a prescription for Methergine, a drug that causes uterine contractions, which clients could take if they experienced heavy bleeding. Staff members advised clients to fill the prescription but not to take the Methergine without talking to someone from the Center first. The aftercare nurse checked to ensure that clients' vital signs were normal before they left the Center.

Sarina told me that she liked doing first-trimester abortions because they were not very invasive procedures. She said that early abortions were more complex than most people recognize though. She described her work as an activity that allowed her to develop adroitness:

> I think actually performing an abortion is a very refined technical skill; it's a very delicate skill—particularly the very early procedures. A lot of people will say, you know, "Oh, those early procedures are a real piece of cake." They're not always a real piece of cake! I think you learn to have an enormous amount of respect for the uterus when you begin to do this because every woman is different. There'll be days or weeks when, you know, everything just goes picture perfectly; you know, you just dilate the cervix and sweep the cannula in and turn on the machine and whoo, you know, it's over in about ten seconds. But sometimes it takes a lot of patience. It takes knowing when to stop inserting instruments, knowing how far to push the cannula and no farther.

Performing abortion, as Sarina described it, involved an interaction between a physician and various uteri: when Sarina said that "every woman is different," she clearly meant that every woman's *uterus* is unique.

Sarina continued to talk about abortion as a purely medical event when she further elaborated on what she enjoyed about her work:

> The thing I like about the procedure is that . . . when you feel like you are indeed a talented abortionist, you can get through the difficult cases. . . . It's getting through a difficult canal; it is dealing with a fibroid in the uterus; knowing what to do if you have an infection on the cervix or if someone has put laminaria in there . . . when they really shouldn't have because the cervix was friable, then knowing how to do this with such delicate precision that you don't injure the cervix. Those kinds of things help me feel like I have really mastered something that I'm very proud of. . . . In the past year, I've probably done close to five thousand procedures, which is more than many people do in ten years of work.

Sarina liked honing her skillful use of equipment to accomplish the emptying of the uterus as smoothly and easily as possible. And abortion, for any abortionist, is obviously a technical accomplishment. I do not mean to imply that Sarina's view makes no sense but want to point out that it is limited. Though she did not talk much about interacting with clients, Sarina did tell me that she profoundly disliked causing them pain. She took pride in being an abortionist; she believed the act of abortion, in and of itself, demonstrated her commitment to helping women.

Health workers' talk, in contrast to Sarina's, centered explicitly on the psychic state of clients. They considered first-trimester abortions to be relatively easy work for them compared with second-trimester procedures. They said that clients having early abortions usually had resolved any emotional dilemmas by the time they arrived for their abortions. Health workers usually were able to manage clients' remaining anxieties routinely. First-trimester abortions were over quickly (usually taking less than five minutes), did not cause clients much pain, and were relatively neat because physicians would aspirate most of the blood and all of the fetal tissue into a covered glass jar. No one I spoke with at the Center described any part of first-trimester abortions as visually disturbing once she grew accustomed to seeing blood. Most health workers did not mind—and some enjoyed—the sterile-room work that accompanied first-trimester abortions. Janice said, "I think it's actually been good for me being in sterile room because now I see it and go, '*This* is what I was worried about?' It's like, I'm sorry, this is not a human being to me, and it never will be. . . . I'm glad that that's my realization." Like Janice, many health workers said first-trimester sterile-room work provided evidence that anti-abortion propaganda relies on deliberate misinformation.

Late-Abortion Work

As pregnancy progresses, though, sterile-room work often became difficult for health workers because fetal tissue looked increasingly "like a baby." Tanya said:

> Health-working, even under the best of circumstances, is a very emotional and stressful job. . . . Most of the time you're working abortions, and, you know, you're dealing with women who are in a real emotional situation. . . . And, as a health worker, you're kind of a sponge for that stress, and there's only so much of it you can take and be healthy. . . . You're going from dealing with people to dealing with what most people here at the Center consider a real hurdle, to do sterile room, because you have to deal with the actual abortion tissue. And for some people that's really hard. They can be abstractly in favor of abortion rights, but they sure don't want to see what an eighteen-week abortion looks like.

When they did sterile-room work and assisted the physician during late abortions, health workers faced what they knew anti-abortionists considered evidence against abortion. This confrontation impelled many workers to do "soul searching," assessing their responses to late abortions in light of their ideological standpoints and reevaluating their ideological standpoints in light of their responses.

69

Abortion clinics can contract sterile-room work with independent labs, but Center procedures included the examination of fetal tissue in keeping with its mission to ensure that clients would be well informed and well served. If sterile-room workers found any indication that an abortion might be incomplete, doctors could reaspirate the same day. Following first-trimester abortions, sterile-room workers strained the contents of the aspirator jar and cannulae to isolate the fetal tissue, which must include identifiable bits of sac and villi and must weigh at least sixteen grams. (The sac, or chorion, is the membrane surrounding the fetus; villi are hairlike projections from the sac.) After eight weeks' gestation, weight should increase according to the doctor's estimate of gestational length, and sterile-room workers looked for fetal parts. If they did not find evidence of a spine, a skull, and upper and lower extremities, the client was called back into an examination room for a reaspiration. After second-trimester abortions, sterile-room workers looked for the placenta (or bits of placenta) in addition to the other fetal parts. (As pregnancy advances, the sac develops into the placenta.) Sterile-room workers packaged the fetal tissue in plastic bags when they were finished examining it. The Center contracted with a funeral home for disposal (incineration) of the fetal tissue.

New health workers knew that more experienced co-workers often found tissue analysis after second-trimester abortions to be a trying task, and they frequently anticipated that part of their jobs with some trepidation. If doing abortion itself can be seen as "dirty work," sterile-room work is the dirtiest part. As Janice said, "I didn't know if I could handle looking at the tissue; that was like the big thing." When I interviewed her, Janice was in the process of training to do sterile-room work for second-trimester abortions; she had observed and helped more experienced health workers but had not yet done it alone. She discussed her feelings about learning this part of the job. "I'm still not there yet. I mean it's hard, really really hard." When I asked what made it hard, she replied:

It's just—I mean it looks like a baby. It *looks like* a baby. And especially if you get one that comes out, that's not piecemeal. And, you know, I saw this one, and it had its fingers in its mouth; . . . it makes me really sad that that had to happen, you know, but it doesn't change my mind. It's just hard. And it makes me just sort of stop and feel sad about it, the whole necessity of it. And also . . . it's very warm when it comes into the sterile room because it's been in the mother's stomach. It feels like flesh, you know. . . . And some people say they've had the fetus dreams, or whatever, which I've never had. I've always—was afraid I was going to have these, you know, floating fetuses in my dreams [laughing] or something, and I've never had them, so I think that's because I'm trying to deal with them when I'm awake.

Just as Janice worried that fetuses might invade her dreams, many other workers acknowledged that this work involved subjecting themselves to unpredictable, perhaps subliminal psychological reactions. I believe these reactions derive at least in part from anti-abortionists' success at spreading their rhetoric of fetal power and presence. (I shall return to this subject later in this chapter.)

Center workers recognized they had been conditioned to think of normal internal bodily workings and fluids as repulsive simply as a result of growing up in a culture that both mystifies and fears the body, cordons off bodily knowledge as the realm of medicine, and, in particular, denigrates women's bodies. Blood phobia might be exacerbated by workers' concerns about HIV and hepatitis infection. As Risa said, "Being in close contact with the tissue was my fear. . . . I don't like blood products. I'm blood paranoid."

Many Center women overcame this disgust as they grew accustomed to the work, though, and described ways in which late abortions might be appreciated as learning experiences:

> HANNAH: I'll tell you something that's really pretty is the amniotic fluid. One time I saw it. . . . [Roger] put the speculum in, and the amniotic fluid just burst. . . . It was like this beautiful gorgeous bubble, and it just looked so—like a crystal ball—but it was floating around, really pretty [laughing] at that point. And then it's like—all over the place.

> TANYA: I thought I would have a hard time with it, but actually I found . . . I was more fascinated than anything else. You know, you realize what your body can do, and to be able to, you know, figure out what's strictly from the pregnancy and what's, you know, endometrial, uterine tissue. I just thought that was really interesting, you know, in a self-help kind of way.

Workers were surprised and pleased when they discovered they could enjoy tasks they had expected to tolerate at best. Many realized they had the power to recontextualize their work; they could deliberately see late abortion as interesting rather than disgusting. They might not always be able to sustain this control: when the amniotic sac burst "all over the place," as Hannah described, it became a sticky mess for workers to clean up. Workers did not always become more comfortable with this work as they became accustomed to it. Diana told me, for instance, that she felt no qualms about sterile-room work during late abortions until one day when she was suddenly shocked by the sight of a fetus with hair:

> Sterile room is so fast-paced. And I'm a person who's really into learning. Like, I'm into the technical and not really into what's there. . . . And so, okay, now I've got the technical down, so now I can, like, get lax in my thought processes. You know, it becomes more robotic. And I think that what happened one day [was] I stepped back *inside* of myself, and I was just like, "Oh my God, what are you *doing?*" when I saw the hair. . . . I have been in sterile room since then, and it hasn't bothered me.

I noticed the range in attitudinal possibilities in my own reactions to what I saw. For example, when I originally observed first-trimester sterile-room work, I was startled by what seemed a surreal use of kitchen equipment (strainers and Pyrex dishes) to examine fetal tissue. I wrote in my field notes: "Lee and Janice said I should have been there earlier because they'd had a 'beautiful perfect sac.' Hard to imagine taking aesthetic pleasure in slimy blood-tinged goop." When I first watched a second-trimester abortion, I wrote, "It was quite disgusting-looking from my vantage point, this bloody gunk spilling out of her." But the longer my exposure, the more I, too, came to see the work as nuanced and fascinating rather than primarily strange or "disgusting-looking."

The procedures doctors used to perform second-trimester abortions at the Center varied considerably depending on length of gestation. As gestation progressed into the second trimester, clients had laminaria inserted into their cervices before their abortions. The number of laminaria inserted increased with the length of gestation; at sixteen weeks, a woman had about four inserted (in one session); at twenty-six weeks, she had about ten inserted (in two sessions separated by several hours). For clients having twenty-one- to twenty-six-week abortions, the insertion of laminaria in two separate sessions reduced the pain they would experience during the abortion. After I first observed a lam clinic, I wrote:

> I watched Vera, one of the nurses, insert laminaria into the cervices of two women very sure-handedly. It looked like it should hurt a lot, but neither one of the women reacted much at all. Vera told me that for the really late abortion clients, it hurts her to keep putting the lam in because she thinks it must feel horrible. She said she thinks, in those cases, the laminaria insertion is more painful than the abortion will be. As Vera was doing the insertion, Lois was telling the client step-by-step what would happen. Lois told me (later) that when she had her abortion at

twenty-four weeks, the lam insertion "hurt like hell," but that this perception of pain varies a lot among women and that having [had] a vaginal delivery makes it easier to take. I've never had such a clear view of a cervix before. The os seemed very easy to stretch, which Vera explained is because it becomes increasingly pliable as the pregnancy progresses. She was very quick; [she] told me that she's done as many as thirty-one insertions in one afternoon so she has to be quick.

For a woman who was between twenty-one and twenty-six weeks pregnant, the doctor injected digoxin into the fetal heart during her last visit prior to the abortion. (A client may make a total of three visits to the Center over the course of two days.[6]) The Center began including digoxin injection as part of second-trimester-abortion protocol when it began raising the gestational limit above twenty-one weeks (during the summer of 1991).

Celia detailed her apprehensions and ambivalence about using digoxin during an interview that took place just before it was incorporated into Center protocol:

It's going to be weird now because you're going to see the sono. You're going to see the heart beating—little hearts, you know—and then, all of a sudden, you're going to put this cardiac medicine in it to make it stop—to kill it. So you're going to see that exact moment when you kill the fetus. I won't kill it, the doctor will kill it. . . . And, I mean, it might be more humane . . . [If] the fetuses do feel something, why not kill it, you know, fast, [rather] than rip its leg off? I don't know if anybody's been this graphic with you. . . . It's just a harder reality check of what we're doing. . . . It's not really sympathy for a fetus. I don't know. It's just a really gut thing. . . . It's like rationally I know this is going to be much better because, God, you know, if it can make a twenty-three-week skull come out easier, you know, God bless this digoxin. To me it will be like a savior. You know, I really see it as like this *good* thing. These women aren't going to have to go to Pavillion and have these induction abortions.

Even as she announced her uneasiness, Celia wryly referred to the antis' fetishization of fetal hearts (as in the popular bumper sticker "abortion stops a beating heart"). This new procedure would be "gross," Celia imagined, but no worse than dismembering a fetus without "killing" it first. Celia did not venture to say whether she thought fetuses "feel" pain, a claim antis constantly make; nor did she dismiss this presumption. Ironically, she draws on the antis' own argument to defend the use of digoxin during abortion. Digoxin, she explained, would prevent fetuses from feeling pain, if they did feel pain. (It always struck me as a humorous semi-intentional parody of anti-abortionist linguistic strategies when staff members thanked God—as Hannah did earlier and Celia does here, calling digoxin a "savior," too—for the magnificence of Center abortions!)

I first observed digoxin injection while Hallie was health-working. She had told me in advance that she disliked this part of the abortion process a great deal and that it nauseated her. In my field notes, I wrote:

> I watched three instances of digoxin injection. I couldn't tell until the third one what was going on on the sonogram and never clearly made out the fetus, but Hallie told me what to look for to see the heart, which is what Roger aims for. One of the women was really scared—hates injections, hates bee stings, which is the analogy health workers use to let women know what the anesthesia will feel like. First Roger locates the approximate location of the fetal heart, makes an x with the sonogram jelly, turns off the machine, and injects the anesthesia. Then he takes a bigger sort of tube needle and puts that into the same spot where he injected the local, turns the sonogram back on and finds the heart, and then puts in the digoxin. The women are lying down and can't see the sonogram. The heart looks like a flashing light. The woman who was really frightened held my hand; Hallie had the job of holding the ultrasound device still on the woman's belly for Roger. Afterwards, when Roger had left, the woman said she felt the fetus moving around. She said, "This is what kills the baby, right?" and started to cry before either of us could answer. I guess she didn't expect an answer. She said she'd "done this before" but never this late and that she had had no idea "how far along" she was.

During the early part of the second trimester, up to about twenty weeks, the physician used a forceps briefly in addition to suction, and the abortion itself took only a moment or two longer than a first-trimester aspiration abortion. Later in the second trimester, though, because of the increase in fetal size, abortions required much more exertion on the part of the abortionist and could be quite painful for clients.[7] These abortions lasted about ten to fifteen minutes. Managing pain was a much greater challenge during second-trimester abortions than in first-trimester abortions both for clients and for the health workers helping them through their abortions.

Health workers tried to assess how women would do in advance, based on several criteria. They told me younger women usually had a harder time than

older women. They expected women who had given birth to hand
more easily than women who had not. And they gave special a............ ..
women who expressed their fear openly during group sessions or women who
had difficulty with the preparatory procedures (laminaria or digoxin). Finally,
they recognized that the way people handle stress and pain varies considerably. In this vein, I was told several times that one could not unfailingly predict
who would have a "bad time," especially because some women, when sedated,
lose the ability to maintain control over their responses. Consider the following examples from my field notes:

> I went in today during two late abortions; one was the worst I'd ever
> seen. But the first woman was the calmest I think. She talked with Roger
> about their mutual favorite football team nearly the whole way through
> and seemed not to notice anything was going on until he started to pull
> with the forceps. Then she did deep breathing and held our (mine and
> Julia's) hands.
>
> The second woman was Japanese and spoke very little English, and
> she had not brought anyone to translate. (The Center requires a woman
> who doesn't speak English to bring a translator only on the first day of
> D&E's, when informed-consent forms are explained and signed.) This
> woman actively *resisted*; I mean actively in terms of energy, not volition.
> She was very drugged up—Demerol and Valium on top of the Sub-
> limaze. She wouldn't keep her legs open and kept sliding up on the table.
> From the second Roger first *touched* her, she looked like she was in ag-
> ony.
>
> What happened was that three people held her down, basically. Julia
> and Toby held her legs apart, and Ilene, who was assisting, held her at
> the waist to keep her from sliding up. I stood at her side and tried to get
> her to do deep breathing, pretty ineffectually. It was horrible to watch,
> and Julia sputtered, during it, "This is so humiliating!" There was a river
> of amniotic fluid that Julia said later she felt on her foot and that I
> pointed out to Toby just in time for her to move her foot out of the flow.
> Roger looked very annoyed during the whole thing. Toby told me later
> that when Julia was first encouraging the woman to take deep breaths,
> Roger said, "This will make her breathe!" and slid in the speculum
> roughly. I had thought of him as very compassionate but apparently not
> when things don't go well. I wonder what that woman was thinking
> during the whole thing. Once in the aftercare room, she immediately fell
> asleep.
>
> When it was over, Toby and Julia told me they felt horrible participat-
> ing in her abortion, holding her down. They said there is no other

recourse, once the cervix is dilated, and this kind of awful abortion rarely happens, but it does happen. They said she had been fine during the lam insertions yesterday and that she clearly wanted the abortion then. Roger said to me, "Well, I guess it's good for you to see the difficult ones as well as the easy ones." I said that it must be very frightening to not understand what's going on or what people are saying during one's abortion. He agreed, and I wondered how he could have made such a cruel remark earlier. But I suppose his job becomes a matter of negotiating a sea of potentially uncompliant crotch-bearers ("difficult ones"). On the other hand (again), he knows that the danger of a perforation increases substantially when a woman resists by moving around a lot.

If Toby heard Roger correctly, this abortion reads like a rape scene. Even if this remark was merely a lapse in the kindness I saw Roger extend to clients, it illustrates how vulnerable women are as clients. Medical workers may, at the very least, not respect clients and, at worst, may abuse their power and victimize clients. Whatever the situation, doctors have ultimate control over the tenor of our interactions with them. The consumer rhetoric of the women's health movement has little power once individual doctors are in rooms with individual clients, especially when those clients badly need the services doctors provide.

Most of the time, because Center workers were so successful at achieving good rapport with clients, it did not appear that their jobs involved manipulating women into compliance as in the abortion I describe above. But all workers who provide a service manage clients so that they will behave in organizationally approved ways (see, for example, Leidner 1993 and Lipsky 1980). The Center could not opt out of performing an abortion once a client had laminaria inserted and a digoxin injection, unless the physician wanted to transfer a client to a hospital for an abortion under general anesthesia. Such a move would involve complex logistical arrangements and would be quite costly for the client (beyond the amount already paid to the Center). During my association with the Center, I never heard of such a case; clients went to the hospital only if something went wrong, such as a uterine perforation.[8] If a client lost control (as in the situation described above), Roger simply worked as quickly as he could to finish the abortion since an abortion must occur.

Iconography, Ideology, and Identification

Beginning with the first interviews I conducted in 1990, staff members told me about their problematic responses to abortion work. Early on, my sense was that several women hesitantly *confessed* to me their unease over staffing late abortions or doing sterile-room work in a way that indicated they would not openly say such things on the job. Echoing Celia's words, "I don't know if anybody's been this graphic with you," many women spoke about the difficult or disgusting aspects of abortion as if they each thought they were revealing something clandestine to me for the first time. However, when I began my ethnographic work at the Center in 1992, I found that workers' perceptions of abortion were not kept secret at all. Health workers spoke openly about their responses to late abortions and sterile-room work. I believe the reticence I first encountered was a result of Center women's uneasiness about discussing this issue with an outsider. Uncomfortable responses to aborted fetuses are, after all, what anti-abortion activists hope for and seek to encourage in their proselytizing. Center workers did not want to risk being misunderstood.

Though their talk about what abortions looked like sounded, at times, similar to anti-abortionists' portrayal of abortions, Center workers' ideological standpoint was dramatically opposed to that of the antis. Rosalind Petchesky describes anti-abortion tactics "used to convey the idea that the fetus is literally a baby from the moment of conception":

(1) photographs of fetuses at different stages of development, revealing recognizable physiological features; (2) photographs of aborted (bloody, gory) fetuses, particularly those aborted late; (3) clinical descriptions of fetal development, with special emphasis on the formation of heartbeat, fingerprints, fingers, and toes; (4) juxtaposition or alternation of pictures of fetuses with pictures of live babies, reinforcing the idea of their identity; and (5) the constant use of language referring to fetuses as "babies," "children" or "unborn children." (1984: 334–335)

Antis believe that once they show people what abortion "is," they will gain converts to their cause; thus antis strive to persuade the public to think about abortion in their terms. Faye Ginsburg writes, "A popular quip summarizes this position: 'If there were windows on a pregnant woman's stomach, there would be no more abortions'" (1989: 104). Center women were disdainful of the antis' literature; they found its rhetoric both offensive and comical.

The anti-abortion pamphlets I collected when I escorted clients at the Center all present women as negligible but pregnancy as imperative. Indeed, the pamphlets insist that the fetus be seen as the central character in the story of pregnancy and that it be considered fully human. Women exist in this literature only in our relationships to fetuses; if we are pregnant, we are good if we accept that we are mothers, and we are errant or sinful if we do not. For example, in a pamphlet entitled *Did You Know* (n.p., n.d.), this text appeared next to a photo of a hand-held fetus:

Did You Know . . .
This is how big you were when you were only 11 weeks old. From then on you breathed (fluid), swallowed, digested, urinated, and had bowel movements, slept, dreamed, and awakened, tasted, felt pain from touch and heat, reacted to light and noise, and were able to learn things.

In anti-abortion lingo, aborting women are simply murderers. (We may be forgiven if we recant and then we can join the organization Women Exploited by Abortion and pass out literature ourselves.) Another pamphlet queries, "Is it really necessary to kill your baby in order to solve the problems caused by your pregnancy?" (*You Have a Right to Know*, n.p., n.d.) And, in *Did You Know*, next to a black-and-white shot of several baby-sized (alleged) abortuses in a garbage bag, captioned "Human Garbage," there is a little poem:

> Did you "come from" a human baby?
> No! You once were a baby.
> Did you "come from" a human fetus?
> No! You once were a fetus.
> Did you come from a fertilized ovum?
> No! You once were a fertilized ovum.
> A fertilized ovum? Yes! You were then
> everything you are today.
> Nothing has been added to the
> fertilized ovum who you once
> were except nutrition.

Look inside the womb (only), anti-abortionists plead, and you will see everything you need to see to convince you that abortion is evil. "Nothing has been added . . . except nutrition."

Center women saw their provision of information, and their approach to abortion, as directly opposing the antis' rhetoric. Center workers *did* see into the womb; they also saw what emerges from it during abortion. And they did not, as their narratives continually attest, abandon ship; they did, however, get a little seasick at times. They did not want their descriptions to be confused with anti-abortion rhetoric, but they realized that the collective consciousness surrounding abortion in American culture has been forged by the anti-abortionists' vehement attempts to frame the "debate" by claiming certain language as their territory, making talk about and images of blood and abortuses their specialty.

Because of the popularization of medical technology such as sonograms, the antis have had a window to the womb opened up for their viewing pleasure. Though they focus on the interior of women's bodies, it is as though we have disappeared—or rather, that they have made us disappear.[9] Celia said, "A lot of it is the politics around ultrasound, I think. That, I mean, maybe that's why some of the abortion stuff has changed, that now you can see that it's a fetus and it looks like a baby, and it sucks its thumb, and it, you know, kicks around, just like newborns do; and so it's like we can personify this fetus as opposed to, like, relating to this woman. This fetus has become God. And once it's born, of course, it's not."

Center women stated that the antis' "pro-life" stance dissipates after birth; antis do not care about the well-being of children or adult women. Most staff members thus doubted antis' sincerity, yet saw that the antis had gained a great deal of credibility for their depictions of fetuses and pregnant women. In the state in which the Center is located, a "certificate of fetal death" was once filled out for each abortion; though the form had been amended to a "certificate of abortion," staff members said that state agency workers still referred to the form as a "death certificate."[10] Workers saw this practice as a potent reminder that legal abortion always stands on shaky ground. Petchesky writes, "The 'public' presentation of the fetus has become ubiquitous; its disembodied form, now propped up by medical authority and technical rationality, permeates mass culture. We are all, on some level, susceptible to its coded meanings" (1987: 281).

Mira talked at length about the danger implicit in honestly discussing late abortions:

I feel some sadness [about second-trimester abortions]. . . . And I think part of the problem is that we don't talk about that. . . . We don't talk about it as much as we think about it. . . . There's part of me that's nervous even now; I mean I can feel my blood pressure and my pulse go up talking to you about this—because there's always that fear that somebody will hear it. That you'll print it and somebody will read it. And an anti will get a hold of it. And that—do you see what I'm saying?—that somehow your pro-choice stance is compromised by saying the word "baby." . . . We don't allow ourselves to say or think that word. . . .

When a woman says, you know, "Does the baby go through there?", we just, you know, alarms go off, and, "Oh my God, is she ambivalent?" And, "Someone needs to . . . talk to her!" And . . . it's like *Yes!* Celia's saying, you answer that woman, '*Yes,* the baby goes through that tube.'" We've been trained to say, "Yes, the tissue goes—" You know what I mean? It's using this language that's in complete denial of the fact that to this woman "baby" doesn't have to mean that she's ambivalent. It can mean that that's the word that she knows. . . . We've *lost* that. It's something that we've had to give up because the antis have claimed that word. It's kind of like the word "God." [In] liberal religious communities, so many people are freaked out by that word "God" because, you know, the Fundies [Fundamentalist Christians] have taken that word and defined it. So it's very hard to claim it as yours and redefine it without having all the emotional red flags and alarm bells go off every time you hear it.

Antis have created a baby-centered rhetoric that robs pro-choice activists of untainted language to use to describe abortion. If you talk about the fetus as a baby, Mira explains, you sound like an anti. If you talk about God, you may be mistaken for a "Fundie."

Pro-choice activists have generally striven to separate our language from the antis', utilizing medicalized or sanitized words, as if they would neutralize the antis' efforts: Center staff members commonly said "the pregnancy," "the tissue," "the products of conception." "Fetal tissue" was the most explicit term I heard health workers use with clients. In Carole Joffe's ethnographic work at an abortion clinic that performed first-trimester abortions, she found that: "the most interesting problem was how to refer to the product of the abortion. Although it was acknowledged that many clients would refer to this as the 'baby,' or the 'pregnancy,' new counselors were, not surprisingly, urged not to use these charged terms, but instead to use the more neutral, though admittedly more awkward, 'product of conception' or 'tissue' " (1986: 94).

When clients used the term *baby* at the Center, I did not hear staff members contradict them, nor did they ever initiate a discussion about the gap in language. I sensed that no matter how straightforward Center women were with me or with each other about resisting the language barriers erected by antis, they seemed uneasy when clients used tainted words. I found this uneasiness to be contagious; for instance, Hallie and I were silent when the client asked us whether digoxin was what "killed the baby." Center workers found themselves in an awkward position. How would one credit the client's view of the situation while also ensuring that one did not exacerbate guilt feelings she might have? Could the client know that she was speaking the language crafted by anti-abortionists? How might feminists reappropriate tainted language?

Staff members might feel that the clarity of their own views about abortion had become uncomfortably muddled because they lacked a way of talking about what they saw that was distinct from anti-abortionists' rhetoric. Carrie described how her exposure to late abortions shook up her pro-choice ideology:

Seeing the fetal tissue and seeing the blood and cleaning up can be kind of unsettling, especially seeing larger fetal tissue. At nine weeks . . . you start seeing fetal parts. And by the second trimester it's, you know, it's a baby, and by eighteen weeks it's definitely a baby. And by like, you know, . . . twenty-two weeks, you go in and you watch someone do a sonogram, and you're like, "*Oh my.*" There it is just moving, moving around. And it's really hard because I always thought of abortion in terms of *just* the woman, *just* her body. . . . It doesn't matter *what* is inside her; . . . it's her body and she has a choice to make whatever decision. And I never even *allowed* myself to think, you know, isn't it a shame that there's something alive inside her that's not going to be alive anymore if she has an abortion? Because somehow I had to make it black and white. Abortion isn't okay unless it's *completely* okay and there's nothing to be sad about. And it's weird because it *is* something alive, and if you have an abortion at any point, it's something alive that's not going to be alive anymore. And it's not the same kind of living being like it's someone who's already born, and breathing their own air, and eating on their own, and not inside someone else's body.

Carrie said she resolved her doubts by "allowing myself to feel both ways." Abortion may be "ending something . . . that is alive that I don't believe is really a human being yet," and participating in that ending might feel sad or strange. Carrie realized that women having late abortions experienced them as necessary acts.

Center women wished there were a way to turn anti-abortion language on its head, to reapropriate words like *baby* so that each pro-choice woman could fully express her own view of abortion. Such language might also defuse the potency of antis' framing of the situation in the way that gay and lesbian activists have successfully appropriated the terms *queer* and *dyke*. *Baby* was never used by antis as an epithet though; it is both an honorific term used to venerate the fetus and an accusation leveled at anyone who supports or has abortions. Because the anti-abortionists have been so successful in stigmatizing the act of abortion, Center women found it hard to imagine that a new way of talking about abortion could take hold. People may talk about abortion as a disembodied political or moral dilemma, but they seldom discuss *having* actual abortions. Greta gave an example of how an acquaintance responded to her own forthrightness about abortion:

I was at a party once, and . . . one of my friends who's pregnant and having a baby . . . said something like, "Well, now that I'm past the throw-up time, everything's going pretty good." And I said something like, "You know, that really sucks. When I've been pregnant, oh my God, I'm just so *blah*," and on and on, and one of the men just looked at me and said, "You don't have any kids." And I said, "Oh, well, I've had some abortions." And he was just like totally shocked. I mean, he just could not continue to have a relationship with me after that.

Antis have been successful at persuading people to view abortion as evidence of poor moral character and a shameful act, if not a sin. To talk about abortion in the way Greta describes, from the antis' ideological perspective, is to profane pregnancy. And because of the prevalence of the antis' ideological system, Greta's acquaintance need not have been an anti-abortion zealot to interpret her casual revelation as unseemly, unwomanly. Abortion may be confessed to in private but not mentioned in passing at a party.

Several Center women reported that the very fact they felt disturbed by abortions troubled them more than abortions themselves. Karen, a summer intern, talked about her original response to watching a twenty-one-week abortion:

> You're looking between the woman's legs; you're seeing, you know, what the doctor's doing. And it's what a lot of people would call kind of, I guess, gruesome—that's not really the word because—it's identifiable. I mean, when he . . . takes the forceps and pulls out a foot, you can see the foot, and my reaction—because I feel so strongly that women who *want* to have a twenty-one-week abortion should be able to have that—but I mean when I looked and was just like, you know, my first reaction was, you know, I was pretty horrified. And I immediately denied that, and said, you know, "No, that can't be my reaction. I'm here for the woman," and just really sort of squashed that down, that what I saw really freaked me out. And it stayed with me, you know, and really upset me. I mean, I'd be in the shower, you know, washing my feet, you know, and . . . the picture would come to me. . . . I just got to the point where . . . I just really needed to sit down and cry, and, like, *deal* with it. . . .
>
> What I've done now is given myself a little time away from it, sort of, I know this sounds weird, but [to] work up to . . . being able to see that. Because I don't really . . . feel that abortion is murder. And for the woman, it needs to be—it's her decision, you know, as to when the fetus is her child, is a baby. And, you know, if it was me who was that pregnant, then it would be my judgment call.

Karen began by distancing herself. "*You're* looking between the woman's legs; *you're* seeing . . . what the doctor's doing." And when she described her reaction, she spoke of "what *a lot of people* would call . . . gruesome" and then denied that depiction, choosing a neutral word, "identifiable." She interrupted her recollection to assert her political pro-choice stance. But as her narrative continued, she told me that she was "horrified," "freaked out," and "upset" by what she saw and that she had a hard time keeping these images (fetal feet, no less—one of the antis' all-time favorites) from popping into her mind when she was not at work.

For Karen, as for most health workers, it became imperative that she both acknowledge and analyze her reaction ("I just really needed to . . . *deal* with it"). After describing her negative response, she again counterposed her distaste for the abortion with pro-choice rhetoric, which ultimately won out because she deemed it more morally pertinent than her reaction to aborted fetuses. Many other staff members reinvested pro-choice rhetoric with moral potency by examining their ambivalences. They continued with their work even when they disliked parts of it because they cared more deeply about clients than fetuses. They believed everyone ought to see women's lives as more important than the loss of potential babies, while they also recognized that observing abortion might mean one sometimes experiences—and aborting women sometimes feel—a sense of loss or sadness.

Carrie said that sterile-room workers often sympathized with the fetus and that this identification was the root of troubling reactions to late abortion. "So by it looking like a baby, you're associating it with yourself because . . . you used to be a baby, you used to be a fetus." This link, Carrie concluded, dissolved when she thought about it rationally because "then you have to realize you used to be Jell-O," and it made no sense to identify with Jell-O.

Many health workers spoke about their attempts to resolve unsettling responses to abortion; in some cases, their talk revealed identification imbued with personal symbolism. Two narratives, those of Mira and Toby, are worth considering in detail: each woman described her difficulty dealing with late abortions as being embedded in her individual history. Each woman told of an association she imagined between herself as a fetus or baby and the late-term fetuses she saw during abortions—that is, she identified with fetuses at the point of abortion as opposed to identifying with them as potential fellow people (as anti-abortionists urge). The fetuses, then, became a reminder of the fragility of each woman's own mortality, reflected onto the past. Mira was adopted and realized that had circumstances been different—had abortion been legal—she might never have been born. Toby sometimes thought about the fact that she had been born prematurely when she handled fetuses from late abortions. Both women eventually recentered the women having abortions in order to achieve a sense of resolution.

MIRA: It's hard. There's a lot of days it's *really, really* hard. . . . I don't know what makes it so much harder at twenty-six weeks than at thirteen weeks. I don't know what makes handling that tissue harder. It's starting to look like a baby. That's hard. To know that she's not going to have that baby. For me, there's a lot of probably some hidden guilt that I'm not willing to look at about my adoption. That this could have been me. You know, had my natural mother had access to abortion, this easily could have been me. And when you're, you know, putting a fetus's feet in over its head in a baggie, there's just that brief moment of "this could have been me," which I fundamentally believe is okay. She should have had the right to choose that, and I, being a religious person, believe that things happen as they're supposed to and for a reason. And that I would have found, you know, this soul would have found another body to come to. I mean, I just have no problem about that. But there's some gut-level reaction when you're handling twenty-six-week tissue. . . . It's very easy with a thirteen-week fetus to dehumanize it. It's much more difficult when you see a twenty-six-week face.

TOBY: When I've been in sterile room all day [during second-trimester-abortion clinic]. . . it's hard.

W.S.: What makes it hard?

TOBY: I don't know. It's just bloodier, and grosser. . . . I think also just that the more you think about what it looks like, . . . it looks like a baby. And you know, sometimes . . . we go farther than we intend to,[11] and then that's really, really hard too because I was premature, and looking at this thing that could have been me, you know? And I try not to personalize it that much because it could have been me, and I would never know be-cause I wouldn't be here, but it's still hard to do. . . . I think I probably cope with it better than some other people who work here who talk about having nightmares and stuff. . . . In the first couple of months [when] I started working here, I'd have images of like, the face, you know, when it comes into sterile room. And I always turn it over. But I don't dream . . . about it. So I don't know if that makes me more re-pressed or better able to cope [laughing].

At first, both Mira and Toby claimed not to know what they found emo-tionally difficult about late abortions and then immediately tried to analyze their responses. Mira spoke of "hidden guilt" that she really did not hide, guilt over the fact that her birth mother did not have the option to abort. She presented an ironic twist on the anti-abortion stock chants that ask one to imagine the unfortunate decisions Einstein's and Beethoven's mothers might have made! The "logic" of antis' rhetoric rests on the assumption that abortion thwarts the possibility of realizing the genius inherent in particular fetuses. Mira reframed it: the lack of abortion thwarts women's potential for self-realization. Mira conflated her birth mother with "the woman" client and her uterine "self" with aborted fetuses. She said that her birth mother "should have had the right to choose" abortion and that "this soul would have found another body." She concluded by again asserting that her "gut-level reaction" could not be fully explained. In other words, she knew why abortion bothered her, but at the same time she could not fully articulate it. Many Center women described their visceral reactions as natural products of the "reality" of abortion, though their comments also clearly suggest that they actively shaped the ways in which they saw abortion.

Toby's narrative followed the same pattern as Mira's. She acknowledged identification and then told about the intellectual work necessary to negate the undesired emotional pull of the fetus. She said, "It could have been me, and I would never know." In other words, it would not matter to her because she would not exist (she would be less than Jell-O, in Carrie's terms). But like Mira, Toby still found fetal faces disturbing. A face made a fetus distinctive, different from other fetuses. A distinctive face allowed Toby and Mira to imagine an attendant, yet terminated, "self" more easily than they could with "younger" fetuses (which do not look particularly different from each other). Like Karen, Mira and Toby did not want to dwell on this identification; but they described it as productive and necessary to think it through as fully as possible.

When I asked Toby if her response made her question whether women should have late abortions, she said:

It *does*. And . . . it's one of the reasons that I'm glad that I do it 'cause it made me really think about whether I thought it was right. . . . I think every now and then I still feel, you know, some doubt. But I think for the most part I've solidified my belief that women have the right to have abortions . . . until *whenever*. . . . That was the thing, balancing the work that I did with women as a health worker and balancing what I saw in the sterile room. . . . And I think about, you know, having been a biology major and how gross it felt to cut up a rat or a, you know, or a frog. . . . And *that* was gross and disgusting. . . . And I think part of the sterile room is that same kind of grossness. . . . I think maybe most of the grossness is just that it's gross! [laughing]—not that it's human.

Toby gradually moved from linking aborted second-trimester fetuses to pree-mies (like she had been) to a more comfortable analogy in which she com-pared her work at the Center to dissecting a rat or a frog. Finally, she presented her troubled response to aborted fetuses as a natural reaction to the inexplicable "grossness" of innards and body parts, whatever the species.

In a *Harper's* piece on the clash between abortion providers and anti-abor-tionists in Milwaukee, Verlyn Klinkenborg (1995) describes his reaction to the limbs of a twelve-week aborted embryo as an almost primordial response, invoking—as Center women often did—a certain "reality" that would rise up and make itself known upon witnessing abortion. Though his language echoes Center women's comments, his response is also clearly influenced by his position as a man observing women's abortions:

> In that instant, I felt a profound and unmistakable kinship with the shape implied by the foot and hand in the tray, a kinship so strong that it was like the rolling of the sea under my feet. . . . I was surprised by the sense of loss I felt. . . . I suspect I was sad for myself, pathetic as that sounds, as though I were somehow looking at a homuncular version of myself scattered in that basin. . . . And in another instant that feeling of kinship was replaced by a visceral understanding of the enormous sym-bolic power of the human form. I realized that it's impossible to see the human form, no matter how minuscule or vestigial or fragmented, with-out seeing also the whole curve of human time, the trajectory of an entire life, without seeing also an autonomy that is only potential, utterly contingent in a fetus or an embryo, but that seems, because of the famil-iarity of the form itself, already fulfilled. . . . If I felt implicated by what I saw . . . it was because I found it so much easier to be moved by . . . a disembodied hand the size of a question mark . . . than it was to be moved by the woman from whom it had come, who was without work, without money, without education, without birth control. (47)

Unlike Klinkenborg, Center women did not have much difficulty moving from the imputed innocence of a fetus to feeling sympathy for an aborting woman. They also developed strategies that made their work easier and en-abled them to desensitize themselves to what disturbed them about it. The women described a variety of ways to handle fetal tissue that made the task less unsettling. Risa spoke about methods of arranging fetal parts: "I hate it when people put it together to look like a baby. I hate that. . . . I don't want to look like it when it's like that 'cause it's like a broken doll, and that grosses me out." She said she deliberately avoided using this "broken doll" configuration when she sorted through fetal tissue. Many health workers told me they "never look at the face" when processing tissue. Some health workers said they wore two pairs of gloves in order to create a barrier of rubber between their hands and the warmth of the tissue and that they tried to use tongs as often as possible, also to keep from having to touch the fetuses.

For several health workers, sterile-room work involved focused psychological preparation and the cultivation of an appropriate solemnity; they did not welcome shifts in scheduling that required them to do sterile-room work without advance notice. As with so much about their style of working, Center women's approach offers a criticism of the medical model. Medical training relies on the deliberate desanctification of the body and body parts. As Hafferty (1991) and Finkelstein (1986) write, the culture of the anatomy lab, from the outset, encourages a display of callousness and joking among medical students; this behavior functions to shield students from the emotional potency of the interior of bodies and the deadness of cadavers. (While Center workers did make jokes about fetuses, these jokes were always directed against the anti-abortionists and never occurred within the sterile room or involved actual fetuses or the handling of them; see Chapter Three.) As Barbara Katz Rothman points out, we know very little about emotional responses to jobs like sterile-room work, such as the medical analysis of amputated or extracted body parts. It may well be that Center workers' stance toward sterile-room work would resonate in other communities performing the dirty work that results from surgery in general (personal communication, 1994).

Self-Protection and Situational Ethics

Health workers strove to resolve their problematic reactions to late abortions by invoking the ideology of the feminist self-help movement: they deliberately focused on the women they knew they were helping and spoke repeatedly about their empathy with these women's experiences. However, a sense of distance often remained; as Greta said, for example, "My experience with women who are having D&E's is they're—I hate to generalize, but for the most part—most of them have lives that are so out of control and tornado-ish, and in a whirlwind. And they experience themselves as victims." Greta saw herself as working to assist women in taking control over this one crucial event in their lives. Once, while I was in the sterile room with Julia, she told me it helped her to cope with her work by distancing herself. "I remind myself that it's not me" having a late abortion, she said.

In an effort to protect themselves from emotional overload, Center women sometimes shielded themselves from the pain they saw in their clients' lives and in their abortion experiences by repressing or rejecting similarities between their lives and those of their clients.

NELL: I understand that these women's lives are even more complicated than [those of] women who are having seven-week abortions.
. . . The women are generally much more uneducated. They don't
have the education; they don't know what's going on. How the hell
are they supposed to come up with $800 in three days? . . . . I un-
derstand that, and that's what I have to . . . pull back to whenever I
go in and examine tissue . . . of a twenty-week fetus. Because it
looks like a baby. That's what it looks like to me. You've never seen
anything else that looks like that. The only other thing you've ever
seen is a baby. . . . You can see a face and hands and ears and eyes
and, you know, . . . feet and toes. . . . It bothered me real bad the
first time. . . . But, you know, I see the tissue, and then I look at the
lab sheet, and I go, "Oh, well that was Judy. Judy's fifteen years old
and raped by her father." And it makes it okay. But I don't think I
could do it, and I say that not being in that situation.

JANICE: I tend to be a little bit more compassionate with second-
trimester women just because in general you'll find that their situations are much rougher, you know. There are sometimes, I guess,
more compelling reasons that they're having this late abortion, like
they're poor and they had somebody who was going to help them
with this baby and they took off or whatever. And I mean, you've
seen the D&E clients, right? You know they're usually indigent and
also young and all sorts of stories. They always give you their story,
it seems like, much more than earlies do. And they're there longer,
and so you get to know 'em. . . . Plus, their abortion's much longer,
so you, you have to feel more of a bond with these people so you
can help them stay in control.

According to Nell and Janice, clients having later abortions were different
from those who had early abortions; their situations were more desperate and
their lives were "more complicated." Lacking education and financial resources, they might even lack a grasp on reality (in Nell's words, "they don't
know what's going on"). In these ways, some staff members perceived drastic
differences between themselves and their clients; staff members' lives might
be dramatic but not to the extent that they would feel completely powerless,
as they said many clients did.

Though staff members talked explicitly about cultivating a nonjudgmental
stance toward their clients (see Chapter One), both Nell and Janice indicated
that they regularly assessed clients' situations. Nell said that she focused on
clients' circumstances in order to quell her uneasiness about second-trimester-abortion sterile-room work, offering a hypothetical fifteen-year-old in-

cest victim as a prime example of just how justified such abortions were. Janice explained that clients having late abortions sometimes had "more compelling reasons" (presumably, more compelling reasons than those that clients offered for early abortions), implying that more compelling reasons for abortions *ought to* exist as pregnancy advanced.

Most Center women concurred that arranging a late abortion indicated that a woman had taken one step toward gaining control of her life, and they respected this decision because it showed a client had taken action. Diana told me, however, that "women should give a lot more—*a lot more*—thought to second-trimester abortions"; not every client she met gave the matter as much thought as Diana believed she should. But she also said, "I'd never stop anyone else because I really feel that's an individual decision."

Thus, though staff members talked about suspending judgment as a central element of feminist praxis and about defending any woman's right to a late abortion, they sometimes framed abortion as an act that required justification. I believe the intensity demanded of them when health-working, assisting, or working sterile room during second-trimester abortions led them to seek explanations for why clients would go through with such a painful procedure as well as why clients would put *them* through it. No matter how they evaluated particular clients' decisions, Center women unilaterally maintained that no matter how saddened or disturbed they might be by late abortion, their reactions did not impinge on their belief that late abortions should remain available. They might evaluate particular aborting women's decision making as less than ideal, but Center women maintained that the outcomes of these processes must be understood as unquestionable in the final analysis.

Lois found abortion increasingly disturbing as gestational age advanced and said that working sterile room during late abortions made her "extremely nauseated." (She frankly acknowledged that her responses were connected with discomfiting memories of her own second-trimester abortion.) Despite her negative comments, Lois also asserted that it was essential that late abortions remain available. She explained why she "hates" abortion:

LOIS: It's like a real challenge to get through the day.

W.S.: What makes you able to get through it?

LOIS: Because these women are going to have abortions whether we provide 'em or not. I hate abortions. . . . I had a lot of problems when we went to twenty-four weeks [twenty-six gestational weeks]. I was like really faced with the reality of what I did.

W.S.: . . . What is it that you hate?

LOIS: The destruction I can't deny. . . . I wish we lived in a world
where abortion didn't have to exist. I wish, you know, people had
day care. I wish everyone had enough money to eat and good birth
control that was a hundred percent effective. You know, but none of
that's going on.

Lois believed, in common with most of her co-workers, that no woman
frivolously decided on abortion. In more aggressive terms than her co-workers used, though, she declared that she hated abortion because, in her view,
"reality" indicts abortion as undeniable "destruction." Staff members often
asserted that abortion would remain a necessity as long as poverty existed and
as long as completely effective and harmless contraceptive technology was
not available. Several workers portrayed abortion as a last resort, a "choice"
no one wanted to make but one that was often unavoidable, necessary to
sustain a woman's psychic well-being or her basic day-to-day survival.

Lois's narrative exemplifies how pro-choice sentiments may themselves be
infused with traces of anti-abortion rhetoric. Most Center workers talked
about abortion as a positive act that might have attendant negative consequences, but Lois's characterization of abortion as absolute destruction
echoes a resurgent trend in pro-choice circles. In an article profiling Charlotte Taft, director of the Routh Street Clinic in Dallas, Sally Giddens (1990:
54) writes:

[Taft] faults herself and the movement for getting sidetracked again and
again into defending themselves and for failing to identify a vision that
people en masse would want to support.
   "Would you want to join on to 'every woman gets to have an abortion'? Right. Come with me to fight for this negative. Now I'm not
saying that abortion is negative. Abortion is like a tool along the way of a
woman being a human being—one of the tools—there are lots of them.
But because it's one of the tools that's so attacked, that's where we've
gone and spent our focus."

Lois, Taft, and other pro-choicers want to find a way out of being cast as
abortion proponents because they fear that there is no way of making abortion appealing to people; this desire for distance may become even more
pronounced among women like Lois, who find the sight of abortions so disturbing.

When I worked at the New York clinic, I attended a two-day workshop
about the stresses of doing abortion work. We were urged to discuss how
awkward it felt to be forced into the position of defending abortion when,

in the workshop leader's words, "nobody loves abortion." The longing for a utopian world without abortion that Lois expressed also got a lot of play at the workshop: we wished our own jobs did not exist. We believed that, ideally, every pregnancy would end in the birth of a wanted child. Such defensive fantasizing allows us to enumerate the reasons why abortion must remain available, but underneath it suggests that with the proper revision of social reality (such as the provision of affordable, accessible childcare; equal pay for women; the elimination of sexism, racism, and poverty; absolutely effective and safe birth-control methods; co-parenting; and so forth) we could ensure that all pregnant women would choose motherhood all the time. Yvette said, "This idea that abortion is . . . a necessary evil seems to be real predominant even among feminists." She saw Center workers as an exception to this trend, but clearly they did not remain immune to the increased defensiveness about abortion brought about by the anti-abortionists' successes during the Reagan-Bush years. Over the course of my association with Center women, the attitude that abortion was a depressing last resort seemed to grow more prevalent among workers. (This observation may reflect my greater familiarity with the women over time or may have to do with the addition of abortion up to twenty-six weeks to the Center's repertoire of services or both.)

Ilene told me that doing sonograms was "hard" for her at one time because she wished she was pregnant, but she did not feel ambivalent about participating in others' abortions because "it always comes down to the fact of living in the world and how it is to have to live in the world as a woman. You know, wanting a baby or not—all this is just—we have to live in the world every day 'til we die, so that's what makes abortion have to be." Risa said that while sterile-room work and late D&E's "sometimes make me feel sad . . . 'cause they [fetuses] look like little babies," she believed that abortion was better than carrying a pregnancy to term and having a child one did not want:

> My main concern is about the woman. What is she going to do? Have it, can't take care of it, beat it up, abuse it, flush it down the toilet, leave it in a gutter? . . . I think of the big picture, that this woman knows what she has to do. She knows that she can't take care of this baby. . . . I always just have to put it in the proper perspective, that, you know, it could have been here and still you would feel sad when you saw the news report about that baby on TV. And every week I have a specific [news] story that I can give reference to, you know.

These women asserted that because of the harshness of some women's life circumstances, abortion would always be the best course of action available to them. The bottom line, for Center women, was that no one ought to be forced to bear a child she does not want. Though workers might have wished to distance themselves from clients' distress or from the "whirlwind" lives they perceived clients as leading, they repeatedly expressed their understanding of every woman's struggle to have children only when she feels the time and circumstances are right.

Several workers said they would not have late abortions, but they usually qualified these assertions as probabilities rather than absolutes; as Nell said, "I say that not being in that situation." Janice's hesitant tone captures the women's awareness that decision making about abortion is unpredictable; she said, "I think, having seen that [late abortions], it would affect my—I think— I say this—it would affect my decision if *I* were twenty-two weeks, or something. . . . But I don't know, you know? That's the whole thing." Julia defended women's right to have late abortions but declared that she would not have one. Still, she spoke in tentative and uncertain terms:

> I think for any woman to have a D&E, whatever her reason is, for her it's a really good reason. I mean, I just couldn't imagine feeling movement and getting the digoxin and knowing that it is dead and it is inside my body. That's really hard to deal with. . . . I think that they should definitely, you know, be able to get those abortions. I just don't think for myself that I would choose to have a D&E. I don't think I would choose to have an abortion. It looks painful. . . . I think if I do get pregnant, I don't *have* to have an abortion. I don't live with my mama. I could probably swing it. It's hard, but I think I could. . . . I hope that I'll get pregnant when the time is right, and I won't have to think about that as an option.

Center workers believed that women's situations, rather than personalities or individual consciences, are the most crucial factors in procreative decision making. Thus, no one woman has absolute agency because none of us has complete control over her circumstances: that is, agency cannot be thought of as an abstract, individualistic characteristic. Petchesky writes that situational ethics are central to a feminist perspective on abortion: though we are "locked in the abstract moral language of 'prochoice' and 'privacy' derived from a male-dominated tradition of liberal individualism and property rights," we predicate our "practical morality about abortion in the real relations in which the necessity for abortion arises" (1984: 327).

Ultimately, for Center women, agency meant the ability to deal with one's situation productively. They thought pro-choice rhetoric inadequate because it portrayed "choice" in an uncontextualized fashion, and for most women opportunity to "choose" freely was severely constrained by social forces.

Tanya believed, along these lines, that abortion would not be a true choice until abortion and having a child cost the same amount of money—that is, women's options cannot be considered equal until their dollar values are equivalent:

> Here we are going around saying this is their choice. Well, in a certain sense it is, but in another way, it's like it's not a choice. I mean, when I had an abortion, yeah, that was what I *chose* to do, but I felt like . . . nothing else was realistic. I mean, nothing else would have worked out for me or for a potential baby. It would have been horrible for me; it also would have been horrible for any life I would have brought into this world. And I couldn't do that to a child, much less to myself. . . . It usually boils down to something along those lines. . . . It's not like most of us have that *Leave It to Beaver* June Cleaver option anymore of standing in the kitchen all day with our pearls and high heels on. I mean, we do have to go out and work, most of us.

We might choose to mother, Center women said, but rarely will we be able to choose *only* to mother and rarely will the conditions under which we mother be perfectly amenable to our mothering. Anti-abortionist ideology fails to acknowledge that the diverse constraints on women's lives have any relevance; to antis, pregnancy *means* motherhood. And, in its idealization of "choice," pro-choice ideology understates the extent to which women's lives are constrained.

Center staff often remarked that pro-choice rhetoric obscured abortion itself with innocuous words. They said it refused to acknowledge what abortions look like and what abortions feel like for the women who decide to have them. Basically, pro-choice language does not speak openly about abortion. Some Center women saw this avoidance as a conscious defense strategy on the part of pro-choice activists in response to the antis' tactics; others, such as Nell, considered it a failure to address the concerns of the general public:

> I think the pro-choice movement has neglected to deal with a lot of the stuff that goes on as far as, like they always say, "It's a choice." . . . Well, it's a hell of a lot more than a choice. It's, you know, one of the most difficult decisions a woman will ever make in her life. . . . It is a very fundamental decision that is going to affect the rest of your life. And I think the antis prey on that. . . . It can be a traumatic thing for a woman. I think the pro-choice movement has just neglected to deal with . . . a lot of the feelings that women actually have about abortion.

Nell indicted the benign neglect of this issue by the pro-choice movement for making aborting women vulnerable to the influence of anti-abortionists. Anti-abortionists have cornered the market on sentimentality with their manipulative imagery and rhetoric, and sentimentality appeals. Meanwhile, pro-choicers have cornered the market on political activism, painting abortion as a cut-and-dried, pragmatic symbol only and always of women's freedom (albeit not exuberant freedom, as in the depictions of abortion as a regrettable but necessary course of action).

Greta, too, called feminists' reticence about abortion dangerous; she believed that maintaining a veil of secrecy around abortion helped to fuel its stigmatization:

> We do everything that we can to retain confidentiality. We treat the woman like no one in her life knows that she's having an abortion. . . . And if they knew, we assume they would, like, totally ostracize her or kill her, you know. We . . . really go about taking confidentiality so seriously. And I think, on the one hand, that's really good that we respect that. But, on the other hand, we're just perpetuating this myth. And we're perpetuating this shame about abortion.

In Greta's view, the pro-choice movement's focus on the right to privacy, along with the inequitable gender relations concealed in such a focus (see MacKinnon 1983), contributed to a silencing of women's voices.

Celia spoke vehemently about the closeting of abortion as a failure of the pro-choice movement:

> The reason why . . . we've been falling back in terms of abortion rights . . . is because we haven't been talking about abortion. . . . We've been so afraid to dialogue honestly about it that when we talk abortion, . . . it's like this constitutional right. We talk about it as, you know, "what can we do to help?" You know, you go and you write your congressman a letter. . . . We have our armor on, like we're ready for this battle. . . . We've just been on the defensive so long that we haven't changed the language about abortion. . . . You know, we still say "products of conception." Well, why don't we say it looks like—you know, a twenty-week fetus *looks like* a baby. Why can't we say that in public? Because that's what the *antis* say, you know. But you know, it's pretty much true, and you'd better say it. . . . The antis have this one extremist language, and then the pro-choice movement has this other extremist language, and there are all these people in the middle, and they don't believe either one.

Most Center women attributed the infusion of anti-abortion sentiment into public consciousness to the persistence and aggressiveness of the antis, whose views were bolstered by conservative misogynist politics yet also abetted by pro-choicers' reticence about abortion. Center workers talked at length about how anti-abortionists' activity, their rhetoric, and their visual props had worked to stifle any honest public discussion of abortion, a discussion they considered essential to continued procreative freedom. Lee said, "I think that legal changes [prohibiting or restricting abortion] will be a lot easier if people are afraid to talk or don't know that they *can* talk" about abortion. Many workers said they had the impression that pro-choice activism did not seem to be "taking" the way it once did, and they could not understand how people could be apathetic about the issue of procreative freedom.[12]

Viability, Recognizability, and Setting Limits to Abortion

Many Center women called fetal viability, the point at which a fetus can live outside a woman's body, the most potent weapon anti-abortionists have to "chip away" at abortion rights because viability shifts with technological "gains" in neonatal treatment. Some babies born late in the second trimester can now be hooked up to ventilators, incubated, and fed intravenously, and they will live. (Physical and mental disabilities are much more common for premature infants than for infants born at term however, and the earlier pregnancies end, the more likely disabilities are.) Several Center women pointed out that capitalizing on earlier viability possibilities would be a promising route (for antis) toward limiting the availability of abortion since public-opinion polls show disapproval of second-trimester abortions, and the Supreme Court has never safeguarded second-trimester abortions. Some of the staff thought about viability rather legalistically; as Rae said, for example, "I feel that every woman has the right to choose, and if . . . the government says that twenty-six weeks is the cutoff limit, I feel that a woman should be able to have an abortion at twenty-six weeks." Others reframed viability in a more radical manner, questioning the rationale behind setting limits.

Carrie talked about how, for women desperate to end pregnancies, viability was often irrelevant. She segued, as many women did, from talking about viability and limits on performing abortion into recognizability—what a fetus looks like as it develops. She said, "I believe that abortion is a woman's individual decision. I mean, I know that thirty-one weeks is harder for me to look at than twenty-six weeks, but I'm not going to tell a woman whether she can do it or not. It's weird because it is arbitrary; any kind of limit is very arbitrary." Watching Lois tell a client she had gestated past the twenty-six-week limit and thus would be having a baby instead of an abortion conveyed the magnitude of this issue to me. The client looked as though she'd been be-trayed—by Lois, by her body—and sat silent, immobile, numb.

Sarina's point of view exemplifies a gradualist approach to thinking about abortion. She did not pretend to draw a line dividing acceptable abortions from unacceptable—or too late—abortions. Women should be able to have abortions when we feel we need them, but, as a practitioner, Sarina distin-guished between abortions she believed she was capable of performing and those she could not do. Length of gestation was the crucial factor that made the difference for Sarina. She did not want to be responsible for ending preg-nancies where the fetus was so close to becoming a baby that it looked like one. Sarina conflated concerns about recognizability with viability; she was distressed both about destroying the fetus and about confronting fetuses in advanced states of gestation. The potential for both recognition—cognitive association of the fetus with live babies—and thwarted viability—the knowl-edge that a fetus might have lived had it been born rather than aborted at, say, twenty-six weeks—increased as gestation advanced.

Sarina, like all physicians, had been medically trained to disengage emo-tionally from clients' bodies, but at first she found second-trimester abortions difficult to observe both because of the emotional impact fetuses had on her and because she disliked seeing clients in pain and recoiled at the thought of "causing" such pain through her actions. Sarina told me that almost from the beginning of her employment at the Center administrators pressured her to "go further" and perform later abortions. She resented "feeling forced" by people who "don't know anything about what . . . it feels like" to do abor-tions. "Fetal destruction is a very different ball game" from the vacuum aspi-ration procedure used in first-trimester abortions, she said. Sarina said that "moving up" should occur only as an abortionist feels mentally prepared to do it. "You have *got* to be comfortable with what you are doing because you have to come home and . . . hopefully sleep at night and not have nightmares or, you know, have it haunt you."

Emma and Nancy told me they had a verbal agreement with Sarina from the outset that specified that Sarina would learn to do second-trimester abor-tions; because the Center paid other physicians per procedure, to have Sarina do them would be economical. Sarina conceded eventually and began doing thirteen- and fourteen-week abortions and then, some months later, fifteen-and sixteen-week abortions. Learning how to do the new procedures was not difficult, but she said it took about a month before she stopped feeling un-comfortable about what she was doing:

I think the tough part was seeing actual pieces of the fetus being re-moved. . . . And in the beginning, yes, I remember looking, standing behind this woman's shoulder [as she performed an early second-trimester abortion] and thinking, I can't do this. . . . There's something emotionally upsetting about this. . . . Features are discernible; you can count five fingers on a hand and five toes on a foot. You know, all the organ systems are formed. You know, you can see ears as structures, and the nose and eyes as structures. It's just, you know that, at that stage of development, the fetus would not live outside of the uterus anyway, but I think the destruction was hard. . . .

I have gotten to the point now that because I've been doing this work five months, four months, I look at it a little differently. I don't see the same things that I did. And, honestly, when I sit down to do one of these now, I am watching to be sure that I'm getting everything that I need to get. It's: Do I have two lower extremities? Do I have two upper extremities? Is there a spine? . . . And the skull? . . . So there is a definite goal to be accomplished. . . . I don't see whatever I saw six months ago. It doesn't trigger in me the emotional response [I first felt]. . . . It does become a bit routine after a while. I don't fear it. I don't dread it when I go in there.

Sarina grew accustomed to abortions that once looked disturbingly unpleasant to her and that she originally thought would be impossible for her to perform. Acceding to management's desire for her to learn to perform second-trimester abortions fueled their pressure on her to go further. She said, "I am always for a woman's choice, and whatever a woman decides to do with her pregnancy, that's her business. But I don't know that I am willing to be the one that helps her terminate a twenty-week pregnancy." Sarina did not believe she had a moral responsibility to participate in abortions once they became visibly upsetting to her; no physician did, in her view. She presented a unique assessment of late abortions, personalizing the issue in a way that other Center women could not because they did not actually perform the abortions.

Though no Center workers ever explicitly said so, I sensed that many nonmedical staff members did believe that doctors—especially feminist doctors—had a responsibility to perform abortions. One of Meryl's remarks highlights the desire on the part of many lay health care activists to disempower any authority that impedes procreative freedom. Echoing the argument voiced by feminists fighting for the repeal of abortion laws several decades ago, she said, "I feel like I am totally at peace with what I believe about abortion—more than I've ever been before. . . . And I've considered it on spiritual levels, on ethical levels, on political levels, and personal experience. And I am more firm than ever . . . that it should not involve anybody [but women]. Not the church, not a doctor, not the state. . . . It's a health issue."

The demand for abortionists far exceeds the supply of doctors willing to perform abortions. In 1991, only 13 percent of the residency programs for obstetrics and gynecology required first-trimester-abortion training. Only 7 percent required second-trimester training, marking a 70 percent decline in six years (Lewin 1992a: A11; Manuel 1994: A3). The number of abortion-providing facilities has diminished significantly; the abortion rate dropped 6 percent between 1980 and 1988 (Lewin 1992a: A11). Workers often reminded me that Center administrators spent two years searching for a staff physician before hiring Sarina. Planned Parenthood began its own training program for physicians in June 1993 (Belkin 1993), a strategy the Center had already initiated. In addition, in 1995 the Accreditation Council for Graduate Medical Education voted unanimously to require programs that train doctors in obstetrics to include abortion skills or risk losing their accreditation (Coleman 1995). Requiring abortion training, of course, will not necessarily produce willing abortionists.

Physicians may choose to avoid abortion because harassment is likely. Indeed, abortionists fear for their lives; between March 1993 and December 1994, anti-abortionists shot twelve people, killing five. Obviously, abortion provision has become increasingly dangerous; simply being inside or near an abortion-providing facility now means one risks an encounter with a gun-wielding anti-abortionist.

Meryl, like other lay staff, considered the shortage of physicians a problem that ought to be solved by allowing other medical workers (such as physicians' assistants, midwives, and, for very early procedures, even lay health workers) to become abortionists. Center women hoped that RU-486, the French "abortion pill," would eventually help to loosen the medical profession's control over abortion, although they acknowledged that the realization of such a goal was remote, given that access to the drug in the United States would almost certainly be mediated by physicians for a long time to come. (The Center became a trial site for the testing of this new abortion method in May 1995.)

Lee offered an extensive theological analysis of viability. Like Carrie, she called viability an "arbitrary distinction" because it was defined by the "medical establishment" and "not by the woman." She pointed out that "in the Middle Ages, abortion was acceptable until the point of quickening, which is something that the woman reports on herself." Quickening, or the point at which a pregnant woman perceives fetal movement, usually occurs between the sixteenth and the twenty-third week of pregnancy. Rothman found that women who had amniocentesis often delayed feeling fetal movement until after the test, suggesting that pregnant women's attitudes about their pregnancies exert a strong influence over when quickening occurs (1986). A good amnio result meant it was all right to feel pregnant. Health workers told me that many second-trimester-abortion clients said they did not feel movement "when they should" or did not look pregnant or "as pregnant as they are." Women who did not want to be pregnant carried themselves differently from women who did; denial or distress could mitigate against all sorts of bodily evidence of pregnancy, workers believed.

Lee preferred a system for evaluating and describing pregnancy based on pregnant women's judgments rather than one devised by doctors who may not care about protecting women's interests. She had worked out what she called "a theology of abortion" that keeps pregnant women central:

> I start with . . . the incarnation—you know, figuring out the dual nature of Christ, being truly God and truly human? . . . That means that the body is a dignified and wholly complete place. It's both autonomous . . . and immeasurably connected to the rest of the created order. Okay? And that's true of women's bodies. . . . It's really a passionate thing for me when I talk about the dignity and completeness of a woman's body and . . . everybody's body being so connected to the rest of creation as to be inseparable and to be completely autonomous at the same time. And how both of those factors play into her having the moral authority that one exercises during an abortion. . . .
>
> If the woman is a complete being, then she has no . . . obligation to involve any other specific person in that decision. But at the same time, she's entitled to the blessings of the community. . . . I don't want to say that the woman should be completely isolated . . . I don't want to say that because I think that the woman has the right to privacy but she also has the right to community.

Deciding to have an abortion, in Lee's view, meant exercising the "moral authority" incumbent upon an autonomous, adult human being: but the liberal notion of privacy as sole justification for "choice" was not enough. Lee believed we were all "entitled to the blessings of the community" to back up our solitary decision making, and, ideally, the two (self and the collectivity of self with others) ought not be dichotomous.

In her theological stance, Lee refused to make distinctions between acceptable abortion and unacceptable abortion because she conceptualized the fetus as part of a pregnant woman's body.

> I never have come to a point where I would say, okay, here's where I'm not going to participate in an abortion anymore . . . or . . . here's where I don't think abortion should be allowed or where I don't think it's accept-

able. Because there's never a point where there's something there that wasn't there before. That's true in the development of the fetus. . . . When you're talking about conception, I mean, that's even a vague term. That's not a moment, that's a process. Does conception start with the genetic material that both of the people got throughout the ages? Life is always a continuum, it's not a series of discrete moments. . . . And that ambiguity used to really bother me, that I couldn't really figure out when the fetus becomes a person. . . . Some people say when the woman consents to the pregnancy. Well, what if she never consents to the pregnancy? Does that mean after she has the baby that it'll never be a person? Maybe in some kind of poetic way that might be true, but I don't think that it means that it's okay to kill toddlers. And so, see, the problem is, I don't want to say that, that a parent has a right to kill their children, and on the other hand I don't want to say that I know when . . . a group of cells becomes a person.

Ironically, Lee's description of conception resonates with the anti-abortionists' portrayal. Lee said, "There's never a point where there's something there that wasn't before"; the antis say, "You were then everything you are today." Lee's argument, of course, dramatically opposed that of the antis. She drew on the presence of potential selfhood at conception to support her contention that women should make decisions about pregnancy because our personhood is clearly evident, whereas the personhood of the fetus is in invisible flux. The antis' reasoning that conception crystallizes personhood could be pushed back to "genetic material" itself, and yet they do not argue that ejaculation or ovulation not followed by fertilization is, along with abortion, equivalent to murder. But, moving in the other direction, Lee explained, we reach a point (birth) where personhood is clearly evident.

Center workers like Carrie, Lee, and Meryl remind us that, in recent U.S. legislative history, pregnant women have been denied the power to mandate—or even to contribute to decision making about—how and whether abortion ought to be limited. The hypothetical pregnant everywoman about whom policies are made does not function well as a guide: she is no one. Policymakers, likewise, do not function well as arbiters of the behavior of real, live women: as Lee queried, Who has the moral authority to limit the bodily autonomy of pregnant women?

Rhetoric and Reevaluation

As I transcribed and read Center women's descriptions of late abortions, and as I thought about the strange similarity their words sometimes bear to anti-abortionists' rhetoric, I remembered the children's parable about the blind men feeling the elephant. Each blind man feels a different part of the elephant—smooth end of the trunk, rough hide, fuzzy tail, and so forth. Extrapolating from these partial "views," each "sees" the elephant itself as a distinct entity, entirely different from what each of the other imagines. And what we have here are similar descriptions of the "elephant"—abortion—with entirely different meanings. The moral, at least as I interpret it, is that we ought not assume we can so easily know what we "see," or, in postmodernist terms, the text (elephant) depends on the reader (feeler). In postmodernism, the elephant's existence as a central common entity must vanish if the ways in which people interpret it are different.

In very unpostmodernist terms, though, the parable can also be read as suggesting that the underlying element/elephant *is* a cohesive whole, the sum of these various fragments. I do not mean to say that Center women's talk of abortions and the antis' talk of abortions are two different readings of the same thing (or, in postmodernist lingo, of the same text). Rather, the thing itself depends on the reader's reading. These readers—Center staff members—recognized the variability of their text. They also contradicted themselves. They referred to a "reality" about abortion that one simply *sees* when one looks at abortions in progress, yet they also talked about the various methods they employed to construct particular visions. Center women said the anti-abortionists were entitled to believe whatever they wanted to, yet they also espoused a feminist moral sensibility they believed to be *the* truth. They both refuted and affirmed the postmodernist relativistic amorality that holds that all texts and values are in flux and flexible.

The anti-abortionists have chosen to make fetuses central: take notice, they say, fetuses look like babies; hence, they *are* babies. Center workers replied that there is a difference between looking like a baby and being a baby. Fetuses get to be babies only if women choose motherhood. And Center women saw choice, remember, as a weak word because most aborting women do not feel wholly pleased about or empowered by their choice: one does not choose abortion over motherhood the way one chooses strawberry over chocolate ice cream, though antis certainly portray women's decision making about abortion this way. This piece of anti-abortionist rhetoric, that women's decisions to abort pregnancies are frivolous choices, may be the most popular and widespread in the current cultural climate.

At first, it may sound like an admission of uncertainty about the justification for abortion when Center women state that fetuses might have some meaning. This conclusion is one that Carole Joffe (1986) and Kathleen Roe (1989) reach in their studies of abortion workers' troubled responses to abortion. And, indeed, misgivings may coexist with pro-choice political views and remain misgivings, or, in Roe's words, workers may hold "multiple definitions" of abortion (1196). Within the organizational culture of the Womancare Center, however, negative responses to abortion—doubts, misgivings, bad dreams, whatever—were bracketed within a deeply felt commitment to furthering procreative freedom for women. Center women believed that one did not negate or compromise one's support of aborting women if one felt disturbed by any aspect of abortion. In the final analysis, Center women found abortion to be more complicated than pro-choice rhetoric allows, but the pro-choice moral framework remained unchanged except for their belief that thinking through the complexity gave their position increased strength.

In an essay about coming to terms with the miscarriage of a wanted pregnancy, Susan Chira (1994) calls for a philosophical outlook on procreation that resonates with the feminist stance on abortion that Center workers articulated; it centers on trusting women. She writes, "We could transplant the principle of pluralism to the abortion debate and concede that this is a spiritual decision that everyone can make for herself. And it is a decision that should be a struggle, an honest battle with moral and emotional messiness" (20). Like Chira, Center workers believed women ought to be the arbiters of what our pregnancies mean, though they were not as insistent as she that the arbitration process be difficult in order to be valid. Chira writes, "For me, a child's life begins when a mother who wants that child makes a place for it in her heart and her life" (20). Similarly, Center women retained the focus of pro-choice rhetoric—the centrality of women—but they also sought to add depth, to show what they believed was the whole picture, to incorporate various feminist realities of abortion.

CHAPTER 3

Anti-Feminism Personified

Encounters with the Enemy

As the feminist health care movement expanded in the 1970s, so did the anti-abortion movement, which had begun organizing even before the *Roe v Wade* and *Doe v Bolton* decisions in 1973. The Womancare Center emerged out of the women's health care movement, and its struggles with anti-abortion protesters are grounded in the growth of an anti-feminist countermovement. After the Supreme Court decisions, anti-abortion groups dedicated themselves to banning abortion nationwide. From several years before 1980 (when Ronald Reagan was elected president) until Bill Clinton ousted George Bush in 1992, the countermovement enjoyed a series of successive triumphs, beginning with the Hyde Amendment (1977), which ended Medicaid funding of abortions in most states, and culminating in several Supreme Court decisions, most notably *Webster* (1989) and *Casey* (1992), which together enabled states to restrict abortions in a variety of ways (including the imposition of parental-notification and parental-consent restrictions and of waiting periods, and the barring of abortion from public hospitals or clinics). The Supreme Court also ruled in May 1991 that workers in federally financed clinics could not discuss abortion with their clients. (Clinton lifted the gag rule on the twentieth anniversary of *Roe v Wade*, January 22, 1993.) Anti-abortionists did not, however, realize their goal of outlawing abortion. Dallas Blanchard

(1994), Connie Paige (1983), Michele McKeegan (1992), and Robert Spitzer (1987) document in depth the strategies, successes, and failures of the anti-abortion countermovement.

Over the years, a number of aggressive splinter groups have developed out of the mainstream National Right to Life Committee (NRLC), which originated in 1973 within the Catholic Church; eventually it became independent of the Church, but most members and funding sources are still Catholic (Blanchard 1994: 62). Randall Terry, a former used-car salesman, founded Operation Rescue in 1986.[1] (For descriptions of twenty-three major anti-abortion organizations, see Blanchard 1994: 61–81.) Terry claims God spoke to him, providing him with the vision that led to the foundation of Operation Rescue (Faux 1990: 140). Terry borrowed confrontational strategies that had been used by smaller groups, groups that never received the publicity Operation Rescue would. For example, Catholics United for Life, a group that formed in the early 1980s, conducted "rescues," in which its members joined arms to attempt to block clients from entering abortion clinics, long before Operation Rescue did. Operation Rescue's tactics include forming human chains to block women's entry into abortion clinics; posing as clients to gain entry to clinics in order to disrupt abortion provision; broadly publicizing "rescues" so that anti-abortionists from outside the targeted cities will travel to demonstrate; gluing locks on clinic doors shut; and picketing the homes of abortion providers. Operation Rescue signaled the emergence en masse of a new sort of anti-abortion activist: fundamentalist Christians willing to dedicate themselves wholeheartedly to achieving the goal of stopping abortion. Other fundamentalist groups such as Rescue America and Lambs of Christ (originally known as Victim Souls of the Unborn Christ-Child) emulate Operation Rescue's methods but have fewer followers and receive less attention from the press.

Operation Rescue claims it does not advocate violence, but Terry's early alliance with Joseph Scheidler (leader of the far-right Pro-Life Action League and author of *Closed: 99 Ways to Close an Abortion Clinic*), along with remarks Terry has made, belie this claim. The Operation Rescue training manual refers to participants as "warriors" who "know if they don't defeat the enemy the enemy will defeat them. There is no stalemate, no middle ground. Warriors don't run into conflict; they run to it. Warriors are prepared to die" (cited in Faux 1990: 141). Terry calls Operation Rescue the "Civil Rights Movement of the Nineties," and likens himself to Martin Luther King, Jr. Americans would take the anti-abortion movement more seriously if its adherents acted more aggressively, Terry writes. "Our cries of 'Murder!' go unheard because our actions are so far removed from our rhetoric. If a child you love was about to have his arms and legs ripped off, . . . what would you do? Would you write your congressman . . . ? No! You would do whatever you could to physically intervene and save the life of that child. That is the appropriate response to murder" (1989: 83). Anti-abortionist leaders depict themselves as heroic masculine protectors of children and "the family" and as protectors of women (from our own unfeminine, unnatual acts). Never do they speculate about how gendered labels like *warriors* relate to anti-abortionist women; in effect, they erase their own women's unfeminine militance.

Anti-abortion activists—usually male—are famous for remarks that implicitly condone violence done in the name of their cause. The response of anti-abortionists to the murder of Dr. David Gunn in Pensacola, Florida, on March 10, 1993, is a potent example. Terry said, "While we grieve for him and for his widow and for his children, we must also grieve for the thousands of children he has murdered" (Barringer 1993: A12). Echoing Terry, Don Treshman, director of Rescue America, said, "While Gunn's death is unfortunate, it's also true that quite a number of babies' lives will be saved" (Rohter 1993: B10). Debbie Dykes, a member of the American Family Association, applauded Gunn's murder. "I think the man . . . should be glad he was not killed the same way that he has killed other people, which is limb by limb" (Barringer 1993: A12). After Gunn's murder, Sara Rimer interviewed participants in a training camp Operation Rescue runs in Melbourne, Florida. Though Operation Rescue members allegedly sign a pledge of nonviolence, several trainees expressed sympathy with Michael Griffin, Gunn's murderer. "'Can you justify killing a murderer?' said Eric Johns. . . . The majority thought it was wrong. No one at Operation Rescue would ever kill an abortionist. But a few people thought it was morally justified. Then someone said, 'If it's morally justified, why aren't we all out killing abortionists?'" (Rimer 1993: A8).

Anti-abortion supporters of Griffin, led by Paul Hill (who would eventually become a killer himself), circulated a petition praising Griffin's act as "justifiable," proclaiming the "justice of taking all godly action necessary to defend innocent human life, including the use of force" (Belkin 1994: 48). Thirty people signed the petition; a similar letter was sent to various abortion providers after Hill killed Dr. John Bayard Britten and his escort, James Barrett, Center women told me. They interpreted such documents as threats, signed by potential murderers.

Dallas Blanchard and Terry Prewitt represent anti-abortion–movement activities with a diagram of concentric circles, narrowing from "education and public opinion" toward a center of "radical violence" (like clinic bombings, arson, kidnapping—and, now, murder) committed by people who have become frustrated with legitimate means of agitating for social change (1993: 255). As more violent activists emerge, Blanchard and Prewitt write, they legitimate less extremist countermovement participants; public perceptions of right-wing extremism and acceptable behavior may continually shift, making Operation Rescue seem relatively tame (256). Bombings, arson, and other violent "direct-action" techniques against abortion-providing facilities increased in the mid-1980s, reaching a peak in 1986 of 183 reported incidents. The number of attacks on abortion-providing facilities increased again in the early 1990s; there were 93 reported incidents in 1991 and 186 in 1992 (Blanchard and Prewitt 1993; Staggenborg 1991; and Rohter 1993). Between 1977 and 1991, there were 1,187 "incidents of violence and disruption" against abortion providers (Blanchard 1994).

Operation Rescue has gained legitimacy within the more established and less aggressive anti-abortion movement; mainstream anti-abortion leaders tend to speak of Operation Rescue the way an indulgent and slightly annoyed parent might scold a naughty child. Dismissals of Operation Rescue's tactics within the movement are rare. For example, Jack Wilkes, director of the more moderate NRLC, describes Operation Rescue's publicity as "bad for the movement" but avoids criticizing Operation Rescue and lays the blame on the media. "They portray those demonstrators as a bunch of kooks, religious fanatics" (cited in Cryderman 1988: 49). Paul Brenton, an anti-abortion pastor, writes about trying out Operation Rescue's method by joining in a "rescue," only to realize that he had become part of a group of well-meaning yet manipulated followers (1992). Brenton sees abortion as "a national malignancy of the first order" but concludes that "this does not justify the use of guilt and manipulation to motivate God's people" (24). Here Brenton speaks of the way Operation Rescue leaders treated their disciples, not about how demonstrators interacted with clinic clients.

While most anti-abortionists avoid criticizing Operation Rescue's methods, Brenton does portray "rescuing" as an ineffective approach that is not particularly Christian. "It is not at all clear that blocking doors to clinics is either saving many babies or putting an end to abortion," he writes (1992: 24). An anti-abortion Catholic priest, Terry Attridge, similarly criticized Operation Rescue for its assaultive tactics in Dobbs Ferry, New York, in 1990. "You don't jam a bloody fetus into the face of a 5-year-old," he said. Operation Rescue members respond to its detractors among the clergy in nasty ways: in Dobbs Ferry, they blocked a funeral procession at a church (Foderaro 1990: A13).

The Catholic Church beefed up its anti-abortion efforts by focusing on public relations, perhaps hoping to counteract the bad press received by Operation Rescue and other fanatical groups. In 1990, the U.S. Roman Catholic bishops hired the public relations firm Hill & Knowlton and a polling company, the Wirthlin Group, to help make its anti-abortion message slicker and more appealing (Goldman 1990). One of the first image-reshaping efforts urged by Hill & Knowlton was the appointment of Helen Alvare, a thirty-year-old lawyer, to be the Church's spokeswoman on abortion. With Hill & Knowlton, the bishops produced an advertisement that featured the Statue of Liberty weeping over abortion; "We try to link the value of life with the value of freedom," Alvare said (Steinfels 1990: A10).

Operation Rescue at the Center

The Center had been targeted by anti-abortion protesters intermittently since its founding, but the attack by Operation Rescue during the summer and fall of 1988 was far worse than any demonstrations staff members had seen before. Upon Operation Rescue's arrival, workers were plunged into an ordeal they described as nightmarish, hellish, and extremely anxiety producing. As they related their memories of this time, participants repeatedly used war as an analogy for what they had been through. An examination of their descriptions of dealing with anti-abortion protesters (both during and after Operation Rescue's 1988 blockades) highlights nuances of the interplay between work and feminist identity, and reveals how the intense emotional labor demanded of the workers both exhausted them and helped to consolidate their self-images as activists. Also, the narratives of staff members who began working after the "siege" of 1988 show that negative reactions to the antis remained strong regardless of the dwindling number of protesters. Protesters continued to function as a reminder that the war over abortion continued. The size of protest groups fluctuated, demonstrating the anti-abortion movement's political vicissitudes; but workers came to feel antis were "out there" even if they were not physically present outside the doors of the Center.

Before its hundreds of adherents descended on Anyville in 1988, Operation Rescue bragged that it was coming to shut down the city's abortion clinics. Center staff members were unsure about what to expect even after Emma gathered them for a meeting to talk about the expected arrival of Operation Rescue and its plans to conduct clinic blockades. Lee recollected, "The administrators really create a constant crisis. You know, there's always some major threat to the Center that's going to drive us out of business, and everybody . . . is supposed to make all these sacrifices to, you know, to pull us through. . . . So I wasn't sure whether she was just, you know, coming up with . . . the crisis of the month club or whether it was really going to be that rough."

Emma also met with other abortion providers, community groups, and city police to try to prepare for what was coming. "The police's response was, 'Well, just shut down to avoid confrontation.' And we were adamant that there was no way that we were going to shut down and that was never going to be an acceptable solution for us. . . . We demanded that they protect us," she said. Fortunately for the Center, as part of advance publicity efforts, Operation Rescue communicated its mission to the police. Until this point, the city police force had refused to promise clinics that it would respond to the planned blockades. Nancy said, "And then Operation Rescue met with the police and were very arrogant—as they always are—and just told the police, 'We don't care about your protest area. We don't care what you say. We're coming to town to break the law.' So the police all of a sudden thought, 'Well, maybe these clinics have something to say here.' "

Tanya took on the job of organizing Center escorts, relying first on staff members and later (when the demonstrations did not abate) on local NARAL volunteers. She said that before Operation Rescue arrived the Center could not count on police to deter anti-abortion protesters who trespassed. "As a matter of fact, the policemen who did come out every once in a while would go and have breakfast with the antis. . . . And the police refused to do anything about the fact that they were *on our property.*"

This time, though, with their authority threatened, police became sudden allies. As Tanya put it, "You just don't go around telling the Anyville police you're gonna break the law, 'will you please cooperate with us!' " Anticipating Operation Rescue's tactic of transporting protesters to demonstration sites without identification (such as drivers' licenses) so they could withhold their names if they were arrested, the police tracked Operation Rescue's vehicles with helicopters. They stopped the buses and asked to see the drivers' licenses. When the drivers produced none, the police refused to let them continue driving. Undeterred, hundreds of Operation Rescue members walked from where they had been pulled over on the expressway to the nearest abortion clinic.

According to Center administrators Emma, Nancy, and Trudy, Operation Rescue's assault took a substantial financial and emotional toll on the Center. During the two months when protesting was heaviest—August and October of 1988—the Center suffered deficits of $23,000 and $61,000, respectively. Emma said in 1990 that the Center had still not recovered from Operation Rescue's activities. "Our business declined 25, 30 percent during that time. And we've never really recuperated. We've had to shrink the size of our organization. . . . We've had to eliminate staff positions and eliminate programs." Emma and Nancy told me that an unusually high number of staff members had quit as a result of Operation Rescue blockades. "When we had our second anniversary party for surviving Operation Rescue, . . . we looked through the employee list. . . . There'd been over 130 employees during a two-year period, and only 11 of us were here during the entire time of Operation

Rescue," Emma said. According to Nancy, in the four months immediately following Operation Rescue's demonstrations in the fall of 1988, "we lost eleven staff. . . . Nobody said it was because of the antis, but it was, you know." Their general consensus was that working at the Center during the blockades was so stressful that it made staff members burn out quickly; workers' commitment to the job weakened because of the relentless opposition of the antis. As Nancy said, "You know, you can only go so far. . . . The real reality of it was that people had just *taken* it. It was really hard. And it's hard to . . . keep saying that it's really worth it."

Nine of the seventeen women I interviewed in 1990–1991 had worked through the 1988 blockades (Emma, Nancy, Meryl, Tanya, Lee, Deva, Celia, Ilene, and Mira). Hannah, whom I interviewed in 1992, had left for about two years during 1989–1990, and then returned to the Center. By the end of 1993, of all the women who had been present during the Operation Rescue blockades, only Hannah remained at the Center; so the reasons for turnover ought not be summarily attributed only to external stresses like Operation Rescue. (There is a lot of turnover in this sort of intensive work.) However, I consider the administrators' conviction that Operation Rescue was behind the wave of resignations at the Center in 1989 significant (though unverifiable) because it bespeaks the power these women felt the antis wielded to thwart the efforts of abortion providers.

Each day during the 1988 blockades, Operation Rescue targeted one of a handful of Anyville clinics. Clinics circulated advance knowledge of their enemies' activities, obtained with some regularity from a "mole" inside the group. But Operation Rescue was not entirely predictable; it might change its itinerary at the last minute or leave one clinic to "hit" another before the police made arrests. And, eventually, Operation Rescue leaders sent groups to several clinics at once to try to confuse abortion providers and confound police efforts to arrest demonstrators. Center workers had to be prepared for the arrival of Operation Rescue masses every day. Staff came to work at about 5:30 in the morning in order to get inside before the antis attempted to block the doors. Emma described the situation:

> There were times when I would say it was the equivalent of a three-ring circus because we had the police, we had the barricades, we had horses and prison vans out here. And then we had the protesters. And then we had all this media . . . [and] all of the pro-choice supporters. So it just made quite a ridiculous scene—to think that anybody was going to get in here! . . . That first week of October was probably the worst of it all because that was the week they did several things differently. First, they went to simultaneous locations and divided up the police resources.

They crawled up underneath the barricades and *crawled* up the street. So you thought you were protected with the barricades, and then, lo and behold, they just started sliming up the street here! Literally, we were all standing there with our mouths open because you just couldn't think that adults would do this. . . . It was just unbelievable to me . . . like something from another planet.

No matter what precautions they took, Center workers were not prepared for the reckless methods or zealous determination Operation Rescue demonstrated in its efforts to confound clinic staff and the police. Emma had not been overreacting in her advance efforts to warn staff. Mira described how staff members dealt with the "rescues" and how they learned to manage chaos:

It was just mayhem. At first we had no idea how to combat it. We'd never seen anything like this, you know. We had absolutely no idea, but we did the best we could about getting women in. . . . We had to pull staff members [from clinic duties] to put on staff t-shirts to go out there. Later, as we started to get more organized, . . . we got volunteer escorts, so that we weren't short-staffed in the building, and worked out systems as the police came. And they had barricades to try to keep these people away. . . . We'd go to the woman's car and say, "You know, I'm going to, you know, take you in with me"—one escort on either side, who would talk to her and try to keep her out of the mass confusion because we had to go through the whole crowd of 250 people screaming at her. . . . But then we got smart and used umbrellas. . . . One of us would hold that [the umbrella]; the other one would take the woman's arm. And if we held the umbrella in front of us, they had to clear the path.

Center workers described how "mayhem" was sorted out and managed pragmatically and creatively. The unusual became commonplace in terms of what workers did on a daily basis as part of their jobs. However, they never completely normalized the emotional chaos the battle with Operation Rescue provoked.

Responses under Attack: Anger, Anxiety, Antipathy, Ambivalence

Staff members all spoke of their anger at antis, regardless of whether they had worked during the Operation Rescue blockades. They were angry at the antis for the views they held, for their methods, for their effects on clients. They were angry that the American public did not in their view understand the danger the antis represented and that the public did not actively challenge anti-abortionist ideology.

Most Center workers believed the antis' moral framework was wrong in several crucial ways: they called it dishonest, insincere, and misogynist. They told me repeatedly that the antis' propaganda and their shouted remarks to women entering abortion clinics were filled with lies about abortion and about what the antis would do to help women if they changed their minds about aborting. Center women called the antis hypocrites who claimed to care about women but who really sought to control our actions. They believed the antis blatantly disregarded the social realities of women's lives because the antis were dogmatically committed to a hateful world-view in which women were denied full humanity.

Staff members repeatedly expressed their belief that the antis were entitled to their views, however distasteful, untruthful, or dangerous Center women found them. They often said the ways the antis expressed themselves were far more objectionable and offensive than their ideology itself. Straightforward, noninvasive protesting that centered on making a moral statement against abortion would not upset them, staff members often said. Many insisted that they considered this kind of action to be an exercise of freedom of speech, a right they enthusiastically endorsed. Yet they also believed free speech should be truthful and that the antis were liars. Center women were angry at *both* the substance and the mode of expression of antis' views. Consider the comments of these six women:

> EMMA: On the one hand, they'll say, "Oh, yeah, love Jesus!" and on the other hand they're praying that I'm dying and that I'm burning in hell. And the women [clients] are sluts and whores, so they're gonna burn in hell. So where are they [antis] coming from? It's not anyplace that I want to be.

> DEVA: They represent everything that is . . . against, you know, freedom of *everything*.

> LEE: It's a series of clichés. It's not a clear argument. It has to do with a lot of just spewing out a lot of . . . really sloppy sentimental stuff. And sentiment is important, but not—not as a—your religion should not be a trash bag for everything you got tired thinking about!

> YVETTE: Is there an honest way to be anti-abortion? . . . To me, no, there's not. It's like, Is there an honest way to be anti-Semitic? Is there an honest way to be racist? There's not. And, to me, abortion's one of those fundamental things in that same league.

111

JANICE: I can really respect the other side of the issue . . . because I was in that dilemma myself [of feeling anti-abortion sentiments], you know? And it's not like I *can't see* the other side. It's just when they lose that rational ability to think and talk about it, and it becomes this other, just *obsessive* thing that they're doing, . . . just crazy, and *scary* crazy.

TOBY: My experience with them is that most of them are sick. I mean, I believe people have the right not to believe in abortion—whatever. You know, that's fine. But from talking to them—sometimes I go out there to figure out where they're coming from. . . . Something's *wrong* with them. . . . Like a woman's body's the same thing as a life-support system.

Many Center women saw the antis as demented extremists (as Toby and Janice did, calling them "sick" and "*scary* crazy"). They characterized antis as obsessed with the desire for power over women's bodies and women's lives. They dismissed antis' religious zeal as false—as hypocritical or blindly dogmatic. To be anti-abortion meant one was against women, in Yvette's view, and it also meant one committed a basic moral wrong like being racist or anti-Semitic. As Center workers reiterated their belief that the antis were entitled to believe anything, however warped, they also came down against the abstract notion of freedom of speech; they were particularly disturbed by the antis' stubborn refusal to examine their ideology introspectively. As a result of their ignorance and misguidedness, the antis remained impervious to feminist truths as workers defined them. Many Center women considered the antis' dogma so inane that they suspected the antis did not truly believe it either; they often described the antis as zombie-like zealots who might as well be considered brain-dead. Janice said, "They're just untouchable people. It's like, I've tried to talk to them before, . . . and it's like you're looking in this glossy face. And, to me, that says something about anti-abortion, personally." In contrast, most Center workers considered themselves open-minded, and many, like Janice, spoke of how they had arrived at a feminist philosophical stance on abortion, how they had "rationally" explored and logically rejected anti-abortion attitudes.[2] Hannah was the only study participant who blatantly acknowledged her inability to credit anything about the antis' position. "I don't see how anybody can *not* be pro-choice. I mean, I really—I *don't* see it," she said.

Center workers acknowledged that antis likewise dismiss feminists as close-minded extremists. This attitude, too, angered staff members because they "knew" demonstrators had seen evidence that contradicted anti-abortion rhetoric. For example, several workers told me about antis who had gained entry to the clinic by posing as clients. Workers believed that the antis' experiences at the Center must have made them recognize that staff members were not profiteers pushing abortion on unwilling clients. Yet the antis continued to shout the same epithets even after their unwelcome visits. Greta described one such incident and its aftermath:

> We thought they were clients, and we treated them as nicely as we treat anybody else. And we were all so angry. . . . They were out picketing . . . not too long later, and I thought, They *know* the truth. I mean, we showed them how humane we are and that we are not, you know, "baby killers"—I mean that we're real people, and we're nice people, and we're decent, and we're human. And I just wanted to shoot them. I just was disgusted. So nothing that we do can ever make a difference . . . to them.

All the women I interviewed said that they considered the antis' most inappropriate behavior their demonstration of hostility toward women: they screamed at and aggressively surrounded clients and attempted to block their way.

The antis' hypocrisy enraged workers, as Greta's comment indicates. Though antis might appear fervently religious (regularly kneeling on the sidewalk to pray, for example, or, at the height of the 1988 blockades, occasionally speaking in tongues), most clinic workers did not credit such displays as sincere. Rather, as Lee's comment indicates, the antis used religion as a "trash bag" they would then dump on others. In Lee's view, "that's not what God is for." The tenor of Lee's criticism of antis' religiosity owes its bite to her own self-definition as a Christian. She acknowledged the awkwardness of her position. "There's something that I share with them that I don't share with most of the other people that I work with." Yet Lee's narrative demonstrates that she and the antis shared Christian identity only nominally. She described the "last" time she had spoken to the antis, in August 1990:

> It was the feast of St. Mary. . . . So I had left work and gone to church during lunch, and then I was on my way back in. And it was these assholes out front again, talking to me. . . . And they were saying something about . . . "Oh, if you *only knew* how much Jesus loves you." And I said, "I am *sick* of your arrogance! You don't *own* God! And it may interest you to know that I just got back from church," and I *wanted* to say,"—so fuck off!". . . . They said something like, "You may *think* that you know Jesus, and dah dah dah," and I just kept walking at that point because I wasn't there to dialogue with them. I just needed to tell them that they don't

own God. And even though they couldn't *hear* that from me, I still just wanted to say it, even though I knew it wouldn't make any difference. So it made a difference to me.

Lee's spirituality was grounded in theology; she believed worship ought to be thoughtful. She struggled with the notion of ecumenical kinship with the antis and ultimately settled on denouncing them as, at best, misguided in their Christian practice. "They may have some rhetoric about . . . putting themselves on the line for their faith. . . . But I think they're really there because they want to feel powerful, because they see that they can intimidate women or at least embarrass women. And, you know, they get a lot of approval within their community for that kind of thing. So they may think that they're bucking the system, but I think they're being very manipulated by their leaders." According to Lee, Christian thinking and practice ought to be built on kindness and inclusiveness, not implacable dogma.

Several other Center women mentioned their anger at what they saw as the antis' misuse of religion. They believed one should not impose one's religious beliefs on others and viewed antis as proselytizing a religious agenda that would do away with the separation of church and state. Also, most Center women considered religious beliefs a personal component of one's individuality. Denying the validity of any but their own beliefs meant that the antis sought to transgress the boundaries that the right to privacy protected. As Julia expressed it, "On Judgment Day, each person . . . will be judged alone. They're not going to be standing up there with me. . . . 'Leave me alone! What—are you trying to save my soul? Let me be responsible for my own life, thank you very much!'" I asked her if she ever actually confronted the antis this way, and she said, "I've talked to this one guy. And, you know, I told him he was gonna burn in hell [laughing]. He was real angry." Like Lee, Julia felt a sense of satisfaction when she challenged the antis' "holier-than-thou" attitude, even though she knew her outburst would not bring about any change.

Audrey, who was raised by fundamentalist grandparents, was the most charitable of all the study participants in her assessment of the antis' religious motivations. "I can understand where they're coming from . . . because I was brought up in that environment, and if it weren't for my parents saving me from the brainwashing, I could be out there too," she said, depicting antis as innocent victims of indoctrination. "That's what they were taught, and that's what they truly believe. They're not doing it to be assholes; they're doing it 'cause that's what they believe is right." Audrey's familiarity with anti-abortion family members meant she accepted their position as sincere (if not valid—she did, after all, call it "brainwashing"). Audrey came to work at the

Center after 1988 and had not "had many run-ins" with antis when I interviewed her. She did not feel personally attacked by the protesters she had seen and thus did not view antis as a significant threat to procreative rights as did workers who had been at the Center during the 1988 Operation Rescue blockades. Audrey declared rather disinterestedly, "I'm almost sorry that I missed out on all that just 'cause, I don't know, it would have been interesting." Audrey's personal experience and her distance from antis' activities softened her stance toward them (as compared with that of others, like Lee).

Except for Audrey, staff members were unified in their definition of the antis' behavior as terrorism and harassment of women. They believed that because abortion has been culturally cast as a "women's issue" and women's issues are disparaged as unimportant or ignored, it follows that antis can get away with transgressions that would not ordinarily be tolerated (both legally and in terms of breaking social norms). In Nancy's words, "It felt very unfair that these people had all the rights, and we had none. You know, you couldn't help but feel like if these people went over to the Burger King and started doing this, . . . they just wouldn't be allowed to do it. It wouldn't happen."[3]

Center workers were all subject to antis' verbal attacks. Until they were recognized as staff, antis treated them as clients, potential aborters. Once the antis learned who they were, they tailored their harassment to staff members. The litany antis reserved for workers ranged from vehement accusations of "baby killer!" to a plaintive rhetorical interrogation: asking them why they wanted to kill babies or begging them not to kill babies; asking them why they did not find other jobs or offering to help them find jobs making more money. The antis also employed religious "scripts" similar to the ones they used with clients, telling staff members they would "burn in hell"; or, alternatively, they adopted a less antagonistic tone and would "pray for" staff members to "see the light" and change their minds about abortion. Operation Rescue leaders claim to have been successful at both changing women's minds about aborting pregnancies and converting abortion providers to their brand of Christian dogma (see, for example, Szykowny's 1992 account of the leaders of the Buffalo blockades, and Terry, cited in Hiskey 1988 and Leber 1989). Workers considered antis' attempts to "connect" with them part of the performance, intended for show and designed to irritate.

The antis reserved a specialized script for minority women. As Anne described, the overwhelmingly white group of antis attempted to engage with women of color by focusing on "race" in a bizarre and insulting manner:

Well, being [I'm] a black woman, the way the protesters handle me, I think, is a little different . . . from the way they handle other women . . . who are not of color. They tend to use my history to try to slash out at me. . . .

They always say things like "the Reverend Dr. Martin Luther King would be very upset because you're creating genocide on your people." . . . They try to make me feel responsible for my whole race of people, as opposed to things that they would say to a woman who's not of color. . . . I don't know if they think that women of color don't care about what happens to themselves, but [they think] we care more about what happens to our people. So they . . . try to lay a bigger realm of guilt on me. . . . If I go in there and have an abortion, I'm going to just stop the whole black race. And that's basically how they say it.

Toby told of a similar experience, when an anti singled her out, saying, "'See those two little black boys over there? Their mother didn't have abortions.' And I can't tell you on how many levels I was enraged by that statement. . . . And I said, 'Don't try to use that shit with me!'" Black and white workers saw antis as ignorant of their own racism in such encounters; rather, antis seemed to feel that such particularized treatment demonstrated sensitivity. The antis' racist rhetoric worked only to infuriate targeted staff members.

In *The Managed Heart* (1983), Arlie Hochschild contrasts the occupations of flight attendant and bill collector to demonstrate the spectrum of emotional labor demanded of workers; Center employees performed emotion-work across the spectrum, being called on to empathize with and nurture their clients and each other while also striving to appear controlled, united, and assertive in the face of an enemy they considered dangerous and frightening. They were enraged, yet had to appear calm. They felt anxious, even to the point, sometimes, of feeling physically sick. They were, in short, emotionally overwhelmed. Tanya's description of coming to work during the 1988 blockades attests to the emotional overload workers experienced:

Oh, it was just like you'd be getting ready to come to the clinic; it'd be 5:30 in the morning, you know, and you'd gotten to bed late because you had to stay late [the day before] because everything went real slow, and so nobody got much sleep. We were all working forty-five or fifty hours a week, you know. You'd get on the highway, and you'd see a police helicopter in the sky, and you'd try to figure out whether it was over the Center or [a neighboring clinic]. . . . For me it was like, you know, you get this adrenaline rush, you know, because you're like, you just get all tensed up, and your stomach is in knots, and you don't know what it's going to be like when you get there. . . . Are you going to have to walk through picketers? Are you going to be able to get inside the building?. . . .

And it was . . . that fearful anticipation. I mean, I used to feel that way before I came to the clinic with just *regular* antis, but this was just like, you know, it just expanded exponentially. It's hard to describe. I mean, I don't feel that way when I come to the clinic anymore. We're so used to the antis, and I feel so secure with my escorts. . . . [Now] I just come, and my stomach is fine. . . . By the time I'm here, I'm ready to go.

I interviewed Tanya in July 1991, nearly three years after the worst of Operation Rescue's blockades had ended; even long afterward, the anger and frustration she had felt were rekindled when she retold the story.

Whether or not they worked at the Center in 1988, most workers expressed unequivocal rage at the antis, along with distress over the intensity of the anger they felt. They repeatedly disclosed ambivalence about anger: a resentment at being provoked into an ugly feeling, the knowledge that in our culture women's anger is considered unseemly, yet a strong conviction that their anger was justified. As Hannah said, "What bothered me the most was that I felt like I really hated those people." They found few ways to demonstrate their anger productively and no way to purge themselves of it absolutely. They spoke of attempts they made to "deal with" anger, both with co-workers and alone, both by confronting the antis and by ignoring them.

In her work on a feminist health center, Sandra Morgen (1983) asserts that emotion must be understood as an element of experience that is interwoven with ideas and actions. Similarly, repressed emotions must be analyzed to understand lived experience fully. Staff members spoke repeatedly of not wanting to let the antis see how they felt, telling of how they often resisted displaying their anger and fear because they worried that these emotions could become uncontrollable. Were their emotions bared, they would risk "lowering themselves" to the antis' level of hyperbolic display. Center women sensed that the antis might interpret chinks in their armor as cracks in their ideological stance.

For the most part, Center women considered avoiding interaction with antis a sensible self-protective measure. Nancy's comments are typical of most staff members' misgivings about direct confrontation: "I've found for myself, personally, that I don't get very far with speaking with them. I mean, it's not that great for me because I'm not real quick-witted—you know, stuff doesn't just roll off my tongue—and also sometimes when I've actually done it, it just allows all this anger to come out. And then I feel really drained." Similarly, Hallie said, "Usually what I do to try to cut down on my stress level is not pay any attention to them and not look out the windows [when they are outside]. . . . It just makes me angry to deal with them." The women wanted to feel they were in control of themselves. Anger was a hot potato Center

117

women preferred not to juggle in front of the antis. As Carrie put it when she explained why she never talked back to antis, "I guess I have so much anger toward them, I don't know what I'd do with it."

Despite their beliefs that the antis' accusations were ungrounded and ridiculous, workers still felt accused by them, and feeling accused often made them itch to respond. If workers ignored antis' provocations, antis might think workers had nothing to say, no words with which to fight, instead of recognizing that staff members meant to convey disapproval with their silence. And thus, they said, ignoring the antis, though sensible, was not always what they did.

Center women strove to appear stoic and calm in the face of adversity. They eschewed any show of emotions that might be characterized as stereotypically feminine to avoid appearing weak or vulnerable. Yet, no one could keep her guard up relentlessly. Celia described the emotional turmoil the protesters' activities evoked for her:

> I just remember this one night . . . I'd walked a client up to her car, and it was like the end of the night. . . . And I walked over the hill, . . . and there they were. And I just had this like *panic*, you know? This complete, you know, feeling of panic. . . . They had gotten under my skin, and that was absolutely the worst thing. . . . I remember those nights, I would just get in the car and get on the interstate, and I'd roll up my windows and just scream. Just scream. You know, you do this whole job of, like, protecting the clients—but who's protecting you? . . . I mean, it's just like this bully in the classroom; you don't want to let them know that they're bothering you. You know, don't—don't cry in front of the bully.

For Celia and many others, the emotional residue of the job could be released only when they were by themselves, away from the clinic. Several Center workers told me their stress took a physical toll (causing insomnia, stomach ailments, susceptibility to illnesses) and, in some cases, led to self-destructive behavior (such as smoking).

Most staff members said that though they occasionally interacted with antis, they found little to be gained from this communication. Most interchanges became sarcastic or angry on one or both sides. A few workers said they enjoyed this hostile repartee, that it satisfied their desire to fight back, at least temporarily. They were pleased with themselves when they could shock or stymie the antis:

> CELIA: I thought they were being so violent [verbally] that I just tried the whole, like, reverse shock thing, and they would say some-

thing to me, and I would go, *"Penis! Penis!"* And it really worked. I'll never forget one time I was, like, out there, and this man and his son—who was probably about fifteen—came up, and the man was, like, saying all these mean and nasty things, and I was just like—to the fifteen-year-old son—I was like, "Do you know your father masturbates?" And the father just looked at me and looked at his son, and they just *left* [laughing].

MIRA: There are days when I go out there just to amuse myself and talk to them. We'll embarrass them if we can. . . . Just get into discussions with them, you know. "Well, I don't understand. I mean, if you believe in, you know, brotherly love and unconditional love . . . is it expressive of that to call me a murderer, exactly? . . . Is harassing women, you know, part of that?"

Trying to silence the antis or poke holes in their rhetoric could be entertaining; Mira called it "playing with" them, and, among the workers I observed interact with antis, she was the one most ready with a sarcastic comeback.

Many Center women said they consciously endeavored to defuse their anger with humor, by finding ways to laugh at the antis:

JANICE: My gut feeling is: *I hate them. I want them to die!* But realistically, I mean, I've come to the point where if I can't deal with it, it's like I want to yell at them and hit them over the head with a fucking Bible and go, "You're stupid! You don't know what the shit you're talking about!" But it's like, okay, I deal with that, and I have that anger at first, and then I just try to be funny about it. . . . And so, I mean, I try just to *not* give it the attention that they want.

MERYL: Saying stuff to 'em can make me feel a lot better as long as it doesn't take any time. And the best thing that I've found is if I can laugh at them, if I can *really* laugh at them, I find it diffuses the anger. It doesn't perpetuate a hostile relationship with them . . . because we empower them within ourselves by letting them get so big.

Trying to rile and annoy the antis made some of the women feel a brief flash of satisfying vengeance; at the same time, it provided comic relief and diminished the threat the antis represented for the time being. One anti, Lewis, was a common target for Mira's acerbic wit. Oddly, he eventually developed a crush on her. She took pleasure in teasing him about his claim to be in love with her, saying things like, "You're in love with a lesbian feminist!

What do you think that *means*, Lewis?" He even claimed to repudiate his anti-abortion past as a result of his love for Mira and gave her information about the antis' tactics for approaching the Center. "He may be crazy and have a totally inflated sense of himself, but he's said, 'You know, well, nobody would ever mess with this clinic. Nobody would ever bomb this clinic. . . . This is *hands off.*'" Mira happily exploited her "friendship" with this man because he said "he was going to give me the inside scoop on Operation Rescue."

Staff members struck out at antis in a variety of ways that were less confrontational than verbal exchange. Tanya played Madonna tapes loudly to drown out the antis' shouting, knowing the antis disliked her music. (As I heard Lewis say when I was escorting clients, years before his alleged conversion to the pro-choice cause, "Madonna—she's a wicked woman!") Audrey described sweeping the dirt and cigarette butts off the porch in front of the Center onto the antis congregating below (where they weren't supposed to gather according to the city injunction against them). Workers conceded that retaliatory actions such as these were rather juvenile, but they did not believe antis merited respectful treatment; indeed, they wanted antis to take notice of their disrespect.

Responding collectively worked most effectively to provide staff members with brief respites from their anger. Clinic workers joked with each other or with escorts about the antis within earshot. They commented on the antis' paraphernalia—"Oh, you brought my favorite sign today!"—or about the little plastic fetuses antis often held in the palms of their hands during prayers—"Look at those cute little fetuses; wouldn't they make nice earrings!" In private (away from antis), too, Center workers made fetus jokes, poking fun at what they considered the falsely sanctimonious positions of the antis and aping their glorification of the fetus. For instance, during a staff meeting I observed, discussion turned to ways of encouraging donations from clients, an idea most staff members scoffed at. It was Emma's idea, and she suggested some sort of "creative display." At McDonald's, she said, patrons could drop money for the Ronald McDonald House into a model of the house itself. Mira turned to Hannah and said, audibly, "How about a model of a fetus?" Her remark met with a chorus of groans.

Center women told me about several collectively engineered jokes at the antis' expense. The most popular one began on a day when, after several hours of picketing, only a handful of antis remained outside the building, all of them men. One staff member brought out a ruler and a large hand-printed sign that read "Small Penis Contest" and posed next to the group of men while another worker took pictures. Mimicking the protesters' sign wielding and intrusiveness was great fun. Meryl said, "Have you seen our pictures from when we've done the 'Small Penis Contest'? And, you know, that made them feel . . . what the women feel when they come in. They could see what it was like having a group staring at their bodies. It made fun of their sexuality." Center staff members particularly liked how the antis responded to the "Small Penis Contest": they sidled away from the Center worker holding the sign and covered their faces, behaving like Center clients who had been assaulted by *them*. "Why don't you want your pictures taken? Aren't you proud of yourself?" workers and escorts would heckle.

Several participants told me about another humorous incident that occurred when antis planned a large "rescue" around Christmas time. Center workers lavishly decorated the building with Christmas decorations, and Elise's husband came dressed as Santa to hand out condoms. The display worked like a charm, scaring the antis off, just as workers had hoped. How could the antis intrude on the holiday spirit with their dour chants and gory signs? Jokes, organized and impromptu, public and private, were stress-breaking rituals that provided a collective way, albeit a temporary one, to dissipate the staff's hostility toward the antis collectively and to reinforce a group feeling of feminist solidarity against the enemy.

Threats of Violence, Desires for Vengeance

Managing anger remained a constant challenge for Center women, especially because antis forcefully reminded them that women were neither safe nor secure in the public realm. Center women repeatedly likened the antis' treatment of women (themselves and clients) to sexual assault or rape. They saw the protesters as violent, invasive, potentially dangerous—as figurative if not literal rapists.[4]

Celia told of a time when the Center was running night clinics, and staff members picked the doctor up from various locations so he would not have to drive his car to the clinic and risk being followed, assaulted, or having his car vandalized. The antis figured out what was going on:

So we would, like, have these car-chase scenes. . . . It got your adrenaline flowing, but I was just—I mean, you know, as women, I think we live with enough of this fear of, like, being raped or . . . assaulted or someone breaking into your house. I really try and, like, not be paranoid about that. You know, I really try not to, like, let my energy be tapped off in that way. But it was really hard, those night clinics, when those men were out there at night and they wanted to follow [us].

121

The antis' presence exacerbated Celia's (and her co-workers') anxiety about physical safety and heightened her anger about the all-encompassing danger to women in a culture where violence against us is an omnipresent possibility.

Many staff members described a desire to retaliate against the antis in ways that would go beyond verbal counterattacks or harmless pranks. Two women, Mira and Yvette, spoke about actual violent acts they had committed—one accidental and one intentional—and of the ambivalence they felt afterward.

Mira spent a lot of time outside the Center during the summer and fall of 1988, escorting clients through the crowds of antis into the clinic. She told me about "the only really violent incident that ever happened" during Operation Rescue's blockades; she and another health worker were escorting a client across the street:

> This guy was all of a sudden under our feet grabbing at the client's feet! And she went down, and Ethyl and I picked her up . . . by the seat of her pants and . . . the arms, and we carried her *over* this man, who kept getting up and rolling, getting up and rolling, and being under our feet. . . . And the woman's mother fainted, 'cause she saw her daughter go down in this horrible crowd of, you know, screaming people. . . . There was cars and people and [police] horses. And I don't remember it clearly at all. It was all a blur. I do remember *stepping* all over this man. . . . And if I felt him grind underneath my shoe between me and the asphalt, it felt good. And I came in here shaking and crying. I said, "That's disgusting!" Not only was I capable of, but I got some sense of satisfaction from, stepping on another human being. "Fine, throw yourself under my feet; I will walk *all over* you!" It was awful. . . . That was terrifying. . . . Physically, we were now in danger.

Mira vacillated between expressing her violent reactions with a sense of vengeful approbation ("It felt good. . . . I will walk *all over* you"), justifying them as appropriate ("Physically, we were now in danger"), and lamenting them as morally repugnant ("'That's disgusting!' . . . I got some sense of satisfaction from stepping on another human being"). No one of these emotional responses eventually dominated; Mira frankly acknowledged them all.

Mira also described a time when antis got into the clinic by posing as clients, months after the huge demonstrations had dropped down to a few dozen antis coming to the clinic on Saturdays. She said she "just lost it" after this incident:

> The feeling of violation, of [their] violating my space, of them *filthying* my space . . . with their presence! Their smirks were just imprinted

forever on my brain. And the ugly stuff that came up—I mean, I realized that I could kill a human being. I mean, I realized that if I got my hands on them, I was gonna rip them apart. . . . I knew I could strangle one of 'em, I just knew it. And that was really frightening. It was horrible, you know, to feel that way.

It's disgusting. You feel soiled and gross and emotionally raped that you've been made to feel this way. It makes you face a lot of things about yourself—that we're not, you know, intrinsically all that different. I mean, that same kind of gross, disgusting stuff that they feel is what I felt for them at that moment, that I was capable of that same kind of hatred.

Mira portrayed unpleasant emotions as effects of the antis' actions that were so potent they occurred seemingly independently of her own will *and* as unpleasant, self-generated monsters for which she would have to take responsibility. Examining her reactions to the antis revealed a commonality between feminists and anti-feminists (all are "capable of that same kind of hatred"), but this recognition did not diminish Mira's conviction that feminists ultimately held the moral high ground. Emotionally charged responses, and the sense of identification with the enemy they provoked, were simply a troubling by-product of the ideological impasse between feminists and anti-feminists.

In 1989, city police charged Yvette with assaulting an anti whom Yvette claimed blocked her entry into the Center. In retrospect, like Mira, Yvette said that hurting the anti felt both satisfying and alarming:

I did feel bad. I felt like, I felt sad that I had—I never have done that, . . . never just deliberately, out of malice . . . hit a person. And so I felt bad. . . . So on one level I felt bad, but, on one level, I felt good. But the good feeling scared me because I don't like violence. . . . I mean, there's just something about beating down people that makes them stronger. . . . And I would hate to do it again, but then, on the other hand, you feel so, you know, violently attacked by other people's beliefs. It's just—I feel raped by all of these people with these viewpoints.

Like Mira, Yvette justified and regretted what she had done. Like a woman resisting sexual assault, she struck out against her attacker; but fighting violence with violence was ultimately ineffectual. And as Mira did, Yvette saw hurting the anti as an act she willingly committed but also as an act she was impelled to do (by the person she hit) in self-defense.

Several other Center workers expressed a desire to harm antis physically, usually jokingly; as Janice said earlier, "I want to yell at them and hit them over the head with a fucking Bible." Similarly, Elise confided:

> When you watch day in and day out and day in and day out people being harassed for choice, a lot of anger builds up inside, you know. And I mean, we work really well here. You know, having time out to talk and cry. . . . But I don't trust all that. I mean, I just—I just—think they'd be afraid to be surprised how angry I really was at some of them. If they took a punch at me, I would take a punch at somebody. . . . Flatten 'em. Which in the long run doesn't help anything but make me feel good! [Laughing.]

Center workers, including the two who committed violent acts, acknowledged that they did not believe violence would further their cause nor that a violent act was morally tenable. Their words demonstrate their frustration with bottled-up emotion; the desire to do violence represents a desire to release pent-up anger. Such comments also reveal their inability to see a way out of a cultural bind: even when we actively condemn a widespread ideology ("an eye for an eye"), we may still have difficulty freeing ourselves from it. And we all grow up cheering the good guys when they "flatten" the bad guys; sad or disturbing as it is, it feels good to imagine exacting violent vengeance on those one hates.

Center workers disliked feeling hatred toward other human beings, especially other women. (Roughly half the demonstrators I observed were women, but the leaders of the group were mostly men.) The feminist ideals in which these women believed were based on nurturance, not hatred. They saw hatred and intolerance as the antis' specialty. Hatred for the antis felt productive only in the sense that it seemed a step above hopelessness. Yet hatred infused by anger sapped energy and became emotionally exhausting, adding insult to injury because the women already experienced their work as draining. Many said they felt such impassioned hatred toward the antis that those feelings themselves became stressful, and they talked about their attempts to gain control of emotions that seemed overwhelming. Mira elaborated on the positive aspects of anger and animosity, even visceral hatred, but she talked in a circle, ending up where she began earlier, with ambivalence:

> You just have to get comfortable allowing yourself to feel it. Women are just, you know, we're not allowed to be angry. We're not allowed to be bitchy. We're not allowed. And allowing yourself to do it, and feel it, as long as you don't act it [is necessary]. . . . As long as I don't act on the feeling of wanting to tear one of their limbs off and beat them to death

with it, you know? . . . As long as I don't level a good drop-kick to their head, you know? . . . Who wants to feel that kind of anger and gross, disgusting stuff?

Center women got angry at themselves for "wasting" their energy on anger and on the antis. In Deva's words, "It just, it just affects me in my emotional *waste*, I think—you know, emotions that I waste on these people. So then I become angry at myself for . . . becoming so emotional about these weirdos." They did not want to face the anger and its attending "gross, disgusting stuff," but they saw doing so as part of the work of being feminist women in American culture.

Everyone who spoke of her uneasiness about hatred or anger (or both) toward the antis said that talking about how she felt was a relief. The Center held monthly counseling sessions when the antis were most bothersome; staff members found these productive avenues for commiseration. But talking did not ameliorate their anger; it merely cleared the air for the time being. Their rage could not be eradicated as long as the antis and what they represented remained potent threats.

All workers, however remote their job responsibilities were from the performance of abortions, had been subjected to shouted insults or affronts, bomb scares, and vandalization of the clinic and sometimes of their own personal property. Many Center workers talked about antis' surreptitious acts of harassment. Hallie said, "I've had four vandalisms to my car. So I feel afraid a lot of the time, afraid about being followed home, afraid of something happening to my car when I'm driving, a lot of fear about being unsafe." They were afraid outside the Center and afraid for the Center. As Tanya said, "Every day we come here, we're never a hundred percent sure the building's going to be here or whether it's going to be burnt or whether there's going to be some damage. You know, sometimes there is. Sometimes there's notes on the door; sometimes there's broken windows; sometimes there's paint on the door."

Center women said they believed the antis were capable of devastating destruction. Many spoke of their attempts to protect themselves from the antis' invasive assaults: some had unlisted phone numbers; some said they avoided discussing their work with people they did not know well; most described being more attentive than they were before to who was around them when they were out alone, especially in transit from work to home. Sarina, the staff physician, described the pains she took to protect herself from the kind of harassment she said all abortionists are likely to get from antis: "I live a certain life-style that I never thought I would live. I have maximal security. I pay an enormous amount of rent every month so that my car can be underground and locked [up]. I have a post office box for my mailing address. No one knows where I live. And all of that had to be instituted . . . before I ever came here because you don't want to have to deal with people on your front door, yelling and screaming at you."

Expressing fear meant conceding vulnerability, so some Center women were reluctant to admit to this emotional response. Ilene, for example, at first told me how she responded physically to the antis' presence. "When there are a lot of them out there, it makes me start—I pour sweat, you know, it's like I'm so hyped up there are chill bumps all over my body." Ilene described her reaction as a mixture of anger and fear, but her emotion overwhelmed the capacity of language to aptly define it. "These people out there, they make me so—I don't know what even the word is for it. Of course, they enrage me. They—I feel pretty powerful when they're there, even though it scares me." Ilene said she felt powerful because she knew the antis could not stop her from providing abortions, but she was, nonetheless, afraid of them. Later in the interview, she said of the 1988 blockades, "I think I was too hyped up to be afraid. I mean, I was of course always afraid, but not really. You know, I was more *wired*, a large . . . amount of adrenaline, so that rather than thinking, I just acted." In this vein, workers repeatedly related their experiences of the 1988 blockades as an unending blur of energy and exhaustion.

Because there was no time for assessing or processing emotions, Ilene directed her energy toward getting through each day. In retrospect, she called what she felt then both fear and not fear because at times she steeled herself against being afraid with such consummate determination that she would not allow herself to think; as a result, she later remembered most clearly the physical signals of bodily distress. Ilene's description of emotional states both contradictory and inexpressible attests to the range and depth of workers' emotional response, including the self-protective denial of emotions that were too threatening to think about on a daily basis.

Caught in the Crossfire: Staff and Clients

Because the antis posed a menacing threat to clients and because staff members saw themselves as advocates for their clients, the confrontation that began with Operation Rescue pushed Center women solidly into the role of protectors. They were called on to shield clients with their own bodies. They tended to clients' exacerbated anxieties and soothed clients' fears, while simultaneously striving to manage their own emotions.

Nell, who was not present during the 1988 blockades, told a story that dramatizes how workers saw themselves as protective forces who were themselves vulnerable to attack. She related an incident that worked as an emotional catalyst for her because it forced her to realize that the antis really did frighten her. Nell was in the middle of health-working an abortion when someone began knocking on an emergency door that was covered by floor-to-ceiling blinds:

> We happened to have antis out that day. So, of course, all of our reactions were, It's an anti out there banging. . . . And the doctor's yelling, "Go away—this is not an entrance!". . . Whoever it was kept pounding and pounding. The doctor left; I helped the woman get dressed. . . . And I kept hearing this noise, and I turned around and someone was *coming through* the wall. I didn't know there was a door there, and so my first reaction was, "Oh my God, it's antis called the power of God down, and they have busted the wall open!" . . .
>
> It was a stupid delivery person. . . . My heart was just going a hundred miles an hour, and I was scared shitless. . . . That is your *worst* thought: that an anti is going to come into the room when you are in with a woman.

Despite their efforts, antis never physically intruded on women's abortions at the Center, but Nell revealed her fears that antis could actually appear at the scene of contention. With all their huffing and puffing, they just might be capable of blowing the house down. What made this possibility so dreadful was not, I think, only fear of what the antis might do once they "busted the wall open." Rather, Nell's story shows how workers' fears and anxieties were bound up in their relationships with clients. As feminist health care providers, Center women sought to erase the status differences between caregivers and recipients, to break down what they saw as counterproductive barriers between women. They strongly identified with their clients; they *were* their clients, in a sense. It could be any woman there on the table. When Nell described "your *worst* thought," she can be understood as both generalizing her worst thought to other abortion workers and as speaking as though she were the woman on the table having her abortion invaded by the anti-abortionists.

When I asked Center women to tell how they thought the antis affected clients, they always spoke first about how upset women became as a result of having to negotiate a sea of antagonistic faces and a barrage of verbal harassment. Deva said that during the 1988 blockades some clients "were crying when they were walking in . . . women shaking, women shaking on the table during their abortion, women crying because of what they had seen. Just, you know, emotional trauma on top of the emotional decision they had made." Center staff members who were not present in 1988 believed fewer antis had the same effects on clients as large mobs of them did, though smaller numbers clearly posed less of a physical threat. Walking through the diminished brigades of "sidewalk counselors" (as the antis termed themselves) might be less intimidating than confronting a large group, but it still traumatized clients.

Staff members told me some women turned back during the 1988 blockades, too frightened to confront the crowd of screaming antis. The Center never closed down, though, nor did other city clinics; thus the antis never achieved their greatest goal. The Center rescheduled some clients and referred others to clinics that were not targeted as heavily. After the larger crowds of antis abated, workers said they doubted whether the smaller groups of antis deterred anyone from entering the clinic. As Greta said, "I don't really know that anybody has ever *not* come in and had an abortion because of them. . . . They're clear about their decision, and they know that those people are telling them lies and that they're wrong and that they're so horrible. . . . It just makes them feel worse about a situation that may already be painful or difficult."

Staff members who came to work at the Center after 1988 were more likely than veteran co-workers to see clients' encounters with Operation Rescue as potentially politicizing. Janice, for example, who had an abortion at the Center about a year before she came to work there in 1991, said, "I think it definitely does happen [that clients are politicized], probably more than we realize just because we don't have contact with them [after they leave]. . . . I mean, it happened for me, and I never told anybody at the Center that after . . . having my abortion there it really politicized me further, you know, and was very empowering."

However, workers agreed that antis' aggressiveness had kept abortion stigmatized. They felt that the general public accepted the antis' conceptualization of abortion as a social problem and a wrongful deed committed by women. Emma said, "I think the anti-abortion people have been very successful in making the public view women who receive abortions in a bad light and also make the women themselves feel really guilty. I think that's been something that's remarkably different here in our clients over the past thirteen years. . . . Women are still getting abortions, but they feel a lot worse about it."

In the mid-1970s, when the Center was founded, the right to abortion was newly won, and "everybody who came for an abortion knew somebody who had had an illegal abortion, or they, themselves, had had an illegal abortion. Women were just really *happy* to be able to have an abortion with more dignity," Emma said. Fifteen years later, young women no longer confronted the dangers of illegal abortion, nor were they likely to know anyone who had; but they did experience the wrath and accusations of anti-abortionists, both directly and indirectly. Women, she said, were "bombarded everywhere they go with this message: 'abortion's murder.' They hear it in school; they see it on TV; they get it in church. Their own lives are less significant than the lives of the fetus in the way that abortion's being debated now." Emma thought that because of the prevalence of anti-abortion rhetoric, clients did not think about their having abortions as exercising a crucial right but, rather, experienced them as covert acts and often the culmination of personal failures.

Some clients reacted angrily, however, when antis confronted them. Tanya said that as Operation Rescue's actions and the political debate surrounding abortion received increased media attention in the late 1980s, clients were more likely than before to stand up for themselves and to denigrate the protesters:

> Before abortion rights became a bigger issue, a lot of our clients seemed to feel less strongly about their decision 'cause . . . it wasn't in the media. Nobody talked about abortion that much. It was, if anything, less okay three years ago than it is now . . . as far as people's ideas about it. Their perceptions are much more positive about abortion with all this anti-abortion activity. . . . But that wasn't . . . the case . . . before Operation Rescue and *Webster*.

Celia disagreed with co-workers who said encounters with antis could work as a politicizing force, explaining that she tried to encourage clients to get involved in the struggle even though she did not expect her advice to have much of an impact:

> Maybe I'm just cynical these days. You know, on one hand, I just expect them to appreciate it so much; these people should just appreciate that they can come in and get an abortion. They don't know how close they are to losing it. . . . I don't know if it's just being Americans or what, but we're just very . . . used to, you know, a lot of comfort. And we're used to being very privileged. And we're used to, you know, getting things when we want them.

For many women, abortion had become too easy, Celia thought; some of us took it for granted. Celia advocated democratic practice to revitalize the pro-choice movement but believed the individualistic consumerism at the core of American culture acted against the demonstration of civic consciousness. Protecting clients' anonymity was essential, workers thought, but also allowed aborting women to hide from acknowledging the political nature of having an abortion. Charlotte Taft, director of the Routh Street Women's Clinic in Dallas, says that confidentiality contributes to the stigma of abortion. "Every time clinics assure women of anonymity, she now believes, they reinforce the shame of all the women who have abortions but won't admit it," Sally Giddens wrote in a profile of Taft (1990: 52). Perhaps only if abortion workers stopped making abortion so easy, Celia said, would clients recognize the salience of procreative freedom and fight for it. "Maybe if they were forced to act, they would have to act."

Interaction with the antis strengthened the commitment of staff members who stayed through 1988. But this interaction also exhausted them and made them feel marginalized because they were feminist. Though most Americans were not members of Operation Rescue—or even anti-choice—Center staff members saw the anti-abortionists' stance as having made an indelible mark on mainstream Americans' thinking.

The Results of the Attack: Strained Relationships, Solidarity, Sisterhood

Outside of work, Center women confronted the same sort of ideological opposition they faced on the job. Sometimes the spillover of anti-abortion sentiments into their "private" lives seemed even worse than facing those attitudes at work because it reinforced their sense of themselves as marginalized thinkers. Many Center women described friends' and family's negative reactions to their work, ranging from standard anti-abortion tirades to complaints that the women were unable to leave their work behind at the end of the day. As relationships outside of work were strained, work could come to seem even more central to women's lives.

Emma, discussing her responses to the 1988 blockades, said: "It really made me more suspicious of people, just wondering who I might be meeting was an anti, who I might be seeing in the grocery store or sitting next to me at dinner or in a movie, because a lot of them just look like very normal folks. . . . And so I felt a lot more alienated just from people in general." Center women learned that seemingly "normal folks" could be antis. Thus, they saw abhorrent views normalized. Possible confrontations awaited them not only immediately outside the Center but everywhere they went. Sarina said she considered all social situations potentially explosive, potentially unpleasant:

I find that when I go out in social circles, people ask me what I do. And I don't give it away. . . . I will say that I'm in outpatient women's health care or contraceptive work or outpatient gynecology or something like that. Most of the time I don't tell people that I'm an abortionist unless

I'm fairly confident that we're not going to get into some heated argument and/or debate over this issue. A lot of times I feel like I can never get away from it.

Two of Lee's sisters and her mother were anti-choice, so her work was for some time a bone of contention that strained relations. She spoke of how "the denial system" in her family allowed for congenial relations, but when abortion did come up, there was no way that any sort of negotiation could be achieved.

Oh Lordy, when I told my one sister that I was back at the clinic again, . . . I told her, I said, "You need to know that I'm working at the clinic, and that I love my job. I'm glad I work there; I'm proud of it. Right now, I really don't want to talk about abortion; I want to talk about you and me being sisters." But she didn't want to talk about that; she wanted to talk about abortion. . . . So she started out going on her tirade about how—she's a nurse too—and she said, well, as I progress through nursing school, I "will probably develop more of a respect for life" [laughing]. . . . As if I simply haven't thought about this, which is really insulting! . . . So anyway, she started out with that kind of thing and ended up talking about things like demon possession. And this woman's a *nurse*. It really scares the hell out of me. . . . So, it was just the same kind of drivel that you can read or hear from any fundamentalist.

Her interaction with her family members taught her, she said, that "there wouldn't be any dialogue" possible with the antis outside the clinic. (Several months after this interview, Lee came to feel no dialogue was possible with her family either, and she stopped communicating with them.)

Relationships with friends or lovers became tense or embittered when they perceived Center staff members as too involved in their work and when they were unable to understand the importance of the battles Center women were fighting. Ilene described this lack of empathy as characteristic of the men she dated and spoke of how her social life suffered, especially during Operation Rescue's biggest protests at the Center.

When I first started working at the clinic, . . . all the men I knew then would say, "You need to get another job. You're too involved in this job." . . . It was really bad when I started there. And this guy, I remember we sat on this couch, . . . and the next thing I knew I was standing up, *screaming* about what had happened during the day. And he was . . . looking at me like, "You need to get another job!" Of course, that relationship didn't last very long. Everyone still tells me I need to get another job, so yeah, it had an effect on my life.

Center women realized that other people might not comprehend the magnitude of the threat to legal abortion nor understand what it was like to worry about this threat on a daily basis. At the same time, their friends' responses made them wonder whether they might be overreacting or be overly absorbed by their jobs. At the Center, though, they reaffirmed each other's assessment of the situation as dire and crucial, and their shared experiences of working through crises provided a sound basis for continuing to see the struggle to keep abortion available as essential, rightfully consuming. Some women said they even came to work on their days off during the blockades to help out. As their views were confirmed through their work experiences, they came to see people who did not grasp the importance of feminist activism for procreative freedom as ignorant of what should be patently obvious. During the summer of 1991, Tanya told me:

> None of my friends thought that it was horrible that Medicaid funding had been taken away or that they kept trying to pass a parental-consent law every year in the [state] legislature. They didn't think that had any connection with them or any connection with *Roe v Wade* being threatened, you know. . . . We had to wait till we had, you know, two crises— OR [Operation Rescue] and *Webster*—before anybody would go, "My God, you're right!"

Painful though it was for them to think about, Center women described positive attributes of the horrible intensity of the 1988 blockades. They felt a sense of daily accomplishment when the antis were unable to shut the Center down. Their experience fighting the antis together was uniquely unifying.

> LEE: To tell you the truth . . . that was kind of an exciting time for me. . . . The staff really got a lot closer, and if you've got, you know, 150 or 200 people out in front of your workplace as you're going to work, that gets your adrenaline going. . . . Health-working is harder when we have protesters because women are upset or they're angry, . . . but people . . . have more to say when they come in. And the staff—you know, we have to support each other more, and, boy, I have never felt closer! We were a really close bunch at that time.

> CELIA: Nothing in the history of the Center had drawn all of the staff together like being under the assault of anti-abortionists. You

132

know, it was the one thing that we could all bond on 'cause you know there are a lot of divisions at the Center. . . . And it was really like we drew together and we fought them off, you know? Everyone was just so committed to winning that battle.

ILENE: Of course, staffwise, we were all much more of a group. We were all together and, you know, I had just started working there, but, still, we were all together as a group.

During battle, the Center was a feminist community where members felt mutual admiration and offered each other nurturant support that was not necessarily available outside the Center. Two years later, staff members who had been there during 1988 waxed nostalgic for the kind of camaraderie they had enjoyed during trying times, and the women who came to work after 1988 spoke wistfully about the collective spirit that had become a staple of Center lore. Thus, in a sense, the antis contributed to job satisfaction. They were a concrete representation of how endangered the right to abortion had become, and their presence gave workers a heightened sense of purpose. Lee explained, "It increased my commitment, and . . . it made my job more appealing because I liked the immediacy of it." She paused, realizing, I think, that she might sound as though she *enjoyed* the antis' onslaught, and continued, "Well, really, well, okay, that's not really the right way to say it. The right thing is that it was a real cauldron for me. That time was really confused with a lot of activity, and I had to solidify my thinking about abortion if I was to continue to work there, so in that way it changed my feelings about my work." For Lee and for the co-workers who endured through 1988, their jobs took on the character of a "calling." The women's intense emotional experiences imbued their work with meaning.

PART TWO

WORKING FEMINISM

CHAPTER 4

Feminist Workplace?

Examining Contradictions in Institutional Ideology

In the mid-1970s, the establishment of a women-run health-care center like the Womancare Center in and of itself exemplified feminist idealism in practice. Emma and Nancy set out to challenge the medical model both through their interactions with clients and in their collective organizational structure. The Center has changed significantly since its early days. The organization exemplifies how professionalization has developed within what was originally a grass-roots movement for women's health care. Many other feminist-founded nonprofit health centers (and other small businesses) have gradually bureaucratized and come to adhere to mainstream models of operating. Suzanne Staggenborg believes these changes are adaptive efforts that have allowed the women's health movement to survive. "The pro-choice movement has been able to maintain itself and grow in strength since the legalization of abortion by acquiring professional leadership and formalized organizational structures. . . . Contrary to some theories of what happens to movements when they become institutionalized, however, these developments actually facilitated, rather than hindered, the growth of grass-roots movement activities" (1991: 5).

Growth made collectivist organizational principles seem inefficient and impractical to members of the Center. But does the power of a larger social movement compensate for structural compromises? More specifically, what happens to staff members' work experiences when the structure of their workplace is transformed—however gradually and however "innocently"— into the hierarchical organizational model the founders originally sought to avoid?

When they examined the conditions under which they worked and when they talked about hierarchy, mobility, and decision making within the Center in the 1990s, many staff members conceded that the Center did not achieve pure feminist goals or ideals. The administrators felt much less ambivalence about how the Center had developed structurally, especially Emma, the executive director. All health workers and supervisors believed that shared decision making ought to be a crucial element of feminist practice, but these groups of women evaluated the governing of administrators differently. Supervisors, sandwiched between the administrators and the health workers, expressed sympathy in both directions. They tended to defend administrators against health workers' complaints, saying that administrators did as much as they could to encourage and incorporate input from both supervisors and health workers. Most staff members said they hoped the administrators would work to repair hierarchical rifts, but several described them—especially Emma—as indifferent to workers' ideas and incapable of adapting their managerial style.

I believe that, as my contact with Center workers intensified and they came to know me better, they felt more comfortable complaining to me about the organization than when they had seen me as a total outsider. This growing intimacy at least partly explains the fact that the women seemed increasingly critical of the Center's organizational practices in the interviews I conducted after 1991. Also, during 1992, the organization was short-staffed; money was especially tight (according to administrators); and morale among health workers was noticeably low. Thus, I happened upon a crisis that accentuated workers' dissatisfaction. I do not mean to undercut the criticisms of the women who were most disparaging of the Center or to suggest that their complaints were not legitimate, but I want to put their remarks into temporal perspective. Within the organizational culture of the Center, it was taken for granted that morale naturally would wax and wane because the work was so intense and draining. Several health workers said that 1992 seemed to them the worst period in the Center's history in terms of worker-management relations. This nadir initiated an unprecedented wave of quitting (along with several dismissals) that, for the first time in the Center's history, eventually reached into upper-level management.[1]

In this chapter, I explore how workers and managers (both administrators and supervisors) evaluated the organizational practices that structured their work lives almost twenty years after the Center's radical beginning. I examine several hierarchical ruptures or managerial mistakes (depending on one's point of view) that workers talked about as exemplifying organizational inconsistencies with ideal feminist practice, and I contrast managers' and workers' analyses of these situations. Some of the issues workers raised may sound innocuous at first (such as the debate over a dress code or incidents of mistreatment involving one or two individuals), but they all allow an exploration of the intricacies of organizational discourse. The most potent example involved a change in protocol for staffing first-trimester abortions. Until 1992, all abortions were staffed by two health workers; one health-worked, or attended to the client, and the other assisted the physician. In early 1992, these two positions were combined in order to reduce the number of staff members needed to run first-trimester-abortion clinics. No health workers were fired but several worked fewer hours as a result of the change. (The old division of labor remained intact for staffing second-trimester-abortion clinics.) The staff's reactions to this amendment of Center procedures elucidate especially well how organizational requirements impinged on feminist practice.

One Big Happy Family?

The Womancare Center's mission statement reads: "Our goal is to enable women to make informed choices about their health care and reproduction through the provision of self-help health education and gynecological services. We work with others locally, nationally, and internationally to ensure that women have the information and power to control their bodies and their lives." Individual sovereignty, the cornerstone of liberalism, here becomes an ideal for an international community among bodily autonomous women, with self-help education spread across the globe. The linguistic division between women inside and outside the Center in the mission statement, though, at least subliminally undercuts the endorsement of the democratization of health care: "our goal . . . their health care. . . . We work to ensure that women . . . control their bodies . . . their lives."

The ambiguous positioning of a Center "we" as both part of and separate from a worldwide "they" recurs, writ smaller, within organizational operations: many workers both felt a sense of community at the Center and felt divided by the hierarchical structure of their organization. They claimed the Center did not and could not live up to its profession of democratic orientation at home because its hierarchical bureaucracy created divisions that eliminated the possibility of "we-ness," even given the best intentions on the part of those in charge. (Indeed, several workers did not believe administrators were capable, *as* administrators, of having the best intentions.) Is it possible for a bureaucratic hierarchy to claim the feminist label?

Feminist scholars have long debated whether bureaucratic structure and feminist idealism are reconcilable or incompatible. Kathy Ferguson's work best represents the antibureaucratic stance; she writes, "Feminists, as individuals and as groups, will often have to confront bureaucracies and to work within them, but if the feminist movement allows its own organizations or ideology to become bureaucratic, it ceases to carry any critical edge" (1984: 180–181). Power divisions are the root of oppression; thus, feminists must eschew power divisions. Other scholars counter this position with the assertion that ideals of shared power and equitable participation through the eradication of structure are pipe dreams. Critics of the anti-bureaucratic position believe collectives are not truly collective anyway. Power struggles and informal hierarchies inevitably emerge in any human interaction, and the view that a group of feminists can wipe out power dynamics with good intentions or long meetings is seen as naive.

In her study of a feminist "counterbureaucratic" battered women's shelter, for example, Noelie Maria Rodriguez draws on the work of Jo Freeman (1972–1973) and Joyce Rothschild-Whitt (1982) to demonstrate that decision making by consensus and the absence of a formal bureaucracy do not obliterate power or status differences among staff members; the outcome is simply unsanctioned hierarchical relations (1988: 221–222). Freeman sees the conflict (hierarchy against collectivity) on which anti-bureaucratic feminists focus as indicative of the tensions between "goal attainment needs and maintenance needs." She recasts feminist resistance to bureaucratic structure as a desire to preserve "a nice family feeling" on the job, an emphasis that she believes can become so time consuming that work itself falls by the wayside, and the organization crumbles (1992).

Using different terms but moving in the same ideological direction, Iris Marion Young depicts the "desire for community" as a moral problem for feminism. She writes that "too often people in political groups take mutual friendship to be a goal of the group and thus find themselves wanting as a group when they do not achieve such commonality" (1990: 312). Community idealism fails, in Young's view, because it relies on conformity and exclusion, and "often channels energy away from the political goals of the group" (312). Young calls cohesiveness a fantasy that postmodern feminists ought to give up if we ever hope to get anywhere. Anti-bureaucratic feminist values can thus act as ideological barriers to organizational accomplishments, whether they are cast in practical or moral terms. Like these feminist scholars, "lay feminist" Center workers also disagreed about whether feminist practice could be realized within a hierarchical setting: most did not hold that bureaucracy always erodes feminism.

In my early interviews (1990–1991), Center workers at all levels of the hierarchy spoke highly of their workplace and rarely questioned its self-presentation as a feminist organization. They felt this label was justified because of the organization's ideological perspective and rarely talked about an inability to realize ideals in praxis. These women said Center administrators encouraged tolerance for differences of opinion or ideology (within a broad range of feminist frameworks) as well as respect for differences of "race," class, and sexual identity. "Strong women" would not always agree with or like each other, but disagreements did not threaten the strongly felt, institutionally forged interpersonal bonds. As Anne, the first black staff member to become a supervisor at the Center, described it, "I think that now that I'm on the inside . . . it's a lot different from what I perceived it to be. I never thought that I could work as a woman in a social setting—in a setting period—just with all women. . . . You know, for everyone, whether they're black, white, Hispanic, it doesn't matter—Asian, . . . heterosexual, homosexual—we all are minorities [because we're women], and we're on an equal plateau."

In these early interviews, Center women continually described what Freeman calls "a nice family feeling." Mira explicitly called the Center "a family" where she knew she could always find a "supportive environment." Tanya said, "I feel like I'm privileged to work here. I'm spoiled now. I don't know if I could work in a regular place where I don't get to work with such a wonderful group of people." She cited one of her mentors, who, when leaving the Center, had said it was "like a home to her and she didn't know what she was going to do without" it. Hallie echoed this sentiment. "We do have some struggles, but I feel we work together well. . . . I think it's wonderful, one of the best working environments. . . . I can be 'out' there. . . . We're real supportive of each other." The women stressed that their organization did not, as many workplaces do, impose false roles or require pretense of any kind because it respected differences. Mira said, "You can be absolutely anybody here." In the workers' view, demonstrating mutual support and respect among women—whether clients or co-workers—was feminist behavior; thus the Center was a feminist workplace.

Not until my interview with Celia in July 1991 did I begin to interrogate organizational structure critically as a research issue. Prior to this point, my focus was on health workers' and administrators' accounts of doing abortion work, dealing with anti-abortion opposition, and thinking about the future of abortion politics. I had not probed beyond the "happy-family" rewards Center women described, which were perhaps the biggest inducement for continued labor: their appreciation of each other kept them coming to work during hard times (such as the 1988 blockade discussed in Chapter Three) and made them love their work. Then, during Celia's interview, she segued from a rather typical discussion of feminist care-giving to a provocative portrayal of Center organizational structure as nonfeminist. "We really try to see eye to eye, woman to woman, as opposed to medical personnel to patient, you know. And that's really unique; there aren't a of places that do that around. But, I mean, the problem at the Center is . . . how does the Center treat the staff? Is the staff being treated in a feminist way?" When I asked whether she thought they were, she replied:

> It's a conflict because we're this hierarchy, and yet we're feminists. And, to me, the definition of feminism doesn't fit into a hierarchy. . . . It's very hard to supervise in a feminist fashion. . . . You know, people call up, and . . . they say, . . . "I'm just too depressed to come to work today." . . . I would like to be able to say, "Well, that's okay." But then you're sup-posed to ask, "Well, do you think you could?" I don't know what you say when people say that, you know? I mean, it's really a conflict.

Celia disliked dealing with noncompliance on the part of the workers she supervised: ideally, everyone would be equally responsible for getting work done, and no one would be put in the awkward position of having to tell other people what to do. Many workers contended that a nonauthoritarian stance formed the core of a feminist ethic of care (as discussed in Chapter One), thus the imposition of hierarchy within the clinic seemed unfeminist. As a friend to the women she managed, Celia would have liked to sympathize with them when their ability to do their jobs was impaired. As an agent of the adminis-tration, though, she could not act as a friend in many situations. Her job required that personal relationships be sacrificed to organizational require-ments when she interacted with health workers as a supervisor. And once she began to act as a supervisor in some situations, her friendships with health workers were affected by her enhanced authority. She might want to only play the role of supervisor, but roles become embedded and active elements of social interactions; one cannot simply shed them at will when one experi-ences aspects of them as false or morally troubling.

More than anything else, my interest in the Center's dilemmas as a feminist organization, first prompted by Celia's comments, made me want to do eth-nography there. Celia questioned the integrity of the Center as a feminist organization because she did not see it struggling against organizational power imbalances in a manner consistent with its founders' mission ("We . . . try to see eye to eye, woman to woman"). Yet Celia said that before the Center was formally defined as a hierarchy, it had not run as smoothly, in part because people did not have clearly defined roles and thus did not know "what to expect" from each other. Though Celia felt the stratification of staff was a more efficient method of organization, it also meant that feminist ideals would not ever be met. "I think the challenge is to create something . . . that's not a traditional hierarchy—that works," she said. But she was not especially hopeful; "I don't think that's going to happen at the Center," she said.

Historians of the women's movement (and of a larger array of 1960s and 1970s leftist organizations) generally agree that the fight against hierarchy and structure ultimately becomes a losing battle: either egalitarianism fails as the informal structure becomes a breeding ground for organizational problems, or the group simply falls apart for lack of direction. It also becomes difficult to deal with conventional institutions that refuse to credit collective principles as a valid basis for running an organization (see, for example, Evans 1979, Echols 1989, Freeman 1975, and Gitlin 1987).

However, several scholars are optimistic about combining a "nice family feeling" with getting the work done (see, for example, Fairfield 1981, Mansbridge 1980, Rothschild and Whitt 1986, and Zager and Rosow 1982). Jane Mansbridge distinguishes between "adversary" and "unitary" democracy, the "adversary" type necessary in situations characterized by conflicting interests among participants, and the "unitary" type appropriate in situations where participants share interests. Mansbridge argues that most organizational situations necessitate a combination of both adversary and unitary democracy. "Relatively unitary institutions [of the late sixties and early seventies] filled human needs that adversary institutions cannot fill," she writes, and "the failures of unitary democracies often derive from their refusal either to recognize when interests conflict or to deal with those conflicts by adversary procedures" (1980: 4). Collectives lack an impersonal method of conflict resolution; achieving consensus is a difficult feat in organizations built on personal ties. Disagreements can be dealt with more easily by relying on a majority-rule system.

Even as its structure became increasingly rigid, the Center loosely incorporated unitary democratic methods. For example, at the health workers' monthly meetings I observed, the supervisors who ran the meetings often urged health workers to raise their concerns. However, this practice did not mean health workers necessarily had a voice in decision making. Administrators' attentiveness to health workers' ideas or complaints was erratic. They always showed concern about staff members' dissatisfaction but had no comprehensive or consistent policy for addressing it. Workers' responses to administrative initiatives might be taken into account when shaping policy or might be summarily entertained and ultimately dismissed, depending entirely on administrators' assessment of the particular situation at hand. Sometimes administrators made decisions after consulting health workers; more often they met with supervisors only, treating them as representatives of the health workers. Other times, administrators simply made decisions and then let supervisors pass the information down to the health workers.

In the interviews I conducted in 1990 and 1991, most health workers seemed to share a basic trust of supervisors' and administrators' intentions to take health workers' concerns into consideration when making and implementing decisions. As their comments indicate, most of the women described the Center as the most flexible, the most congenial, and the most mission-infused workplace they had ever experienced or imagined, and they believed that a hierarchy, though not a morally ideal structure, was the most practical best fit between achieving feminist goals and running a business. It was seen not as an idyllic community but as a benevolent hierarchy that strove to carry its feminism into its internal workings as much as possible. Mansbridge writes that if a group of people share interests, power differentials may not be counterproductive "since each will promote the interests of the others" (1980: 5); this description may well apply to much of what went on during the Center's history until nearly a decade after members of the collective formalized its structure.

"A Very Large Dysfunctional Family"

In the interviews I conducted after 1991, workers' described the Center as everything from a benevolent hierarchy to a ship sinking under the weight of hypocrisy. Most of the women were much less pleased with their workplace than they had been a year or two earlier; the buoyant camaraderie staff members described in the earlier interviews seemed to have eroded. Health workers spoke repeatedly of feeling overworked and underappreciated. They detailed internal resentments and antagonisms that they felt resulted from poor morale. Many acknowledged institutionalized racism as an undeniable facet of Center relations. Robert Zager and Michael Rosow write that "if managers go through the motions of asking workers for advice but do not take account of what the workers tell them, it is better not to begin involving them at all" (1982: xiv). Health workers often voiced this objection to administrators' participatory gestures in the later interviews: no participation would be better than inconsistency or hypocrisy because at least they would know where they stood.

Center workers who criticized the organizational hierarchy seemed to share Ferguson's dream of anti-bureaucratic structures, tempered by the cynicism expressed by critics of the anti-bureaucratic stance. Ellen, interviewed in 1993 after she had quit her job as a part-time nurse-practitioner at the

Center to move out of state, said she felt the Center had become "a male type of organization." She cited increased bureaucratization, increased formalization of the hierarchical structure of power, and reinvigorated adherence to rules (such as the dress code) as reasons for her belief. She felt the Center's internal structure ought to be consistent with its philosophical approach to care-giving, or both the structure and the care-giving would suffer and not realize feminist ideals. By the time she left the Center in 1993, Ellen felt that administrators were not even attempting to run the Center in a feminist way and that a "business focus" had begun to affect the quality of treatment clients received:

> I think that the administration and the supervisors are not as willing to . . . deal with people's issues. . . . People have issues and that takes time. That's what we're there for! . . . . That has always been my problem in health care. . . . When you see a patient, and you go and you deal with a patient, people expect you to turn them out in fifteen minutes. . . . I really feel strongly that the only way you can deal with a patient is to know them personally. . . . You can't just say to somebody "you have gonorrhea" like you tell them "you have high blood pressure."

Ellen used health care provision as an analogy for what she believed had gone wrong with the Center organizationally. By disregarding workers' "issues," administrators reduced them to instruments of the organization and manipulated them in ways that contradicted "what we're there for!"

Health workers complained that administrators did not know what their work was like because administrators were rarely "in clinic." Emma wanted to move the offices out of the building altogether, into another location about a mile from the Center (and eventually did so, in late 1992). Health workers cited this desire as evidence that administrators did not care about what it was like to be doing the actual nitty-gritty work of the Center. They also complained that administrators were not good managers, asserting that they did not care about workers' satisfaction and that they played favorites. Several excerpts from the interviews represent the range of this sort of complaint:

> LOIS: I see the clinic as a very large dysfunctional family. . . . The problem is, I think they had a great idea when they started it out as lay health workers, but I don't think they've been trained in management, and I don't think they know a whole lot about it. . . . They really don't care if the staff turns over. . . . They want the work done . . . as fast as possible for as little as possible.

145

JULIA: I think for all the good intentions of the clinic, they don't understand—and they *need* to . . .—just where we're at now, and where we're coming from. How tired we are, or how hard we work. . . . They're going to have to [listen] or what will end up happening is that people will get burnt out, and people will *quit*. . . . I don't care what they did fifteen years ago. I'm talking about what's here and now, and I'm *tired*.

CARRIE: It's hard to think of a structure that would work, . . . a feminist structure, because there aren't that many in business. . . . I think I would want the divisions between management and not-management to be a lot less harsh, a lot less sharp. I think I would want the . . . people actually managing the clinic to be *in* the clinic . . . instead of being supervised by somebody who doesn't spend any time in the clinic and doesn't know what your concerns are.

ILENE: They [administrators] have this pin that says . . . "The Womancare Center: Working for the Lives of Women" or something. They do. But not for the lives of the women that work there. They exploit women who work there, and they abuse them. . . . It's just like working for men. I mean, it's just like working for somebody who's sexist, except you don't have to worry about sexual harassment. You have to be "in" with them in order to be treated fairly, . . . which I think is not right. Course you can imagine what side I'm on since I'm saying this.

The administrators originally devised the work routines at the Center, so charges that they did not know what was going on seemed ridiculous to them. Administrators told me they thought health workers were not willing to work as hard as they themselves did in the clinic's early days. Administrators—and often supervisors too—cast health workers' "constant complaints" as evidence of health workers' lack of commitment to the Center. Circularly, they often cited health workers' lack of commitment to the Center as evidence that their complaints must be overblown.

One need not consult ethnographic accounts of workplace interactions to know that workers and managers complain about each other and that hierarchical divisions produce at least occasional conflict even in the best of situations. The conflicts Center women described exemplify friction typical of management-worker relations in capitalist work structures. Most fascinating to me was the fact that all this infighting was cloaked with a sleek premise of ideal sisterhood. By 1992, this cover had been badly frayed.

In her first interview, Rae described the contradiction she saw between institutional image and reality. Arguing along the same lines as Freeman, Rae said the "nice family feeling" proffered by the administration was merely a facade; underneath was a purely impersonal business.

> I think that the fact that the Center is losing that primary focus on being a feminist [workplace] is because of the almighty dollar. . . . It's about business, and the Center doesn't want to say that, and that's what they [administrators] should say. . . . They shouldn't say other things to contradict that because that is what they're about. And that's why they have so much problems at the clinic . . . because they always make people feel like they have that space to say how they feel but please know that it won't . . . make a difference.

Rae, unlike Ellen, did not worry about achieving feminist goals organizationally: she said she simply preferred that administrators be straightforward. When I interviewed her a year later, in 1993, she said administrators were being more honest and that by plainly acknowledging a business orientation they had activated a wave of turnover in staff that she saw as potentially positive:

> I like this much more because it's not that—*lying* is the only word to use. . . . It's no gray area anymore. It's like, "This is a business, and the main thing of this business is money. Yes, we care about women, but money is the big issue." . . . A lot of people didn't leave [before this acknowledgment] because of the comfort level they had at their job. A lot of people stayed because what other job could you call off because your cat died? Do you know what I'm saying? Or because you're just having a hard time with your boyfriend and you just can't get up today? What other job would understand that? . . . I don't think that anyone would have the gall [to use such excuses now] . . . 'cause those things aren't accepted anymore. . . . I think that that's fair. But on the same token, because of the workplace that we work in, I think there should be other compensations . . . for individuals.

Rae was willing to play by the administration's rules, but she wanted bonuses in reward for her hard work. Capitalism was fine with her, as long as she got rewarded for her hard work (as she naively assumed she would). When I asked her about what sorts of improvements she would make in organizational structure, Rae said (in both interviews) that she thought relations between staff and administration would improve if staff were treated appreciatively and more instrumentally. "We're living out their [Emma's and

Nancy's] vision for them. . . . If I had a vision and someone was living out that vision for me, I think I'd be more appreciative monetarily!"[2] As she described it, her job consisted of doing the will of others, realizing "their vision." The founders never thought of what they did at the Center as a job in these terms because it was first a dream to which they devoted all their energy, and then, eventually, it became a career for them: it was always *theirs*. Workers often said that Emma—and, less often, Nancy and Trudy—"owned" the Center or that it was a "mom and pop" business (with Nancy as mom and Emma as pop). They knew this characterization was technically untrue (since the Center was a nonprofit organization) but used this language to convey how much the administrators retained control over the Center. Many workers portrayed the administrators' possessiveness as unhealthy and antithetical to the communitarian ideals they believed should be a part of feminist practice.

Decoding the Dress Code

Both "sides" of the worker-management divide wielded examples to demonstrate their righteousness and the other's intractability. The dress code was a recurrent theme in workers' and the executive director's assessments of what was wrong at the Center. For example, Ellen said administrators had lost sight of their feminist ideals. She talked about this phenomenon broadly, then specifically mentioned the dress code as one piece of supportive evidence. "It's becoming a male type of organization. . . . I think there are people who call themselves feminists who get sucked into that because they think that . . . if we're going to compete with the world, we're going to have to be like the world—down to the point where, you know, you can't have hair on your armpits showing or you can't have hair on your legs showing because you're going to offend other people." Ellen used the dress code as an illustration of management's attempt to control workers to the point of unnecessarily meddling in their self-presentation. The administrators' determination to enforce a dress code indicated to Ellen that they did not trust workers' abilities to judge what clothing was and was not appropriate. She also believed administrators were "selling out" by making staff members conform to sexist notions of what women's bodies should look like (clean-shaven or with contested hair-growing areas hidden from view).

Other workers shared these interpretations of the dress code. Ilene cited her own violation of the rules as an example of how unfairly administrators maintained power over health workers. She said, "Did I tell you I got written up on my yearly evaluation because of my tattoos? I was marked down [by Emma] . . . for my tattoos, but, yet, no one ever spoke to me about them." Ilene was told not to wear any clothing that did not cover the tattoos on her back and arms, which were deemed inappropriate and potentially offensive sights for clients. Being written up without warning indicated, in Ilene's view, that the dress codes simply bolstered an unpredictable disciplinary system in which administrators—in this case, Emma—condemned women who were out of favor without warning. Ilene said that administrators considered her a troublemaker because she spoke her mind and that the tattoo incident was a way of reprimanding her. To Ilene, this incident exemplified the way in which power divisions eroded any chance of sisterly community at the Center.

Workers especially scoffed at administrative censorship of dress that characterized certain clothing as too revealing. They considered this hypocritical because they felt that feminism should counter depictions of women's bodies as dirty, unseemly, or distracting to others. One hot summer day when the air-conditioning system was on the fritz, Polly, an administrative worker, told me she had been advised by Emma not to take her jacket off because her nipples showed through her blouse. Diana and Rae recounted another time when an administrator warned an assembly of health workers, "If you could wear it to a nightclub . . . don't wear it to work!"[3] To workers, the most offensive aspect of this line of rule making was that allegedly feminist women were policing the self-presentation of other women and using sexist criteria to determine what would be acceptable. Women's bodies were thus cast as offensive and inherently provocative or inappropriate.

The meaning of the dress code shifts dramatically when seen through the eyes of administrators. The Center's leaders justified hierarchy by talking about how political changes necessitated organizational transformation and conservatization. Emma cast workers' resistance to structure as resentment toward the professionalism she felt was a necessary component of the Center's survival. During our 1993 interview, she repeatedly offered the dress code as an example of workers' misguided rebelliousness. Emma thought workers' complaints revealed intransigence rather than the thoughtful analysis and practical action she believed ought to be central to feminist thought. Emma, like the workers who discussed the dress code, saw it as a relatively inconsequential issue that, when analyzed, revealed the other side's dogmatic stubbornness.

When I asked Emma to evaluate the Center's structure in terms of feminist practice, she began with a broad defense. Like Ellen and the health workers cited above, she offered the dress code as an example in support of her position. She said:

> I don't think that you can run an organization as a collective at this size. I think that . . . there's a certain amount that happens, given the size and the demands, that requires structure. And I don't feel that structure is

bad. One of the things that has certainly been a tension here . . . is just looking at increased professionalism . . . and what does that mean? And is that contrary to feminism? And does feminism mean that you have to be able to just wear whatever you want and have no rules? Or can you be feminist and wear a business suit?

In Emma's view, a hierarchical structure connoted professionalism, which she believed was necessary and mature in the 1990s. Emma elided "wear[ing] whatever you want" with "hav[ing] no rules," depicting the rebelliousness of younger employees as juvenile and self-indulgent.

In language similar to Freeman's characterization of conflict between collectivism and hierarchy as a struggle between goal-attainment needs and maintenance needs, Emma described arguments at the Center over feminist practice as arising out of "competing needs," acknowledging that her needs and goals and those of the health workers differed. But when she spoke about her concern with preserving the organization, she portrayed her needs as the only route to success. She invalidated workers' "needs" as merely petty or selfish impulses:

People think that because this is a feminist organization—they come with . . . so many expectations that we can never meet. And that's unfortunate, but that's reality. . . . It is a workplace as opposed to a social organization. And so the combination—or the juxtaposition—of having a feminist organization and a workplace creates a lot of inherent conflicts. And people often get really caught up in the tension of what that is and can really be very blaming.

Consider the contrasting ideologies: for dissatisfied staff members, "deal[ing] with people's issues," as Ellen declared, was "what we're there for!" Emma saw instead unreasonable "expectations" on the part of the staff, which could not be met because the Center was not a "social organization."

For Emma, the dress code perfectly illustrated the power plays that plagued the Center: her portrayal highlighted the staff's ignorance of survival strategies and the administrators' sensible use of authority. Emma elaborated on the relevance of the dress code from her (reasonable) perspective and, again, described workers' resistance as ultimately leading to chaos:

In terms of trying to provide services and be respectful for the clients and reach a diverse audience of clients, I think a dress code is absolutely necessary. . . . If someone comes to work here and their definition of feminism is that I can wear whatever I want, then they're going to be in a clash. Or "My definition of feminism is, well, I don't really need to prove my work. Don't give me a deadline. People should just trust that I can do this. I'm really a good person." And so their supervisor says, "Here's a deadline, you need to have this in." There's a clash there. . . . And so it's just a setup for some of those kinds of clashes.

I asked her, "What was it like to be on your side of it? I mean does it bother you when people raise these complaints?" She replied, "I've gotten really tired of it. I feel like if I have one more discussion about a dress code, I'm just going to . . . scream. . . . Can we just move on to something else?"

In Emma's view, the context for feminist action had shifted, and some health workers refused to recognize this change. Hiding body hair or wearing stockings may have once signaled compliance with sexist norms, but in the 1990s adherence to these norms could be seen as a service to *women* (clients) because they expected "professional" attire and might be put off by armpit hair or unstockinged legs. Emma felt workers' desires to avoid this sort of regimentation meant they were undisciplined: messy, lazy, and maybe even incompetent. Emma's feminist methods were practical, businesslike; she considered rebellious health workers methodless, unstrategic, and dogmatic. Unsurprisingly, Emma resisted movement toward sharing power with health workers. She may have interpreted such demands as further evidence that staff members did not understand how best to accomplish the work of the Center.

A Pregnant Pause

In discussions about rifts between workers and management, several women brought up the administrators' treatment of pregnant co-workers. During the period of my fieldwork, three staff members were pregnant: Hannah and Glenda (both supervisors) and Audrey (a health worker). Audrey experienced nausea and vomited almost daily well into her second trimester; she and several of her co-workers complained about management's reluctance to make special arrangements for her or to show understanding for her coming in late or missing work. As Audrey perceived the situation, administrators disapproved of her pregnancy because she had left a woman lover for a man not long before she got pregnant; she believed they saw her decision to have a child as impulsive and frivolous. Nor, she thought, did they approve of the way she was managing her pregnancy. Audrey chose an obstetrician (Roger Alton, who performed second-trimester abortions at the Center on Saturdays) over a midwife. She openly expressed her preference for the conventional medical management of pregnancy over midwifery. Trudy and Nancy (and every other pregnant Center worker in the past, to my knowledge) had chosen midwives as birth attendants and simply assumed any right-minded feminist would do the same. Audrey felt administrators showed no compassion for her all-day morning sickness because they didn't respect her decision making.

Janice described the predicaments of her pregnant co-workers:

> Audrey hasn't been getting the support she needed after she got pregnant, and she felt like people didn't want her to be pregnant by this guy because she was a lesbian before, and that she was totally confused, and just all that kind of stuff. . . . And then Glenda, before she got her job as a supervisor, apparently they asked her if she was planning to get pregnant or not, because if she was, then she was going to have to take leave, and it was going to totally mess up the supervisors. You know, that kind of shit. It's just like, *please*, if somebody wants to have a baby, then we need to be supportive and work around that, you know, but not let that interfere with their career tracks. And I think that part of that [lack of support] stems from the fact that they [Trudy and Nancy] . . . have already had their babies. You know, they used to have a *nursery* here.

Though Center administrators took pride in their respect for "choice" as a central tenet of feminist health care practice, the Center had no policies that demonstrated support for employees who decided to procreate. The Center's stance was basically a liberal feminist one. Pregnancy was not officially treated as an impediment to work; when it became one (as in Audrey's case), administrators disapproved. Women typically took two or three months of unpaid leave when their babies were born. (The Center's nursery days ended during its transformation from collective to bureaucracy, when Nancy's and Meryl's children were old enough for preschool.)

Janice believed that the Center ought to have extended the same respect to staff that it offered to clients; like Ellen, she believed the principles that structured the work ought to be consistent with the way in which the organization was run. Thus, staff members' decisions to have babies ought to have been easily incorporated into Center routines, rather than treated as impediments to Center goals. (Audrey's case was one example that several staff members gave of the administration's unfair handling of employee's particular situations. For instance, some women complained that managers were not willing to accommodate their school schedules or their responsibilities to their children, whereas in the past other workers had been able to make special arrangements.)

As director of administrative services, Trudy oversaw the implementation of all personnel policies. She frankly acknowledged the divisions that hierarchy had created. Her awareness might have surprised the more critical health workers, who tended to see administrators as oblivious to their tribulations. Trudy thought everyone suffered from the power imbalances at the Center:

There definitely are things I miss about [a collective]. . . . I miss the idea of everybody working having the same—at least in theory—having the same level of responsibility for decisions that are made because what happens in a hierarchy is that, I think, from the point of view of people that are on the upper end of the hierarchy, it's a heavy burden to bear to have that much responsibility. And, from the point of view of people that are on the bottom end of the hierarchy, it's, you know, feeling more powerless.

Trudy also spoke about how the hierarchy limited the depth of interpersonal bonds, which were once the central elements holding the Center together, as well as about aspects of the organization that had been immensely satisfying for her:

I think the other part that I miss *a lot* is the self-help approach to . . . our own lives. . . . You know, for example, if somebody was getting married, you would sit down and have a big meeting about . . . how not to get screwed, you know, in the marriage situation, you know, from a feminist point of view. You know, if somebody was having a health problem, we would meet . . . and help them really try to figure out what to do about it. . . . Try to figure out if there was a holistic way versus a . . . traditional medical way to deal with the situation. And I think that . . . felt very supportive. And I think that that is one thing that we've really lost. . . .

I think it's because of the hierarchy and because of the times that we live in—but the hierarchy in some ways is because of the times too. . . . In our organization [now], there's very little emphasis on holistic health. . . . none, really. . . . I think people who work in this organization—because we don't have that supportive structure, you know, where, you know, you really can talk to each other in an open way about your health concerns—are as likely as anybody else to go and get the most traditional care available, which may not necessarily be the best medical care. . . . As a manager, you know, it's none of my business, whereas in the collective structure I might go to somebody and say, "Listen, do you really think that's the best thing to do? You know, maybe you should try—" It would be very inappropriate for me to do that in the structure that we have.

The hierarchical structure made connections that were part of the original purpose of the Center impossible to achieve, Trudy said. Trudy alluded to Audrey's pregnancy as she described the lack of camaraderie between workers and administrators that prohibited her from talking to health workers about their lives. In the past, what might have been considered an exchange of viewpoints would now be colored by organizational divisions between workers and management: Trudy thought her opinions could appear to Audrey to be only judgmental criticism, not kindly advice. Trudy thus echoed health workers' wistful desire for a tighter community, one that could not be fashioned out of a hierarchical structure. Ironically, while Audrey considered administrators to be disapproving and unsupportive of her pregnancy, Trudy perceived management as merely silent, unable to offer advice. Audrey and several of her co-workers believed administrators behaved in an anti-feminist manner; Trudy described management as well-intentioned but stymied, unable to accomplish the feminist goal of ideal communication founded on an ethic of care. As Trudy told it, Center women were snagged in different ways by the same trap. Yet, as health workers saw it, administrators operated the trap and had no one to blame for its limitations but themselves.

Center women all argued forcefully in favor of their own polarized assessments of whatever the problematic situation at hand might be. Each side painted the other as the impediment to the realization of a satisfying work life for everyone. On many occasions, I found myself feeling alternately sympathetic to both perspectives on the same day, shifting back and forth with the passion of administrators' and workers' appeals. No one view need be seen as more valid: my point in airing opposing positions is not to pick a winner or identify a compromise position but rather to show how these hierarchical divisions often resulted in an impasse. Each woman's position within the Center's structure, and the degree to which she had become personally invested in the structure, shaped her particular "take" on what the organization's problems were and how they should (or should not) be addressed.

Anatomy of a Procedural Change

I turn now to what I perceived as the most telling cause of workers' dissatisfactions and the most dramatic example of how administrators transformed the Center's goals. As in the conflicts discussed above, in this dispute staff members usually allied or argued with each other in keeping with their hierarchical positions within the organization—health workers and medical workers versus administrators, with supervisors caught in the middle.

Everyone at the Center—at all levels—agreed that administrators poorly executed their decision to combine the tasks of health-working and assisting into one job, "advocating," during first-trimester abortions. Administrators and some health workers even said that workers would have easily adapted to the change were it not for the style of implementation. However, several other health workers declared that the whole incident—in both style and content—confirmed their view that administrators had abandoned feminist ideals at the Center.

In her second interview, in July 1992, Lee was the first to tell me about the implementation of advocating, which had first begun earlier that year. (I had been observing abortions staffed according to the new routine and did not know that protocol for first-trimester abortions had been changed.) Lee described what had happened, along with her outrage about the change:

> When they instituted this change, they instituted in within the course of *two days*. Two days to revolutionize the entire philosophy of the Center. . . . They told us it was because of OSHA [Occupational Safety and Health Administration, which is part of the U.S. Department of Labor]. And then they told us we were going to experiment with it and phase it in, and have health workers develop it and talk about it and see which systems worked best, and that they wanted our cooperation. And then two days later everything was set in stone, and if you argued with it, your alternative was to quit.

Administrators, in the view of many health workers, sought to slip in the new protocol under the guise of an OSHA requirement to institute "universal precautions" for handling bodily fluids (and potential blood-borne pathogens in them). Eventually, health workers were told that the new system was financially necessary and not substantively connected to procedures mandated by OSHA. Administrators told supervisors (who, in turn, told health workers) they had decided to reduce the number of health workers necessary to run first-trimester-abortion clinics in order to save money. Mira, a supervisor, defended the administrators' decision making. "They were looking at how other clinics did it. And they discovered that . . . we had excess, and we needed to eliminate one position from the clinic. It just wasn't cost-effective to do it the other way. . . . We can't afford to run a clinic this way when we can't raise our abortion fees. We're not going to be here in a year if we don't eliminate one body from our abortion clinic."

Several health workers complained that defenses like Mira's were smoke screens for administrators' true motives. These critics said administrators constantly proclaimed that the Center was on the brink of destitution. They believed administrators exaggerated, and they refused to credit their repetitive doomsaying. Instead, they formulated it as a ploy on the part of administrators to get them to work harder. During my fieldwork, administrators announced that some workers' hours would have to be cut, and several health workers volunteered for these reductions. No one was fired or forced to cut her hours, but this occurrence challenged health workers' view that administrators' fearful threats were all a ruse. Several health workers maintained that it served management's best interests to keep health workers always worried that their jobs could shrivel or disappear, that insecurity and instability ensured compliance on the part of workers. Other health workers dismissed this characterization of administrators as deliberately manipulative.

All the health workers I interviewed about the issue of advocating saw the old way of staffing first-trimester abortions as preferable, both for their clients, in terms of achieving feminist goals in health care provision, and for themselves, in terms of job satisfaction. Several health workers adamantly declared that administrators had simply abandoned their commitment to woman-centered care because they had lost touch with the work itself as they gained status and focused more on the Center's financial operations.

Lee, the health worker who first told me about the new advocating procedures, highlighted the ways in which health-working differed from advocating:

Health-working for fifteen years was—the *core* of your experience at the Center was—going in the room with women during the abortion, and . . . you weren't there as an advocate for the medical system, which is what you're doing now. You were there as an advocate for the woman. You wore street clothes. A different health worker [the assistant] assisted the physician. The physician talked very little, not to seem distanced from the woman, but the communication was facilitated through the health worker. So the health worker stood beside the woman, near her face, offering a hand to hold, and . . . in the past, before we had Sarina [the staff physician], . . . depending on which doctor was there that day, you really did have to defend the woman from the doctor because some of the doctors could say really awful things or be very rude. . . . Because of where you would stand in the room, you were the only person . . . who could see the woman's face, the doctor, and the assistant. So you were really counted on to facilitate any communication that was necessary.

Health-working in this manner meant championing each woman's needs even in the face of medical opposition. When Lee considered the new protocol in light of this feminist ideal, it could only fall short because an advocate was truly the doctor's assistant. Lee felt one could not maintain a double alliance and work for both the client and the doctor. The health worker's visible alliance with the doctor coopted her ability to dedicate herself fully to the client. Thus, the health worker ended up doing a job that ideologically opposed feminist health care practice. To Lee, the "core" experience of being a feminist caregiver had been negated:

> Now . . . you health-work and assist at the same time, which is more similar to what other clinics do. . . . You have to turn your back on the woman. You're wearing latex gloves, so there's not the personal contact. I don't feel as free holding women's hands or touching the women with the gloves on just 'cause it seems so impersonal to me. In some ways it seems *more* impersonal to touch the woman with gloves on than it does to not touch her at all and to have a closer verbal contact with her. . . . I cannot focus in on the woman nearly as well as I did. And emotionally, because I know that I have to . . . assist and health-work at the same time, I don't have the personal resources to really be available to the woman. So she's pretty much having her abortion alone. . . . It's still not as bad as it would be at another clinic, by any means, but even so, they've really destroyed the core of the Center.

Lee called the changed first-trimester-abortion procedures "the worst mistake they [administrators] could have ever made." For her, it meant that the principles she wanted her work to exemplify were deemed irrelevant by the very institution that had instilled them in her. "I don't love my job anymore," she said.

Many other health workers recapitulated Lee's criticisms of the new system. They described their inability to connect as effectively with clients as they had before because their attention was now divided, and they were required, as advocates, to look different from clients; they no longer looked like lay health workers. Wearing gloves and scrubs and taking responsibility for even minor tasks associated with the physical performance of abortion meant they were allied with medical personnel and thus in the Center's own reasoning, distanced from clients. Lois said, "You really can't . . . watch what's going on with the physician the entire time *and* take care of the woman. . . . So what's kind of happening is you're doing a half-assed job on every level."

Because they were now advocating more clients than they had health-worked previously, health workers saw themselves as doing two jobs instead of one. They found advocating much more physically exhausting and emotionally draining than health-working had been. Ultimately, they said, the clients were no longer getting the best care possible. Carrie said, for example, "I used to never have trouble trying to remember women's names, and, now, because I don't focus in on the woman enough, sometimes I have to keep myself from calling her the name of the woman who was there before." Engaging clients in conversation became one chore among many, she explained. "I don't learn as much about her because it's hard to think of that many things at once and keep up the conversation."

Like Lee, many health workers described advocating as working with the doctor rather than *for* the woman, as they felt they had done previously. Toby said, "They don't want to call it assisting, although that's what it is because you're not focusing your attention on the woman, because you have to make a decision what's more important, that Sarina get the instrument or that you talk to the woman. And she won't have that abortion unless you give Sarina the instrument. So that's the bottom line."

Administrators and supervisors described the old system as predicated on the assumption of an adversarial relationship between lay health workers and physicians. Defending the new procedures, they characterized such animosity as an impediment to efficient work. (In other conversations, though, administrators lamented the Center's reliance on medical professionals and described it as a longstanding and seemingly insurmountable problem for feminist health care activists.) Sarina, the staff physician who performed all the first-trimester abortions when the change was initiated, considered herself both a feminist health care activist and a doctor. Managers cited Sarina's presence as the reason why health-working and assisting could be conscientiously condensed into one job, while also holding that what remained was really health-working. As Lee's and Toby's comments illustrate, the point was not whether Sarina (or any doctor) was feminist or not. Assisting her negated health workers' ability to attend only to their clients' needs. They had to achieve a balance, and, in their view, this requirement diminished the relationship between client and health worker. Advocating meant doing tasks that were unrelated to the original conception of health-working—that had been *truly* advocating, Lee said. Interestingly, Sarina sided with the health workers (and also echoed their view of the change as having been instituted dishonestly). She said, "I think that to sacrifice what made us unique was . . . real upsetting."

As with the other conflicts among workers and managers at the Center, two disparate views of this situation emerged. Most health workers regarded what transpired as an example of outright deception, unforgivable because it indicated that administrators could not be trusted. They saw the move to advocating as evidence of an unacknowledged and hypocritical ideological shift on the part of administrators. Managers called the change the necessary outcome of reasonable economic decision making; thus, any problems with the new system were not their fault. They believed health workers' dissatisfaction was essentially the result of miscommunication, for which they apologized and believed they ought to be forgiven. Nancy (the clinic administrator) responded angrily to health workers' charges that administrators acted immorally or in bad faith:

What we said we wanted to do was, if we could, you know, eliminate one staff position in clinic. Then we could take that money and give it to the health workers. It wasn't, like, "Okay, now good. Now we can go to Hawaii!" You know, it was, "We'll have a bigger pool to spread among the health workers. . . . They always have got to have something to be focused on to be grumpy about. . . . That's not just them, I think I've found that's true in a lot of workplaces.

Nancy described measures that were implemented to facilitate the new system for the advocate. For instance, because of health workers' complaints, instrument trays were set up in advance to include a wide range of tools that Sarina might need, so advocates were no longer required to hand her each item. What health workers described as a combination of two positions into one Nancy spoke of as an eventual substitution of one job for both. "They thought it was compromising the care. In reality, I just disagree with them. I don't think it did. . . . If it did, it's because they were paying too much attention to the doctor. . . . The position that we eliminated was not the health worker. We eliminated the assistant."

Regardless of administrators' conceptualizations of the shift to advocating, health workers asserted that the change led to lowered job satisfaction on their part. They said they could not productively express their unhappiness because they would be labeled uncooperative and possibly negatively sanctioned (written up or fired)—that is, voicing their disapproval might be called insubordination.

After the initial backlash against advocating had been suppressed, administrators and supervisors simply refused to listen to complaints, Carrie said. She said their intolerance of dissent demonstrated that they were concerned only with perpetuating their own power. "To be told that you can't even be unhappy about [something you don't like] or express that—I don't know, I think women have been told enough what they should think and what they should feel, and that they should make other people comfortable. I resent having it done to me by a group of women under a place that's *supposed* to be a feminist workplace. That bothers me." Carrie saw administrators as silencing workers and imposing their own perception as the only acceptable reading of

159

the situation. She believed feminists ought to dedicate themselves to resisting the denial or misconstruction of women's realities by any authority; thus, administrators were not, in her view, true feminists.

Most health workers were less harsh in their assessment of administrators' motives than Carrie, Toby, Lee, and Lois. But even in their more generous portrayals, staff members described administrators as indifferent toward health workers' complaints or, slightly more positively, as inconsistent in their responses and thus not completely sincere about addressing workers' concerns. For example, Risa said she believed there was opportunity for health workers to voice complaints, but she saw this opportunity as ambiguous. "I couldn't complain . . . working at Acme Whatever Company. You know, I couldn't complain about it because that's your job. You do your job or you get fired. But, you know, I feel like the organization presents itself as a new and different work environment, and that they need to be held to that standard." When I asked whether the Center was a new and different environment, she replied, "Hell no! It's like it is in a way because I can be vocal about how I feel, yet . . . I'm still feeling that threat like they might call me and I might not have a job tomorrow." Risa saw herself as unable to restrain herself from speaking up when she was upset but said she never knew what the consequences would be. Was honesty tolerated—seen as valid and useful feedback by management—or deemed insubordination, as Carrie alleged?

Along with increasing health workers' duties, the change in protocol entailed a marked decrease in the number of breaks they were allowed. Now that there were fewer health workers assigned to first-trimester-abortion clinics, there was no one to fill in for health workers taking breaks. Health workers consistently reiterated the need for breaks to restore psychic well-being and simply to rest. Lois told me that by denying health workers breaks, she thought that the Center was breaking state law.

Exhausted, burnt out, and frustrated, these women saw the change from health-working to advocating as ushering in a pronounced decline in their spirits and in the quality of their work. They differentiated this sort of burnout from the natural exhaustion of working with clients (managing emotions); they believed this drop in morale resulted directly from administrative decision making. Lee described how she felt the change to advocating had destroyed the sense of community health workers once enjoyed:

> We're more isolated from each other. There's not the camaraderie—all I can think about at work is just . . . making myself stand up long enough to get my job done. . . . We sort of see each other in passing, but we don't work simultaneously on the same job task. . . . With the old style, assisting was really a treat because you were relieved of the demands of indi-

vidually attending to the client. You got to really observe the abortion very carefully, and you learned a lot that way. I mean, you got to see cervical polyps and what it looks like when someone's had a cone biopsy, and lots of neat stuff like that. . . . It made you a much better health worker because you could watch somebody else health-work, and you could go, "What a great thing to say. You know, I'll use that next time" or, "Oh, no! Do I look like that when I do that?" You know?

Because they were no longer members of a team during first-trimester abortions, Lee said health workers had lost valuable contact with each other and, thus, a sense of unity. Gradually the mistrust of administration became pervasive; no one felt at ease with anyone else, Lee said. Without this sense of connection, Lee felt health workers would be unable to mount any serious challenge to administrators' objectionable policies in the future. She thought the administration had effectively divided and conquered health workers. Fragmentation prevailed. Similarly, Sarina said, "The atmosphere that used to be there last summer is lost. . . . It feels like [the Center is] about to fall apart." Like Lee, she attributed this decline to fallout from the shift to advocating.

Again, some health workers did not assess the situation in such dramatic terms. Julia called the change a "betrayal" of staff and clients on the part of management but also felt that health workers should pragmatically adapt to (and accept) the situation since the decision would not be reversed: "We all griped and moaned about it, but I think we all had to get to a point where we're going, 'Okay, if we're going to have to do it this way, why don't I just try and change my perspective?' . . . You kind of got over it. . . . I still don't like it. . . . [But] there's nothing I can do about it. It's not changing."

Risa resented the way administrators instituted advocating: "I hated the presentation," she said, "the way they gave it to us was messed up." But, like Julia, she said she had gotten "pretty used to" the new system and had worked to adapt to it. "I manage to advocate and still do my health worker thing where I still pay a lot of attention to the woman." Risa was, of all the health workers, least critical of the new system; she said she felt that, practically, workers must accede to reasonable demands made of them. And though she found advocating difficult and less than ideal in terms of feminist practice, she understood why management considered it a sensible, cost-effective change. Even Carrie conceded that "going back would seem a real luxury because I've gotten used to things" the new way.

Dissatisfied health workers like Lee and Lois thought that newer health workers, like Julia, Risa, and Carrie, eventually found it easier to advocate because these newer health workers did not have years of experience with the health-working/assisting way of staffing first-trimester abortions. Veteran health workers believed the ideological training that newer staff received was not as radical as theirs had been, that it was watered down because the administrators had become more conservative. However, the newer staff members saw the more experienced ones as impractical for resisting the change; they felt that these women made their own work lives more miserable by clinging to ideals that administrators clearly no longer held as salient.

Conservatism versus Conservation: Sellout or Self-Preservation?

In their discussions of how feminism and organizational structure meshed and clashed, staff members formulated philosophical standpoints that transcended specific issues and events at the Center. They interpreted organizational behavior, and they spoke of alternative internal and external circumstances that would help them realize their ideals. They elaborated feminist utopian visions and described how capable they felt real feminists were of carrying them out. Many workers, even those most critical of management, believed that people themselves impeded the realization of ideological perfection. They did not invoke human nature per se but thought that interactive patterns mitigated against conflict-free tranquility. Ideals might be achieved in small groups, but once a collective reached a certain critical mass, they said, one should expect a level of conflict that demanded restructuring.

Hannah and Toby both worked in collectives before coming to the Center (Hannah at an AIDS-services organization in Anyville, and Toby at a women's center at college), and each drew on her experiences to evaluate the Center's performance as a feminist organization.

> HANNAH: We spent so much time discussing everything that, meanwhile, people are *dying*. . . . [We spent] hours over, like, something that was so teeny-tiny. I mean, I think it [a collective] sounds good, . . . and I think that, yeah, people should have more say; . . . but all that stuff delays everything else. And this is a *business*. . . . And we're here to perform a service the best way that we can, and with a collective . . . we'd have to close three days a week to meet!

> TOBY: I used to work at a women's center in college, in a structure that I consider really feminist. It was a pain in the ass, but I think it was a fair way of doing things. . . . There were seven student coordinators, . . . and we all had different job descriptions. . . . And so we each had our own jobs to do, but we also made joint consensus decisions. . . . I don't know if it would work in a large group setting.

I mean, seven was pretty much the maximum number for that kind of thing. I mean, I think consensus can be a problem sometimes! I think it happened to work there because everybody . . . was willing to make compromises, and they weren't going to force their will, you know. But if you got somebody like that, or a few people like that, . . . it would fail.

Like administrators, Hannah (a supervisor) and Toby (a health worker) questioned whether solidarity (or, in Mansbridge's terms, unitary democracy) could be maintained as an organization expanded. Hannah had seen a collective in action that she felt was ineffective; Toby participated in one that worked well, perhaps because it did not provide urgent services, as Hannah's collective was supposed to do. Because she held a more authoritative position in the hierarchy (as supervisor), Hannah sounded a lot like the administrators when she described the organization's intent ("this is a *business*"). Both women believed compromise could be achieved between a collective spirit and a hierarchical structure. Hannah thought the Center attempted to incorporate workers' input in most of its decision-making processes, but Toby disagreed. "People have been making . . . suggestions [all along], but they haven't been implemented. . . . We meet about [whatever the current issue is] . . . and everybody says how they feel, and then nothing changes." Several health workers, like Toby, believed that administrators deliberately worked in this manner: they utilized gripe sessions as a safety valve that allowed health workers to blow off steam, and then they resumed business as usual, acting as if the problem had been resolved, and pleased that workers' anger had, through the act of expression, dissipated.

Workers who lamented what they saw as the inevitable truth that collectivist businesses could not survive might see people as flawed (whether greedy, status-conscious, and power hungry, or immature and rebellious), but for the most part they attributed these flaws to structural roots and societal ills whose resolution lay far beyond the limited power of one small feminist clinic. Like the scholars who debate the practicality of collectives, most health workers believed the current structure of the Center—however unfair—served practical purposes more than a collectivist structure would. Most would also have liked to see it loosen up a bit, to incorporate some collectivist elements. Ironically, most administrators and supervisors (especially Emma, the executive director) already felt such openness existed at the Center. They defended the status quo as the proper balance between authoritarianism and participation.

Despite their mutual complaints across the hierarchical divide, managers and health workers did attempt to interpret each others' positions. Managers, supervisors especially, tended to do this more often than health workers, though not necessarily in a way that led to reconciliation. Hannah and Mira, who both talked of how supervisors got caught in the crossfire between administrators and health workers, defended the women at the top. Hannah prefaced her remarks by talking about how other work environments fell far short of the Center:

> I really believe that they [Emma, Nancy, and Trudy] do everything they can for the staff. . . . I've never seen or worked with people who've devoted so much time to the staff. . . . Like, if there's a problem, you know, having a therapist come in or having a retreat or something like that. I mean, that makes me feel really good. And I have such a *trust* with them now. . . . It's not perfect, but I wouldn't want to work anywhere else. . . . I have such a respect for them, you know, starting this clinic . . . and what they do on a day-to-day basis. And I think a lot of people . . . don't see what they do on a day-to-day basis.

Mira defended Emma in particular, offering her assessment of a division of labor that protected health workers from taking their work home:

> Emma works *much* harder than *any* health worker in that building. And I'm not saying, you know, that on a given day . . . Emma's feet hurt as much as a health worker's or that she gets bleach on her clothes and deals with sucking up the emotional overflow from clients, but Emma doesn't *stop* working. . . . Once they [health workers] punch out, they're out of there. . . . Their workday is over. . . . Emma is the one that wakes up in the middle of the night . . . wondering what's going to happen if abortion is made illegal.

Supervisors contested the view several health workers expressed that administrators did not care about the well-being of clients or workers; Mira rebutted this notion by saying that administrators concerned themselves with loftier issues than the day-to-day events of Center life and that they worked in ways that might not be visible to health workers. Supervisors believed administrators' energies were devoted to safekeeping procreative freedom and that through their efforts they shielded health workers from the stresses resulting from laboring to maintain the Center's existence in a hostile environment.

Emma (and other administrators) spoke about how the political waters through which they had steered the Center demanded conservatism on their part. They hoped to maintain the gains that had been achieved in the 1970s; changing the world in radical ways seemed unlikely during the Reagan-Bush years. Yet some staff members criticized administrators for their conservatism, even describing them as betrayers of feminist principles. I believe the women's structural positions within the Center led them to formulate conflicting definitions of conservatism.

Administrators saw themselves as conservationists who adopted a sensible defensive stance in order to respond to deeply threatening political developments. They felt they had been forced to narrow their political agenda and to conform organizationally in order for the Center to survive:

> EMMA: When we started, it was much more exciting times in that you really felt like you were making social change. And that you could . . . take new turf. And now we're just spending most of our energy working to maintain what we have, and that's really different. And it puts a different slant on what you can see as goals. If your goal is just this year, well we're going to make sure that we don't have parental consent [in the Center's state]; I mean that's really different than saying we're going to advance abortion rights or we're going to advance women's rights in this different way. And all of that's very conservatizing. . . . When you're working for any kind of social change in a real repressive conservative climate, what's considered progressive is all relative.

> W.S.: So do you feel like you've become more conservative as a feminist?

> EMMA: I feel like the Center has become more conservative, and what I see that I can do is more . . . conservative. And I certainly feel like I've had a lot of conservatizing influences. . . . Being in a position of being a *boss* is very conservatizing. When you have to juggle a lot of different competing needs. That, in and of itself, is inherently conservatizing. . . . When we started, when you think, okay, here are some grass-roots activists going to open a clinic and going to provide abortion services and well-woman services with a feminist perspective, in a women-controlled clinic, and now when you start thinking about, well, what does it take just to keep your doors open, it's a very different type of discussion. . . . Yes, there's more power in that we've become an institution, but in terms of where women controlled clinics are in this country right now, it's a more weakened state and a more conservative place.

Emma did not see herself as choosing a conservative course for the Center but merely as reacting to the inescapable "real repressive conservative climate" of the 1980s. Emma stressed that her desire to keep the Center open functioned as the primary motivation behind her management strategies. A participatory structure, in Emma's view, would not have endured.

Many workers, though, felt that conservatism had taken such a hold on administrators that there would be no going back, even in better times. They saw conservatism not as an adaptive strategy but as an erosion process that had sent the Center into a downward spiral. To them, conservatism signaled an alliance with reactionary, anti-liberal, and anti-feminist forces, and ought to be fought at all costs.

During the same period that Emma described as provoking conservative organizational strategies on the part of Center administrators, several scholarly anthologies carried debates about the implications of various compromises between bureaucracy and power sharing. Zager and Rosow's collection, *The Innovative Organization* (1982), opens and closes with unbridled optimism about the potential for reformatory measures in organizational practice. The editors state, in their introduction, "The American workplace is undergoing a sea of change. . . . Employers, employees, and unions have experienced the results and found them good" (xi). The volume closes with D. L. Landen and Howard Carlson's proclamation: "Where the process of workplace innovation will end, no one can accurately foretell. But as long as people at all levels of organization have the opportunity and competency to help shape the nature of their work and their working lives, the future of American institutions will be in good hands" (1982: 334).[4]

Other scholars question the range of participation or beneficence possible as long as capitalism undergirds the workplace. Rosabeth Moss Kanter (1990), for example, writes that the current innovative strategies ultimately highlight "organizational contradictions" inherent in corporate worlds. Giving workers greater influence in decision making leads them to question "the legitimacy of the traditional hierarchy" (283). Administrators who encourage employees' "entrepreneurship" undercut their own authority. Kanter writes that a "mutual adjustment" system can erode management's "command system," creating an unresolvable conflict as long as the bureaucratic status quo remains the basis of organizational structure. "Once having tasted the freedom to participate in decisions, work across organizational boundaries, and envision alternatives, workers find it difficult to accept management by command," Kanter writes (297).

Indeed, at the Center, an idealized collectivist past lived on in the staff's imagination and exacerbated the constraints of hierarchical power relations. All the women at the Center who had been there when it was a collective had become part of the administration; they disagreed about the possibility of reincorporating participatory methods. Nancy, the clinic administrator, had gone to graduate school for a master's degree in management. She had learned about strategies (appropriated from Japanese companies) that she believed would enable everyone in an organization to participate productively in decision making. She described how she hoped to put Total Quality Management, or TQM, into practice at the Center:

> You *invert* the hierarchy. . . . And then the whole role of management is how can you help the health workers do their job better? And you also set up problem-solving teams. . . . The thing that I was just getting ready to work on were the phones. . . . We had had problems with the phones, like there were always too many calls coming in [for the staff to answer]. We had wanted to put together this whole, like, phone team. . . . First, you do sort of an investigation. . . . You gather your information about what are the problems. And you don't *define* the problems; you try to really *assess* what the problems are, you know, by talking to clients. . . . You can even . . . have some of the people on the team call, you know, and see what their experience is. And then you . . . look at the whole structure of the thing. . . . And I think that with that team . . . we would have . . . ended up with a decision that probably wouldn't have been very different than if I'd come in and just said, "We're going to have partitions here. . . because you don't have enough privacy; it's too loud in this room. We don't have enough people [on phones]." . . . But they would have at least felt like they . . . were more included in the decision.

The rationale behind TQM sounds quite similar to the collectivist mentality that prevailed at the Center during the 1970s and early 1980s, yet Nancy said, "I feel like this was a real leap in my analysis and management skills." In order for such a system to work effectively, Nancy stated, people must trust each other and agree to abide by the decisions made by the teams. But, as health workers like Lee and Carrie saw it, such groundwork had already crumbled at the Center because of the hierarchy.

Ultimately, Nancy did not have the opportunity to put her plans into practice because, as she described it, Emma began systematically to purge everyone who disagreed with her actions to make the Center viable "for the nineties," including Nancy and Trudy. Nancy's revived interest in progressive strategies for decision making may have challenged what many workers described as Emma's dictatorial tendencies. But, to Emma, shaping the Center into a more traditional health care provider with a distinctly businesslike orientation was the only route she could conceive of taking. For Emma, feminist praxis condensed ultimately into doing whatever she thought it would take for the Center to survive. In the view of many staff members at all levels of the hierarchy, Emma found it increasingly difficult to trust other people's judgment or to involve anyone else in decision making because she had worked so hard and long to keep the Center afloat.

Emma believed chaos was the logical extension of what she saw as the naive feminist idealism of her underlings. And this chaos erupted, despite her vigorous attempts to repress it. In the time that has passed since my fieldwork at the Center, Emma, Nancy, Trudy, Celia, Ilene, Greta, Lee, Audrey, Toby, Risa, Nell, Ellen, Carrie, Mira, Lois, Diana, Tanya, Rae, and Sarina have all left the Center, some by choice and some not. Emma resigned not long after Nancy and Trudy resigned—or, as Nancy described it, after Emma forced them out. Notably, Lee, who had lost complete trust in the administration, was dismissed for insubordination. And, ironically, Rae (who had earlier hailed the administrators' honest proclamation of a business mentality) was fired, allegedly for failing to give notice of an absence, shortly after a new executive director (the third to take over after Emma's resignation) asked for her frank assessment of the Center's problems. Rae told me (in a series of phone conversations) that her dismissal was handled in such a backhanded way that she was shocked into recognizing that dishonesty and racism still undergirded Center operations. Everyone else listed above quit; some were moving on to other endeavors, and some were simply burnt out and felt they had to get away. The Center continues to function, though. While the cast of characters has changed significantly along with even more changes in management practices, the conflicts produced by the unhappy marriage of hierarchical power divisions and feminist ideology persist.

CHAPTER 5

Purging the Enemy Within

Feminists Approach Racism

During my fieldwork at the Womancare Center, I participated in a currently popular ritual in organizational management: the collective acknowledgment of "difference" or "diversity" and the attempt to ameliorate tension among people of different "races" through therapeutic group interactions.[1] In the 1990s, black health workers began urging the administration to take steps to purge racism within the organization. Developments in feminist scholarship and national trends in corporate management also facilitated the Center's endeavors to undertake self-examination focused on diversity. In this chapter, I explore the ways in which formal practices and individual agency shaped discourse on "race" and racism at the Center.

Hester Eisenstein writes that feminists must address internal conflicts if we are to have any hope of achieving our ideals. Feminists are understandably reluctant to air such grievances, she states, because "there are too many actors on the scene . . . with an interest in exploiting conflicts among women" (1991: 38). Feminists may want to present a united front to prevent such "actors" from attacking, but repressing internal disputes may ultimately exacerbate discord. "We would be better served if differences could be examined so that we had a better sense of how they arose, in what structural contexts they erupted and then—oh, unattainable ideal—if we could find ways to mediate them and restore solidarity," Eisenstein writes (39). Solidarity, in her terms, need not mean leveling heterogeneity but might emerge from

169

frankly acknowledging why and how we diverge. And progressive activists must attempt to bridge the distance between acknowledgment and solidarity, she believes.

Eisenstein writes rather idealistically. Solidarity never truly existed among feminists or any other diffuse group of social-movement activists; thus, it cannot be restored. And though I find the thought appealing, I doubt whether internal analysis necessarily produces solidarity. As Eisenstein states, maintaining fictitious harmony can backfire, yet the airing of grievances may unearth entirely new layers of conflict. It would be nice to think that we could look forward to a happy ending in which everyone loves each other and we rejoice in our commonalities and "celebrate difference," but I don't expect such sisterly bliss. Indeed, my study of the Center has made me cautious about entertaining idyllic fantasies. Nonetheless, I undertake my analysis of workers' discussions of "race" in the optimistic spirit Eisenstein recommends; I believe, as she does, that without self-examination we are likely to stagnate.

Like many feminist organizations founded by white women, the Center faced charges of institutional racism leveled by women of color working in the organization. Black (and some white) workers said that racism had always been a problem, that when black women entered into a white power structure from the bottom (as they did at the Center, as health workers or low-level administrative workers), clashes between black and white staff members were inevitable. In other words, white women tended to re-create covert power dynamics similar to those they professed to despise, treating black women in a manner comparable to the sexist treatment of women by men.

I believe certain conditions must develop for a white administration to consider "race" a relevant issue for examination. First, blacks must achieve a critical mass—must feel they have enough of a presence to protest. Second, whites in positions of power must be persuaded to initiate action; therefore, they must credit as worthy of action the evidence of racism that the women of color accumulate. Third, the organizational climate must be ripe for self-analysis; white staff members must recognize (or be persuaded to recognize, at least superficially) that racism is a problem worthy of attention. All three of these conditions converged gradually, and the Center formally took notice of "race"-based rifts in the organization in 1992. Eventually, the Center moved from a state of denial toward a rhetorical recognition of racism as a sort of virus, or internal enigmatic enemy, which it sought to eradicate.

Philip Cohen presents popular "theories of racism" that help make sense of Center women's talk about "race" and racism. He identifies two reductionist "hidden narratives" underlying common theoretical discourses on racism; he calls them "radical holism" and "methodological individualism." Radically holistic explanations consider "the actions or attitudes of particular individuals or groups, and the meaning of particular events, as the expression of an over-determining social totality" (1992: 77). In this view, racism works as an omnipotent *structural* force. This theoretical stance holds that revolution would be necessary to eradicate racism and tends to dismiss individual agency or any sort of group effort short of state action as an ineffective means of achieving social change of any kind. "Methodological individualism," a dichotomous mode of analysis, "seeks to disaggregate all larger institutional and historical entities into the practices and relations of the individuals or groups who compose or inhabit them" (77). Racism, presented in this manner, boils down to "individual prejudice which, even when institutionalized, is ultimately sustained by the attitudes and actions of racists" (78). Methodological-individualistic theory holds that, ultimately, racism may be overcome through strenuous re-educational efforts, yet it also portrays racists as unremediably pathological. Center women learned to talk about race using both these "narratives," even simultaneously.

Cohen believes that both the holistic and the individualistic models limit constructive dialogue because they essentialize racism and then reify it as essential.

> [They] explain racism in terms of an 'ideal type' or model which makes certain a priori assumptions about its origins, causes, meaning and effect. These assumptions correspond to particular forms or experiences of racism, which are translated into universal criteria defining its "essence." Types of racism which do not conform to this model are either ignored, marginalized, or "redescribed" in ways which deny their independent significance. . . . At the same time, at a micro level an assumption is made about who is racist and who is not in terms of a set of essential defining properties or predispositions. (83–84)

Cohen's deconstruction of these common strategies for understanding racism warns against oversimplification and the reification of oversimplifications that have become common in formal examinations of "race" relations, from sociological analyses to "diversity-training" seminars. The appeal of such formulations lies, I believe, in their ability to wrap up the loose ends of the problem neatly, to tell one of two stories—or a bit of both. In story number one, racism equals false consciousness—that is, irrational beliefs instilled in people through the workings of capitalism (and sometimes patriarchy as well). Racism may be overcome by overthrowing the system(s) that cause(s) it. In story number two, racism equals individual pathology induced by bad culture, bad parents, and so forth. Racism may be cured by altering the pathological individuals, one by one. These theories fail, in Cohen's view, because essentialism takes them in circles and because they ineffectually generalize. But they also work because they provide simple frameworks for examining messy situations.[2]

At the Center, I heard women express a wide range of attitudes on "race" and racism, varying from the reductionist strategies Cohen describes to more nuanced and nondogmatic analyses. They presented racism both as a culturally produced structural evil and also as a personal devil. In the diversity-training exercises, they learned to see racism as so entrenched as to be ineradicable, yet also as open to individual attack: they learned that if one were armed with goodwill and the proper techniques, racism could be "managed" and perhaps even conquered.

Discovering "Race," Deciphering Racism

Beginning in 1991, the number of black health workers at the Center increased to five (out of about twelve total); these women formed a cohesive subcommunity. The black women I interviewed in 1992–1993 reported that they never felt embraced in a cozy sisterly work environment as Anne, the first black supervisor, had described the previous year. (Anne said differences among staff members were rendered irrelevant by the feminist camaraderie of the group; see Chapter Four.) The black women I interviewed after 1991 said that while some white staff members might welcome their participation, covert racism and subtle exclusionism pervaded their work lives. In their view, the Center was a clinic run by white women who were part of a white feminist movement that was itself suspect because of its history of racism.[3]

Emma, the executive director, said that as the Center grew during the 1980s, the staff became varied in a number of ways; as she portrayed it, the influx of women of color was just one dimension of the growing diversity among staff members:

> When we started as a collective, and for a certain period of time, people were really hired based on having similar political views. And then it became a much less common denominator; you had to be pro-choice, but . . . you didn't have to be anti-racist, and anti-imperialist, and anti-capitalist, and have a real clear understanding of the patriarchy. Those things weren't employment criteria [any longer]. So already there was more diversity in opinion of what did it mean to be a feminist. . . . There were people having widely different views of capitalism, of politics in general. So it was already [operating] along this continuum of diversity. Then we added racial diversity.

As Emma described the staff, it lost solidarity as members' conceptualizations of feminism varied and, she implied, became less rigorous. No longer was a "real clear understanding of the patriarchy" an essential prerequisite for employment; in other words, you did not have to understand feminism to work at the Center.

Emma called "race" one factor in this expanding "continuum of diversity" that she both applauded and denigrated. At first, she said, the white administrators took "a simplistic view" toward the inclusion of black women.

[We thought,] "Well, we're going to try to get our numbers right here," but not understanding all the things that really need to change institutionally and looking at what types of things are institutional racism. How are policies made? How are people more included? The leadership has been white women; how can other women—of color—get into that inner circle? . . . We were looking at the fact that black women would start and then end up leaving soon. . . . [So we asked], "Well, what's happening with the training? Are we doing the training right? Do we need to do something like they do in colleges where you recruit people of color but you have special orientations and buddy systems?" . . . There also were some real direct personnel [incidents] where, in a period of time, several women in a row who were fired for a variety of reasons were black. And so it's like, well, what's happening? Is it differential treatment? Is it incorrect hiring? What all is going on here?

The administrators' consideration of these questions became the driving force behind the Center's formal examination of "race" relations, according to Emma. The administrators invited one of the Center's board members, Connie, to work with the staff on "race" relations, and thus began the self-examination process. Administrators commissioned Connie to conduct an inventory of staff members' views about "race" and racism in preparation for a diversity-training seminar to be held at an unspecified date. Connie interviewed staff members individually and prepared a report that summarized views about the "racism problem" at the Center. "Diversity consultants" frequently employ this sort of formal inventory taking as a preliminary to group workshops and then tailor the content of the workshops to the specific group involved (Ellis and Sonnenfeld 1994, Mobley and Payne 1992).

Black staff members told Connie that covert and sometimes overt racism was prevalent at the Center. They said that white managers gave preferential treatment to white health workers (by delegating the most desirable tasks to them), that white managers expected black health workers to work harder than white health workers, and that black health workers fared worse than white health workers in the formal evaluation process because of white managers' biases. When Connie interviewed the white staff members, many told her that they could not understand what their black co-workers saw as the problem. Many denied black women's contention that racism was a potent problem at the Center. Connie's report revealed that the staff was divided in some ways according to race; that is, all the black women believed racism was part of the institutional fabric of the Center, while many—but not all—whites denied this contention. The report also recorded workers' complaints about the division between (black and white) staff and (white) administration.

As they spoke to me about the manner in which the Center came to contemplate racism, staff members told different stories depending on their place in the hierarchy. Health workers spoke in greater detail and were much more likely than administrators to give specific examples of what they felt was wrong. Health workers described the genesis of the organization's formal attention to "race" matters slightly differently from the way Emma (and other white managers) did. They considered the Center's enlistment of Connie's expertise to be a relatively inconsequential move on the part of administrators. They believed that administrators took action only after black women demanded that the organization do something to counter racism. And many staff members expressed doubts about whether administrators sincerely cared about remedying "racial" rifts.

Black and white women often, but not always, told me conflicting stories about how racism worked and was worked on at the Center. For example, during the summer of 1992, Allison, a black, unpaid college intern, was fired after several staff members and two clients reported that money had been stolen from their wallets. Several weeks after the first theft, Trudy (the director of administrative services) fired Allison over the phone. These facts were undisputed, but their interpretation varied considerably among the staff. All the black women and several whites said that the administrators had no concrete proof that Allison was the thief and called her dismissal discriminatory. Allison's firing mobilized the women of color: black staff members (four health workers and one supervisor) staged a walk-out during a clinic. They met with Trudy and demanded an explanation of Allison's firing along with a promise that intensified action would be taken against racism at the Center.

Several health workers told me about Allison's firing because they saw it as crucial to the administration's formal recognition that racism was an issue with which the Center would have to contend. (Administrators politely evaded my questions about Allison's firing.) Risa, a black health worker, clearly viewed racism as the reason for Allison's dismissal.

Allison was not the best worker in the world, I need to preface it by saying that. . . . She was really young, and she didn't like to work. . . . Stuff started [to be] missing, and even though it was missing before Allison came, it was just that it seemed to amplify, I guess, you know, when she was there. . . . On her day off, they called her and said, "The level of mistrust at the clinic is such that you can't return and work here." . . . Bottom line is they got rid of Allison 'cause they thought she was stealing. . . . If they would have fired Allison because of her job performance, we could've understood it. . . . A lot of the black women who've left in the past have left under some suspicious, funky circumstances. And I'm not saying that they did it or they didn't. I don't know. . . . It just turned into a black thing. It was like, look, just because somebody's black, are they automatically, you know, suspect? . . . You need to prove that they did it or prove that they didn't, but don't just let it be out there, you know, floating around in the air 'cause that's going to cause some bad feelings. . . . We got mad, and we went and we talked to them about it. . . . But nothing came about. They said that they were going to have to speed up the cultural-diversity training.

Lee, a white health worker, told me the story without ever explicitly invoking racism:

Allison was a really horrible person to work with. She was very rude and, I mean, just *really mean* and very critical of people. . . . Personally I felt like she was probably doing it, but that wasn't based on any direct evidence. Mostly, frankly, it was based on the fact that I didn't like her and that the stealing started when she started to become employed . . . and knowing that she just had no affection at all for the Center. . . . I was told that it was presented to her that she was being fired because they had suspicion about her stealing. I think that was the wrong . . . approach for them to take because they had no evidence, and that's a pretty serious accusation. What they should have told her when they were firing her is that they were firing her because she was a bad employee, which they had plenty of evidence of that!

Risa and Lee's accounts differ about whether thefts occurred before Allison's internship at the Center began, but both portray her as a less than ideal worker. Risa (and the other black staff members I interviewed) held that administrators suspected Allison because she was black; thus, firing her constituted a racist act. Lee discussed Allison's dismissal as a mistake (because of the

lack of proof that Allison stole) but did not characterize her firing as necessarily motivated by racism. Administrators may have suspected Allison simply
because they (rightfully) disliked her as a worker, Lee felt.

Some white women did consider Allison's firing to be "obviously" racist. In
such cases, white staff members often assessed the behavior—and the intentions behind the behavior—of white co-workers by judging the accounts of
black women. These accounts involved both the quest to discover the intent
behind a particular act and an assessment of the outcome of the deed. Black
Center women were less likely to seek the input of white co-workers than
vice versa but often discussed such matters with other black co-workers.
They were much more likely than their white co-workers to have done this
sort of analytic work before coming to work at the Center and described it as
part and parcel of traveling in white environments. They felt they had become students of white people's behavior out of necessity. Survival and self-
respect were at stake.

In her interviews with African American women in the United States and
black Surinamese women in the Netherlands, Philomena Essed described
methods participants in her study utilized to determine whether whites' comments or actions (or both) ought to be defined as racist. She writes, "One first
tests the acts against *norms of acceptable behavior or acceptable reasons for unacceptable behavior* and then against notions of racial dominance in society"
(1991:124). Black staff members' interpretive work included such tests for
assessing whites' behavior and speech. Risa, for example, placed Allison's firing into a context Lee did not discuss: Allison was one in a series of black
women who left "under some suspicious, funky circumstances." Risa wondered whether a norm had been established in which black women were "automatically . . . suspect." Lee, however, sought to interpret the incident
without invoking racism: Allison deserved to be fired, but administrators
mishandled her dismissal.

I do not mean to suggest that Risa's and Lee's narratives represent "black"
and "white" archetypes for evaluating behavior, where blacks always find racism to be a potential underlying motivator and whites always avoid the
search. Though the black women were more united than the white women in
the way they decoded questionable incidents, they did not all speak about
racism in identical ways. For example, Julia (a black health worker) told me
about why the black women united and planned group action after Allison's
firing; her comments may be read as justifying white administrators' "race"-
based suspicions of Allison:

It was just that we felt that we needed some answers, that the action
taken against Allison was unjust because they had no proof of anything,

and they fired her under suspicion. And they *said* they fired her under suspicion. And it just was [that] the last *three* people that . . . left there were black women. . . . No one ever said they had proof that any of these things happened. . . . Given the fact that that has happened, I know, being a human being, . . . for me . . . that would raise my doubts. I would not feel so trusting toward black women because the last three people that left here, it was like an alleged criminal thing. So that would just lead me to be cautious. I mean, I figure that's just a natural thing. . . . My problem is that I think that the clinic higher-ups have not dealt with their feelings about what has happened and the way that they feel toward black women.

Julia generalized white administrators' responses as "human" reactions to which she could relate, and she said she understood why they mistrusted black women. For Julia, the administrators' suppositions about Allison based on her "race" might be an example of what Essed terms "acceptable reasons for unacceptable behavior." But while Julia willingly acknowledged that the behavior of administrators might make sense or be "natural," she also denounced it as "unjust" and proclaimed that something must be done to remedy a situation in which white people made judgments based on generalizations about black people. And, thus, though she claimed such judgments made sense to her, Julia finally concluded that neither logic nor "nature" justified racism.

Discussion of incidents like Allison's firing began to take place more openly at the Center once the issue of racism had become an officially sanctioned topic. But having the opportunity to talk about racism did not necessarily alter the terms of the discussion or the character of the debate. According to black staff members, openness often proved illusory. They felt that even after various formal efforts were made to consider how racism worked at the Center, significant progress had not been achieved.

In her 1994 interview, Diana, a black health worker whose first day of work at the Center coincided with the initial diversity-training seminar (which I discuss later in this chapter), described an impasse in the dialogue about racism at the Center. She talked about the difficulty inherent in interpreting the words of white women because meaning is "not written in stone. . . . You can interpret it any way you want to." Diana said she had experienced "subtle" rather than "outright racism" at the Center, which she attributed to the fact that by 1994 black women held the majority of health workers' positions. She and Rae debated an example Diana offered as open to interpretation: the remarks made by Amanda, the acting director at the time of her interview, to a group of health workers about applying for newly designed supervisory positions (Amanda took over after Emma's successor resigned in 1993 and has since left the Center):

> DIANA: She says, "Well, we encourage everyone to apply, and it's not based on, you know, experience, or how long you've been there. . . . [But] I personally feel like no one in this room is actually capable of handling [it]." . . . The only four people that applied were black women, but at the time that she made the statement . . . she didn't have a clue who was going to apply. That's why I say it could have been . . . interpreted any way. . . . She [also] said that . . . if you could wear your clothes to a nightclub, . . . then you can't— you shouldn't—wear it to work.
>
> RAE [imitating Amanda]: "Remember, if you would wear it to a club, don't wear it to work!"
>
> DIANA: Right, and that's how she wrote it on a memo. . . .
>
> W.S.: And you think she meant black women when she said that.
>
> RAE: Well, since there are only black women who go to clubs.
>
> W.S.: Right.
>
> RAE: Even the white women were like— [she gasps].
>
> DIANA: But nothing like concrete- and stone-specific.
>
> RAE: How much more blatant do you want to be? Diana wants them to call her a nigger!
>
> DIANA: No, I don't, but . . . my point is that if she said *that*, then that's slander, and . . . then we can take her, you know, to the EEOC [Equal Employment Opportunity Commission], right?

Rae cast Amanda's remarks as obvious examples of racism, whereas Diana maintained that they could not qualify as "concrete" examples. Rae argued that the four black health workers who did finally apply for the supervisory positions had worked the longest at the Center, were thus most likely to apply, and were undoubtedly the women Amanda had in mind when she made her comment. Rae felt sure that Amanda knew the applicants would all be black women.

Both Rae and Diana considered Amanda's comment about appropriate clothing for work to be a clear example of racism. For Rae, this remark clinched the evidence in the first case; Amanda's racist remark about clothes confirmed the racist intent in her talk of workers' lack of qualifications for supervisory roles. But as Diana pointed out, no action could be taken against remarks like Amanda's. Both women believed that it would be foolish to jeopardize their jobs in order to bring veiled racism out into the open and that Amanda would simply deny that she intended to single out or insult black women in either instance. Indeed, Amanda was never told that black staff members found her remarks offensive.

Confrontation, Denial, and Confession

Black women at the Center realized their claims of racism would be met by the counterclaims of white women, whom they saw as acting defensively to protect themselves from even engaging in such confrontations in the first place. Returning to Essed's theoretical framework, norms of acceptable behavior vary, and "race" may make the difference in how a person judges whether racism occurs. For a white woman to accept black women's assessment of her behavior as racist would be extraordinary and unlikely, black Center women felt. Among staff members, the "racial" gap loomed large even as staff members supposedly addressed racism. As Rae put it, "They say they want to know, but they really don't want to know." A majority of her white co-workers, she said, felt "they're better equipped to do something; you're not as adequate as they are. . . . [They feel] like they're smarter, superior to you because of skin color."

The black women referred to Connie's inventory of staff attitudes as damning evidence of racism at the Center and yet as evidence they suspected many white women would miss.

> JULIA: When Connie was reading back her report, . . . it really opened my eyes to how a lot of people really feel. . . . Someone made a statement like "it's just black people getting their way again." I know someone at the clinic said that, and I know it's someone that I talk to and that I wouldn't think would say that, but they said that. So now it's like I know that people have these feelings: that black people are troublemakers; they start stuff. . . . One black [staff member] got a scholarship to go to an Ivy League school, and . . . [a white women said], "And I can't go, basically because she got my scholarship. *I* should be there." I mean, and people said these things!

> RAE: One woman came right out and said that she was very upset that a black woman got to go to an Ivy League school because of

the fact that she was black and not because of her academic record. And that was a *lie*. Because this woman has an academic record out of this world.

Black women were stunned that white women made what they considered to be blatantly racist remarks such as these to Connie because she was both black and an outsider. They found white women's resentment toward the Center's efforts at diversity training as disturbing as white women's overt racist comments. They believed many white women saw the diversity-training seminars (and its preliminaries) as personally threatening and thus attempted to turn the situation on its head by charging that black women constituted the real problem. Julia and Rae interpreted Connie's report as evidence that many white co-workers could not be trusted. Rae felt that on an interpersonal level barriers between blacks and whites could sometimes be broken but, for the most part, white racism worked as an intractable force in American society in general as well as at the Center (a version of Cohen's "radical holism"). She believed her white co-workers' reluctance to acknowledge a problem represented only the tip of the iceberg of white resistance.

Risa, too, spoke about Connie's report as a discouraging encapsulation of her white co-workers' denial of racism:

> There's really a lot of racist women at that clinic that don't even know it. . . . Like one of the things that somebody said on the report was, "The black women at the clinic are causing trouble." "The black women at the clinic are very defensive all the time over stuff that they don't need to be defensive about." . . . "I'm sick of the black shit." I mean, you know, what is that saying? I don't get it. But yet, still, every day people are saying, "Everybody's the same, and we just need to love each other and get over the color thing."

Risa did "get it" really; she openly described her white co-workers' hypocrisy. Their defensiveness reduced racism to individual pathology (as in Cohen's "methodological individualism"), a pathology the white women acknowledged in others but disavowed for themselves. Risa reiterated Julia's conviction that such hypocrisy served as evidence that white women's intentions were dishonorable or, as Julia put it, that certain (anonymous) white women had "a hidden agenda": to protect themselves from the taint of racism (by denying it to Connie and then disingenuously giving lip service to efforts at achieving unity). The situation often seemed hopeless to black Center women: white co-workers' unacknowledged racism was transformed into an offensive tactic of attacking black women for drawing needless attention to "race." Thus, black staff members often reached the conclusion that they had nothing to gain by exposing racism. At the same time, they felt it was their moral duty to remain vigilant.

As Risa continued, she questioned the content of white women's rhetoric (such as "everybody's the same, and we just need to love each other and get over the color thing"):

> There are still some very real differences that we have to deal with. In my neighborhood, it's offensive for you to put your fingers in my face. In your neighborhood, you don't talk to people by yelling and jumping around, but that's how I talk to people. I get loud if I'm angry, and I use a lot of hand movements, and I jump around. That will be scary for a lot of white people . . . because it's a cultural difference in the way we deal with things. So for them to say that the whole racism problem does not exist and the black women are blowing shit out of proportion is a *racist* statement. . . . It's going to take a lot of hard work because people don't get it. . . . If you're not willing to 'fess up on your stuff, you can't take care of it. It's just going to grow and fester or get bigger without you knowing about it, until you say some dumb shit.

In Risa's view, white staff members knew differences existed according to "race"-based culture; when they denied this separation, they denied *her* culture's validity. By contradicting black women's view of "race" relations, white women perpetuated a pattern of interaction where only whites could decide what mattered—indeed, what was true—and established an ideological apartheid.

Black and white women at the Center spoke frequently about racial discord as originating from "cultural differences," as Risa did. When black women took this cultural line of argument, they focused on how white co-workers were ignorant of cultures other than their own. The black women emphasized that white staff members tended not to acknowledge that their expectations about behavior were culturally grounded rather than "objective" or "normal."

When white Center women utilized the cultural line of argument, however, they indicated that "cultural" clashes might be conceptualized merely as innocent misunderstandings. For instance, Lois and Janice both credited black women's allegations of racism, but they explained white women's behavior as innocent ignorance, and, thus, they disregarded the moral dimensions of racism as their black co-workers perceived it:

> LOIS: A lot of the women of color at the clinic—and I'm trying to
> figure this out and—it's just like phrases that are used or things that

are said that if I . . . heard them, I would not be insulted. But being from their culture, they do find it insulting. I don't know if it's not being educated in the difference in the culture—in what would be offensive or not—or someone blatantly being racist. . . . I don't really know. . . . A lot of it just seems to be *feeling*.

JANICE: Well, it's like little things that just sort of—I mean, I think they're largely cultural . . . —pissed off the black women. Like we were in a health worker meeting one time, and I think Julia raised her hand like this [she demonstrates a fist], like "I have a question." And Mira's like, "What's that, black power?". . . Everybody sort of laughed at the time because it was uncomfortable, but they [the black women] were talking among themselves. They were like, "That was really offensive."

Lois reiterated several of the black women's complaints, asserting that she had difficulty assessing whether racism "really" occurred or whether black women misperceived it. Lois wondered whether white women's intent must be taken into account or whether the fact that black women felt insulted sufficed as evidence, in and of itself, that racism had occurred. Racism might be reducible to gaps in understanding. The very same act or comment might be interpreted as offensive or completely benign, depending on the color of one's culture. As in the discussion between Diana and Rae quoted previously, the recognition of racism remained the core interpretive issue: Lois's and Janice's comments indicated that they believed that, at times, the racism of white women at the Center could be read as a naive cultural misunderstanding.

As Cohen (1992) and Paul Gilroy (1990, 1992) write, essentializing racism as cultural makes white individuals almost incapable of nonracist behavior yet excuses us for our racism: we are always culpable, but we deserve forgiveness because we are trapped by culture.

The culturalism of the new racism has gone hand in hand with a definition of race as a matter of difference rather than a question of hierarchy. . . . Culture is conceived along ethnically absolute lines, not as something intrinsically fluid, changing, unstable, and dynamic, but as a fixed property of social groups rather than a relational field in which they encounter one another and live out social, historical relationships. When culture is brought into contact with race it is transformed into a pseudobiological property of communal life. (Gilroy 1990: 266–267)

Ironically, anti-racist ideology may support the same cultural rhetoric as what Gilroy calls the "new racism." Anti-racist behavior, in this context, becomes a simple matter of sensitization to the different cultures of others. Gilroy warns that to evaluate racism and understand "racial" dynamics, we must understand that culture and cultural identity may complement, but ought not be substituted for, politics and history. He writes, "'Race' needs to be viewed . . . as a precarious discursive construction" (1992: 50). Risa, Lois, and Janice come dangerously close to conceptualizing "race" as a static—even if elusive—essential force.

Janice agreed with black women's allegations of racism at the Center, and, like them, she saw the instigators as often oblivious to the offensiveness of their comments or actions. But she evaluated this obliviousness differently than the black women did. In describing such incidents as "largely cultural" "little things," she minimized them, letting white women off the hook, rather than denouncing whites' ignorance as a strong indication of how entrenched racism was. Risa, however, allowed for cultural confusion, while she emphasized that white women must be held responsible (and must accept responsibility) for racist assumptions in order to make progress. Janice agreed that whites should take responsibility for racist behavior, and like most white Center women I interviewed after Connie presented her report, she claimed that many white women at the Center had undertaken this task with goodwill. The black women were less optimistic about white women's commitment to anti-racist work because they believed that hypocrisy and denial ran so deep that many white women would be unwilling to take on—or might be incapable of—the analytic work necessary to cultivating an anti-racist stance.

Essed's black respondents' reports of confrontations with whites resonate with black staff members' remarks about racism at the Center. These black Surinamese women in the Netherlands reported that whites typically resented charges of racism and tended to deny them.

> Because the Dutch have strongly internalized the idea that they are a tolerant people, . . . they are more reluctant than Whites in the United States to acknowledge that racism is a Dutch problem as well. They even *feel offended* . . . when they are confronted with "their" racism. Pointing out racism is seen as an *accusation* and, therefore, as an *offense* to the other party's personality. This leads to strong emotions, which subsequently makes it almost impossible for Black women to confront perpetrators with the racist implications of their behavior. . . . In other words, opponents of racism are accused of victimizing innocent Whites. (1991: 274)

Substitute "white feminists" for "Dutch," and this quotation aptly applies to the Center. White feminists at the Center, like the Dutch whites about whom Essed's participants talked, often resisted the notion that they were capable of racist behavior because they saw themselves as ideologically pure and decent. After all, many defined feminism as a politics of liberation that fights against power imbalances. A portrayal that painted them as linked to oppressive practices challenged their sense of themselves as feminists.

Essed writes that in the United States, whites' responses to charges of racism are "not as emotionally charged" as in the Netherlands, but whites, nevertheless, consistently deny black women's allegations:

> Rather than using emotional blackmail (you are hurting me), dominant group members deny the extra knowledge and perceptiveness Black women have about racism and claim that it is the intention that counts. They either go on "denying and protesting too much," . . . which lets you know that they refuse to admit it, or they might "look you dead in the face and say 'no, that is not what it means at all. You cannot read my action.'" (275); quotes are from Essed's study participants)

White Center women sometimes also responded to charges of racism in this manner. Such a reaction demonstrates that they viewed their own self-images as the only admissible evidence of the true nature of their characters.

Mira called the Center's focus on "race" an impediment to getting work done. She presented racism as an obstacle to the accomplishment of her day-to-day responsibilities as a supervisor. Her comments illustrate both the strategies Essed describes:

> I think there are definitely things that go on that are simply about racism, but I think the managerial waters have gotten really muddied by it. You know that when I make a decision—what I wound up doing was, you know, reverse kind of bullshit. . . . [For instance,] all the supervisors needed to be in a meeting, and we wanted somebody to cover the front, and what happened was we picked a less experienced black woman to do it over a more experienced white woman to do it because we wanted to give the black woman an opportunity and not be seen as racist. . . . And what happened was the white woman . . . was in tears. . . . It destroyed her. I mean, so you know, that kind of stuff. . . . Now was that really smart? To upset a Level 4 [advanced worker] that much, who's been there and served loyally for how many years? Or should that just go ahead and happen because that white woman gets privilege everywhere else? You know, I don't know. I'm tired. . . . I don't want to deal with it. I don't want it to affect my clinic and how it flows, and become this big, you know, screaming large issue.

Mira portrayed management (herself included) as bending over backward—too far backward—to avoid charges of racism. In Mira's view, Center managers were enlightened whites whose good deeds went unappreciated by the black women who benefited from them. Rather than evaluate the credibility of charges of racism, Mira presented counterevidence: administrators like her who tried too hard, showed unmerited preference to black workers, and ended up exhausted and frustrated by continuous undeserved accusations.

Of all the white staff members I interviewed, only Ilene expressly questioned whether racism was a problem at the Center; she saw administrators' attention to diversity as a smoke screen designed to shield them from having to address health workers' complaints about structural divisions:

I worked there so long because I liked most women I worked with, and I learned things, and it was fun to be with them. It was fun to work with them. And then when all this *racial* stuff started, it was like that was *bullshit*. Not to say there's not racism there, but most of it was bullshit because I feel a lot had to do with this other stuff, about them just not appreciating anybody. Didn't have to do with you're black or white. . . . There is preferential treatment, but it doesn't have to do with black or white. So then that became unpleasant—to even work with some of these women that I liked.

"Race," Ilene believed, had become unnecessarily divisive. Administrators benefited from the tensions generated among the staff by the focus on racism because it allowed them to evade hierarchical problems. Other staff members, white and black, concurred with Ilene's characterization of administrative motivations as insincere but did not dismiss charges of racism. They agreed that focusing on "race" had enabled administrators to avoid attending to the rift between staff and management, yet they believed that the attention was warranted.

White women often portrayed themselves as having made progress in dealing with racism: moving from denial to acceptance. I saw a definite shift in white women's publicly stated opinions at the Center between the time of Connie's report and subsequent interviews I conducted in 1992. The notion that feminism ought to be immune to poisonous influences like racism had been disavowed in favor of the position that feminist action against racism was incumbent upon white feminists. The white women expressed this attitude as fitting in with self-help principles, saying, in effect, "We will examine ourselves and do whatever is necessary to make the situation equitable."

After Connie's report, white staff members commonly voiced the notion that because whites were privileged in the United States, whites were auto-matically racist. Whites could be educated, could do self-analysis, could act to repudiate racism, but could not escape the fact that whites were racist. As Deborah said, "No white person gets to be nonracist; you only get to be anti-racist." Hannah and Carrie discussed how their thinking about racism had shifted over time:

> HANNAH: I didn't see it, you know, like months ago, and when a lot
> of the women were talking about it, and I was being, "Well, I don't
> understand this. I'm not racist." . . . I think it opened up my eyes.
> There was a . . . health worker meeting one time, and the women
> of color were talking about how they felt, and it was just like this,
> "Holy shit!" It was like Julia was saying, "You know, when I come
> to work and I'm the only black woman here, I feel . . . I'm being
> treated differently." It was horrible. And it—I am privileged that I
> can turn it on and turn it off. It's like, "Well, I'll think about racism
> now. *Oops*, I don't have to think about racism."

> CARRIE: No one's color blind. And there's so much denial going on,
> to say "I'm not a racist" in a society where you're raised to be rac-
> ist—I don't know how you *can't* be a racist. There are degrees of it,
> but don't say that you're not a racist. Say that you're willing to
> work on it. . . . It also makes me feel defensive because whenever
> racism's talked about, as a white person, I do feel this, like digging
> my heels in, like, well, I want to say I'm not a racist. And I know
> that I have things to work on, and I do have racist things that are a
> result of being in a racist society. And the more I work on it, the
> more I see it.

Both Carrie and Hannah "owned" their own racism; but this acceptance was tinged with ambivalence. Hannah discussed how her original denial of black co-workers' claims of racism at the Center shifted into regret when she learned to appreciate the black women's position and to recognize her own "privilege." Carrie asserted even more vehemently that whites were "raised to be racist," while also acknowledging her own resistance to being categorized as such. As Carrie and Deborah presented it, racism never ends, it only di-minishes.

Black women were less likely to promote this depiction of white racism as a bottomless pit. Rae, for instance, questioned what eventually became the in-stitutionally sanctioned line on white racism, "I had to be corrected last week because I didn't realize that just because you were white that you would have racist tendencies. . . . I didn't think that everybody who was white had to be racist in some form, you know, and I don't know if I necessarily agree with that."

Black women did, however, call for vigilance on the part of whites and blacks, depicting racism as an opportunistic virus struggling to make inroads wherever it could. In this way, they, too, reified a view of racism as a pervasive poison in social interactions. In the anecdote that follows, Risa discussed the intransigence of racist ideas by describing how racism can infect black communities:

Even among black people, you know, we have internalized oppression, you know. That stuff . . . where we choose each other based on color of skin, meaning the lighter is better and the darker is worse. And, you know, I had one of the black women at the clinic say something to me like, "Denzel Washington was married to a jungle bunny." You know, I'm like, "Girl, you can't say that shit! Who taught you that?" . . . "Well I got it from my mama. It's not offensive." I said, "Yes, it is! Especially coming from a lighter skinned woman. That's very offensive for you, as light as you are, to say to me, as dark as I am, that somebody my complexion is a jungle bunny. Girl, you *know* that's taboo. And if you said it in my neighborhood, we'd beat you up." She didn't get it. . . . So I had to break it down to her. . . . "That is not our term for each other. That is someone else's term that is negative and derogatory, and for you to use it . . . is wrong. . . . You can't do that." And she was like, "Okay, I'm sorry." But . . . she didn't get it.

The internalization of racist ideology among blacks may be as intransigent as its cause, white racism. Risa puzzled over how racism could be so obvious to her but invisible to this black co-worker. She was not surprised by white women unable to understand racism but expected more from black women.

Indeed, many of the white women I interviewed after Connie's report continued to express uncertainty about how to identify racism. Their denial shifted into a repressed mode. Instead of saying, "There is no racism here" or "I am not a racist," some white women said, in effect, "Black women experience racism, whereas I, a white woman, cannot. But I would also like to be able to see it concretely because I am unwilling to simply take their word for it."

White staff members endorsed confrontation as a strategy for ameliorating racial tension at the Center because they realized they could be discredited by a charge of racism. They needed to be confronted with their racism, they said, so that they could respond to charges by explaining themselves. Hannah and Carrie insisted that they wanted to be informed if they did or said something a black co-worker perceived as racist:

> HANNAH: If I'm doing something, then I want someone to tell me, "Hannah," you know, "you're pointing your finger in front of my face, and I consider that racist." . . . Then tell me! You know, I need to know *then*, to correct that behavior. Instead of like, "Well, let's keep waiting and waiting, while Hannah's a racist." And I don't know why or why someone's not talking to me. . . . With doing schedules I'm having a problem right now, and unfortunately it involves a woman of color and her school schedule, and she feels I didn't give her the same consideration [I give white women] because she's black. And I'm being real defensive about it. "Well no, like, Tanya and Nell and everyone who's gone to school has done this and this and this," but it's not being seen. . . . Obviously this woman doesn't trust me with a hill of beans. So I'm, like, demoralized.
>
> CARRIE: I guess what I would like to have changed is this sense I have that if I do say something that offended someone—a black woman at work—. . . she would feel free to say to me that she was offended and to talk to me in detail and tell me what was going on, and we could have a discussion about it. And I could say what I had meant to say and be able to examine that. And now I feel that because the game we're playing at work is nobody's racist and we have to not say anything racist, . . . you're never going to learn anything. It feels like going around wondering if you're going to say something wrong. And I know that a lot of white women at work feel that way.

Hannah explained that white women at the Center found themselves in an awkward position: they wanted to say the right thing but were not always sure what that was or how to articulate it. Black women must tell white co-workers immediately when they erred, she said, because white women were not likely to realize it themselves. And sometimes, Hannah believed, as with the scheduling dispute, one could do the right thing and be charged with racism anyway. Hannah portrayed herself as a victim in the scheduling situation, and she saw the health worker as dogmatic in her view that Hannah had short-changed her because she was black. Carrie presented an ideal confrontation about racism as an exchange in which white women could explain what they *really* meant. She, at least, would never *mean* to be racist. Carrie echoed Hannah's concern that white women were afraid to say something "wrong" for fear of being labeled racist.

188

White staff members repeatedly made intent central in their discussions of racism. They said, in effect, that black women should initiate the dialogue and then whites could defend their good intentions. Perhaps white women felt threatened because the developing discourse on racism at the Center suggested that whites could not control the interpretive process. These invitations to confrontation were at once sincere gestures meant to convey white women's openness to participating in a dialogue on racism, expressions of trepidation at being discredited through such participation, and denials of black women's definitions of racism.

White staff members often disengaged from each other when talking about racism, as Deborah and Carrie both did when they proclaimed that whites who denied racism could not be anti-racist. They wanted to distinguish themselves from unenlightened whites who refused to engage in introspective work. Some white Center women stressed strong ties they forged with black co-workers to demonstrate their attempts to understand the situation at the Center from the standpoint of the women of color:

> JANICE: For whatever reason, I ended up being closest with the black women in the Center. . . . And so I'm probably a little bit more in tune with what happens and understand their perspective [better] than the average health worker. . . . When I came there, the black women were the most open to me and the most supportive of me, and it was almost as if they had had a bad experience there, and they didn't want that to happen to the other new people who came.

> ELLEN: Some of these [black] women have said to me, "You know some of these white chicks are so uptight." And I totally agree with them. Some of the [white] people who work there get really uptight. They get too politically correct; you can't open your mouth. I mean, you can't make a mistake.

Unlike many white staff members at the Center, Ellen did not talk of feeling policed or on guard against black women's charges of racism. Rather she allied herself with the black women who had to deal with "too politically correct" white co-workers. And Janice recounted discussions with Rae that led her to accept black women's positions on racism, although this acceptance was mitigated by her allowance that white women were innocently ignorant. Ellen and Janice did sympathize with black women more than many of their white co-workers, but, in highlighting their friendships with black women, they also—perhaps unconsciously—set themselves apart from other white women as ideologically superior. After all, if whiteness serves as evidence of racism, feeling not-white or less-white by association may mean one may consider oneself less blameworthy. Their talk of affinity with black co-workers demonstrates that these white women wanted to indicate their opposition to racism, but it also may be seen as a self-serving assertion of ideological purity.

I confess my own sense of absolution when black women confided in me, sometimes using "we"/"they" language that seemed to suggest I was one of them rather than part of the "they" made up of white co-workers. For instance, Rae once told me over the phone that a black friend of hers was right when she said that whites couldn't be trusted. She paused and said, "You know what I mean." She wasn't talking about me but about the other whites—the bad ones; I was one of the worthy white few. My point is that whites who care about mending the rifts caused by racism like to feel we are exceptions to this overarching rule of white racism promulgated by the trendy diversity rhetoric. It makes us feel good about ourselves, and, thus, it helps us believe we are good. Rather than feeling guilt by association with other whites, we may feel at least partially vindicated by association with blacks.

Dilemmas of Diversity

Connie's report was the first step in the Center's official examination of diversity, and, along with events like Allison's dismissal, it generated formal didactic exercises. I participated in two of these activities: a staff meeting devoted to viewing and discussing an *Oprah* episode about racism, and the first of three mandatory two-day diversity-training seminars in which Center staff members participated during 1992 and 1993. In these forums, participants negotiated the meaning of "race" and collectively lamented the ideology and effects of racism. Like participants in the pioneering (and largely white) feminist consciousness-raising groups of the late 1960s and early 1970s, we sat in circles and revealed ourselves. Indeed, examining "race" and racism together made black and white staff members feel closer to each other, at least temporarily. But these didactic explorations only occasionally questioned the processes that construct "race" (racialization); they often treated "race" and racism reductively and essentialistically.

The *Oprah* exercise exemplifies this reductionist tendency. Staff members watched a videotape of an *Oprah* episode in which the film *The Eye of the Storm* was shown. The film concerns a kindergarten teacher who devised an exercise to teach her class about racism to commemorate the death of Martin Luther King, Jr. (in 1968). She divided her white students into two groups by eye color ("blue eyes" and "brown eyes") and lectured them briefly on the differences between them. She told the children that people with blue eyes were smarter, nicer, better, and so forth. By the end of the day, the blue-eyed children had become arrogant tyrants, and the brown-eyed children were dejected and resentful. The teacher herself appeared on the *Oprah* episode along with some of her former students, now adults. She demonstrated her technique on the studio audience, which had been divided into a favored and oppressed group while they waited to get into the studio: the oppressed were angry, and the favored were incredulous at the oppressed group's fervor. The episode culminated with this polarized audience discussing racism.

Staff members enjoyed this exercise. It was easy, in that attention could be focused outside the Center and onto the ignorant people in Oprah's studio audience. The *Oprah* episode reduced racism to a straightforward matter of indoctrination, like the collars the teacher had the children put on to differentiate the "blue-eyeds" from the "brown-eyeds." The teacher's game offered comfort because it implied that if racism could be so easily learned, it might also be easily discarded (with the proper counterindoctrination). Yet, it also frightened Center women because it showed how quickly and easily people— and not only children—can be influenced. Staff members focused on this aspect of the experiment in their discussion, talking at length about how shocking it was that people gave in so easily to discriminatory attitudes. The former students testified that the kindergarten experience had had profound effects on them. They claimed that the teacher had taught them how to put themselves in others' shoes and that they had learned how to be nonracist. Thus, the *Oprah* episode confirmed the idea that communication, in and of itself, offered a solution to racism. It promulgated racism as both structurally embedded and psychologically based, but it leaned more heavily toward endorsing individual action as the primary escape route from dangerous ideology.

Many Center workers experienced the *Oprah* exercise as a reassuring preliminary to the diversity-training workshop. Indeed, many said the exercise made them look forward to the workshop. This first foray into the analysis of racism went well: the discussion proceeded amicably; there were no explosions and only minor disagreement. Everyone agreed on the crucial issues: racism was ideological poison; people were easily swayed; something should be done.

Administrators and some workers viewed the diversity training workshops as evidence that the Center was adopting innovative, cutting-edge management techniques. But such training programs are not a new phenomenon in the United States. The U.S. army began attempts at easing relations between black and white workers as long ago as the 1940s, when blacks were first allowed to enlist (Nordlie 1987). Training programs had become quite common in the army, police departments, and social service agencies by the 1970s (Hunt 1987, Nordlie 1987, and Smith 1987), as the Civil Rights Act of 1964 "opened up a floodgate of federal dollars to support race training" (Coffey 1987: 116).[4] The most well-known model for "race"-relations programs emerged from the work of Judith Katz, author of *White Awareness: Handbook for Anti-Racism Training*, who held that whites must be held responsible for dismantling racism and that we could do so by participating in well-designed programs for self-examination (1978).[5] Most 1970s and early 1980s programs drew on Katz's premises and techniques, and were designed to sensitize whites to the presence of blacks in work environments. The wave of federally funded "race"-relations educational programs fizzled as Reaganism and the white backlash against liberalism gained momentum; Peter Nordlie argues also that "race"-based civil rights efforts were edged out. "The national interest had turned from race to sex, age and handicap as the primary issues in civil rights" (1987: 121).

In the 1990s, corporate managers in the private sector began reviving "race"-relations programs, which, in their present incarnation, are commonly referred to as "diversity-training" or "diversity-management" workshops. Journalists and business analysts enthusiastically debate the intentions, efficacy, and aftereffects of these workshops (see, for example, Caudron 1990, 1993; Ellis and Sonnenfeld 1994; Lee 1993; MacDonald 1993; Mobley and Payne 1992; Murray 1993; Reynolds and Pope 1991; Sivanandan 1990; Smith 1987; Taylor 1987; and Torrey 1992).

Evaluations in the popular press range from laudatory treatments proclaiming diversity-training seminars to be the indisputable wave of the corporate future, to cautionary tales, to outright condemnations. Melissa Lee, a *Wall Street Journal* reporter, cites small-business owners and diversity consultants who see workshops and follow-up workshops as the perfect way to reduce job-related stresses, to do business, and to increase production (1993: B2). Taking a more moderate view, Kathleen Murray, writing for the *New York Times* (1993: P5), warns about "The Unfortunate Side Effects of 'Diversity Training,'" like "blame-and-shame programs" that alienate white men or the deleterious purging of inappropriate emotions in work environments. But Murray basically endorses diversity proponents as well-intentioned and on the right ideological track.

At the other end of the spectrum, Heather MacDonald lambasts "The Diversity Industry" in *The New Republic*. She portrays diversity consultants as ineffectual—if not incompetent—opportunists. MacDonald considers diversity training to be a counterproductive strategy for organizations. She argues:

Despite the grand rhetoric of its advocates, there is little evidence that diversity management can solve the problems it purports to address. In fact, it may make them worse. . . . Nor will converting the workplace into an arena for the practice of identity politics do much to improve competitiveness or help minorities advance in the business world, where a deficit of business skills, not a proliferation of racism is the overwhelming reason many minorities fail to advance. (1993: 25)

MacDonald turns the diversity advocates' position on its head and makes "minorities," not racism, the problem because she believes minorities lack the skills necessary to compete with whites: whites do not need consciousness raising; rather, everyone else needs remedial education.

Management literature reiterates this range of opinion about diversity training, tending toward a middle-of-the-road position and lauding companies and corporations for their good citizenship, while cautioning against common pitfalls (like one-shot training sessions; "biased" diversity consultants; and insincere managerial participation in programs). Many articles in managerial publications read like promotional material, designed to convince administrators that an investment in the right kind of diversity training will pay off; for example:

Organizations that learn to use diversity as an asset will stride ahead of those that don't. The payoff will be in productivity (greater output), quality (fewer errors), flexibility (faster response to change), and innovation (more creativity).

Organizations that don't learn to respect, value, and utilize individual differences . . . will continue to be socked with discrimination and harassment lawsuits, low morale, high recruitment costs, high turnover, and a lack of creativity. (Mobley and Payne 1992: 52)

Organizations that fail to make appropriate changes to more successfully use and keep employees from different backgrounds can expect to suffer a significant competitive disadvantage compared to those that do. Alternatively, organizations quick to create an environment where all personnel can thrive should gain a competitive cost advantage over nonresponsive or slowly responding companies. (Cox and Blake 1991: 47)

These writers present diversity-training programs as sensible and forethoughtful strategies for building businesses, especially given that the workforce will certainly become increasingly "diverse"—that is, less white—in the future. Employers are assured that they will win (profit) if they join the game, and lose (money, staff, and perhaps the whole shebang) if they do not. Other management specialists are less adamant, but they agree that diversity-training programs may be "beneficial to employees" in ways that benefit employers—"may enhance their communication and morale," may make them "feel invested in the firm and motivated to contribute to the firm" (Ellis and Sonnenfeld 1994: 102). These articles urge whites in positions of power to make room at the top, but they also imply that happy workers will be compliant workers.

Shari Caudron asserts that the diversity-training "movement" no longer targets personal bias nor strives to achieve assimilation. Instead, she writes, "companies are moving toward *managing* diversity, a process by which the company—not the employees—makes the effort to embrace differences" (1993: 56). In "Monsanto Responds to Diversity," Caudron cites a "human resources employee" who explains that the company learned that "diversity was not just a black-white, male-female issue"; diversity was every little thing. "We discovered that any differences—in speech, dress, culture, religion, and age—can create biases that get in the way of effective working relationships. . . . We realized that subtle discrimination will always be there; it's part of who we are as human beings" (1990: 75). And, thus, some diversity programs— and the management literature endorsing them—*level* difference: if the content of difference does not matter, difference itself does not really matter either. Diversity-training proponents reify "discrimination" as natural, normal, part of human nature. This rhetorical strategy portrays the ability to perceive difference as the definition of discrimination and strips the word of its negative connotations.

In this vein, Emma told me, "The Center can't solve the fact that we live in a very racist society—you know, that we all come in with a lot of baggage. I think that there are things that we can do. . . . I think that we can concentrate on diversity." She said that she thought it would be a good idea to hire someone as "director of diversity," who could "expand" the Center's focus on difference. "There's all these different components besides racial components, and I think that it would really be helpful to have someone who really handles that . . . in the organization."

What does it mean to "handle" diversity? This managerial rhetoric reminds me of the "obstetrical management of pregnancy," a euphemistic expression for the control of pregnant women (see Rothman 1982). The phrase abstracts and obscures the women's bodies that do the work of pregnancy, just as "managing diversity" abstracts and obscures the bodies of workers that do the work of organizations. Diversity consultants (and the writers who promote them) claim that corporate culture can change, can welcome everyone and make all workers happily "pursue organizational goals." Workers will not only meet but exceed organizational goals. Paradoxically, then, the organization "changes," but its goals do not. Center women pointed out that corporate culture *creates* organizational goals, and so it will not be so simple to excise the racism institutionalized there without overhauling the institution. This sort of observation resonates with Marxist treatments of racialized discourses, in which anti-racism is shown as maintaining order rather than disrupting capitalist structures (Gilroy 1990, Mullard 1985, and Sivanandan 1990).

A. Sivanandan calls "race"-relations programs instruments of the capitalist state and considers the popular workshop approach (derived from Katz) to be incapable of achieving significant social change:

> It is the sort of psychospiritual mumbo-jumbo which, because it has the resonances of the political movements of its time . . . and [because], by reducing social problems to individual solutions, [it] passes off personal satisfaction for political liberation, and then wraps it all up in a Madison Avenue sales package promising instant cure for hereditary disease, [has] claimed the attention not just of Middle America but of a grateful state. For what better way could the state find to smooth out its social discordances while it carried on, untrammelled, with its capitalist works? (1990: 104)

Sivanandan emphasizes that capitalists do not sponsor touchy-feely consciousness-raising sessions because they intend to raise workers' consciousnesses but because they expect this tactic to make more money for them.

Diversity Training at the Center

Many of the interviews I conducted in 1992 took place after the first diversity-training workshop had been scheduled but before it had occurred. Workers' attitudes about the upcoming workshop varied drastically; expectations ranged from excitement, hope, and optimism to apprehension, wariness, cynicism, and resentment. Each woman's preliminary comments encapsulated her public stance on the Center's handling of "race" and racism, and her view of her role in the "racial" politics of the Center.

Sarina, the white staff physician, talked about the upcoming event as informational, straightforward; she felt it could potentially lift morale:

> I had cultural-diversity training in [my last job], and it was incredibly informative, and very needed, and also is needed in this clinic. . . . I'm

really proud of the fact that this clinic is going to do this. I think it scares the hell out of a lot of people. . . . Everybody is going to learn from this and I think grow in the process. . . . I think all the staff wants to learn from this. . . . I have walked in there and could actually feel the split, which you *can* feel. You know, you can definitely feel the tension some-times—you can cut it with a knife—between the black staff and the white staff. That, to me, signifies something that has to be fixed, quickly.

Sarina indicated that she recognized a problem and that she would enthusi-astically do her part to "fix" whatever was wrong. She underscored the so-phistication of her own awareness: she had already been through "cultural-diversity training" and knew it was "needed" at the Center. Speaking about racism, Sarina separated herself from the staff members who were producing the tension she told me about; she was not afraid but, rather, ready to grow and learn. Janice shared Sarina's optimism and excitement about the work-shop, lauding the Center for its efforts: "I think it's great that we're doing all this work on racism. I think that's much more likely to happen in a feminist environment than a male one." Janice portrayed feminists as predisposed to take on the necessary work involved in confronting racism.

The upcoming workshop troubled Hannah, who said she wanted to learn more about herself and how she was implicated in black co-workers' charges of institutional racism but added that she dreaded the experience because she already felt personally accused:

I just feel like the total picture is that there's a racist current. I mean, I don't know how to solve that; I don't know what I'm doing—you know, I don't *know*, I don't have any answers. I just know that I'm being, like, portrayed as being racist, and I need to find out why. You know, what am I doing? . . . When I do have a conflict with a woman of color, that's what's brought up. And I know I've had it. You know, I mean, I'm like so *tired* of it. . . . And I'm feeling, "Well, maybe she's right," and I'm not going to know anything until September 28 [the workshop date]. And I don't know what kind of answers I'm going to get then either. I don't think it's going to be a miracle, like, "You're not a racist." . . . I think it's depressing. . . . If this is happening *here*, you know, with my little safe haven, you know, then, God, it's got to be really hard out there.

Hannah expressed dismay at the discovery that she had been ignorant of a vital social dynamic at the Center and at the thought that her "safe haven"—and she herself—might be polluted by hypocrisy.

Deborah, another white health worker, countered Hannah's and Janice's view of feminism as automatically anathema to any form of oppression. She explained that white feminists were perhaps more likely (than nonfeminist whites) to find ourselves struggling with problems like racism because our focus on gender could become so single-minded that we might unintentionally fall into the trap of ignoring other forms of oppression.

> I don't think that being feminist in and of itself makes you look for racial contradictions. . . . In fact, sometimes it works the other way. I'm a woman. I'm oppressed . . . as a woman, so I don't want to *hear* about these other things. Or somehow that's an equalizer. I don't believe that's true. So I think that, as there started to be a bigger percentage of black staff, . . . the quantitative level of tension just started to rise because there really wasn't a built-in programmatic way to try and identify problems when they existed. . . . I've heard [white] people say, "Well, we've always had black women working here, and it hasn't been a problem." But actually I think there's always been a problem, but there haven't always been people who've been able to articulate it as forcefully as some of the women who are here [now].

Deborah, like Sarina, had high hopes for the workshop; she also had prior experience with formal "anti-racist" endeavors that enabled her to look forward to the workshop without trepidation.

Black women, unlike many of their white co-workers at the Center, did not fear exposure or condemnation at the workshop but felt that it might achieve nothing and then be hailed by administrators as relevant action. They hoped that, at the very least, the workshop would provide them with the opportunity to express themselves in a public forum but did not expect that white staff members would go beyond paying lip service to addressing racism at the Center.

> RAE: I doubt very seriously if anything will change. I'm excited about being able, you know, to have a space to vent.
>
> W.S.: Why don't you think things will change?
>
> RAE: Because to have change you have to really *want* change. And to really want change, then you have to be able to see the problem clearly, and there's a lot of people who still don't want to see the problem. . . . I don't want to *hear* a white woman say to me, "I know I'm a racist and I'm working on that every day." That's not what I want to hear. I want to *see* that—that you know you're a racist and you're working on it every day.

JULIA: I think that people are willing [to try]. . . . A lot of people just don't, they've never had to think about it, they've never had to deal with it, so they don't think past what is obvious. . . . It's going to be really hard to hear the things they have to say, and it's going to be equally hard for them to listen to what I have to say. . . . I just want to know, you know, really just to admit that you do have those [racist] feelings because I think it's important for them to come to terms with that, and I need to be able to hear them say that.

Black staff members hoped that white staff members would credit their definition of the situation but feared many of the whites were too defensive to be able to truly listen to them. Toby was more optimistic than Rae or Julia, saying, "I actually have more hope about that [racism] getting better than I have of clinic politics getting better. . . . Because I see a certain critical number of people working to make a difference."

Several staff members said they did not believe administrators were sincerely motivated to combat racism and looked at the workshop itself as yet another arena in which management sought to display its control; they called it a performance where workers would be competing for administrators' approval. Lee said, "You have to participate, and I somehow get the feeling that you'll be penalized if you don't jump through all the right hoops." She believed that relations among staff members had become so strained that the workshop might cause more damage than doing nothing at all. "I just don't trust the Center to proceed with integrity on it, because I've yet to see them proceed with integrity when making major changes. . . . We don't have the unity for it now. . . . We don't trust each other well enough to argue." Lee predicted that the diversity-training workshop would turn out to be a farce in which health workers and administrators would fake group cohesion in order to get through the ordeal.

While Lee resented the mandatory attendance policy because she saw it as an example of administrators policing the staff, Rae found the requirement insulting because it underscored white resistance specifically to the training seminar and in general to recognizing the importance of taking action against racism. "If you . . . heard how many times [administrators said] this thing is mandatory . . . and mandatory this and mandatory that, and what it would result in if you don't show up! There's already a buzz or a sense in the clinic that everyone wouldn't show up if it didn't have to be mandatory. So that right there, in itself, lets the black women know where they're coming from."

Workers' trepidation, resentment, and enthusiasm did finally collide at the event itself. After months of discussion, everyone dragged herself out of bed on a cool September Sunday morning to begin this enigmatic corporate ritual of diversity training. We convened in a bland hotel conference room. An air of crisp neatness pervaded the morning activities. We each received a name tag and a notebook when we arrived. The notebook opened with a concise agenda of the workshop activities, followed by several articles and exercises (to be read at home in the evening). The four facilitators (one of whom was Connie) introduced themselves and then asked us to do the same. They asked that we each say our name, tell what we did at the Center, and share something unique we contributed to the Center. They asked us to state an expectation that we had for the workshop. People phrased what they said carefully, and the expectations expressed fit in nicely with the diversity-training rhetoric that would emerge over the course of the seminar (as if participants were anticipating a formulaic, proper outcome). Unanimously expressed, it seemed, were the goals of "gaining understanding" and achieving personal and collective "growth." Whites tended to stress openness and hopes for unity ("to work on myself," "to do team building"), while blacks emphasized their hope of gaining release and relief from the stresses of a racist environment ("to get rid of anger," "to relieve tension").

One of the workshop leaders drew diagrams to chart the realm of appropriate discourse for the workshop. She began with a series of concentric circles: she labeled the innermost circle "values," the middle ring "attitudes," and the outer ring "behaviors." Values, she explained drove everything else, thus their central place in the diagram. They were also the most "intangible" of the three components of human action. We would work on behaviors and attitudes, the parts one could see or hear. She presented four more circles, this time interlocking. These circles were labeled "ideological," "personal," "organizational," and "cultural": the categories out of which values, attitudes, and behavior emerged. "We are here to focus on cultural differences," she said. "Extracultural" realms, such as "policies, practices, and procedures of the Womancare Center," were "out of bounds." These are all, of course, "cultural"; everything is cultural!—I remember thinking at the time, but I did not interject. No one did (though I noticed some scowling and rolling of eyes). It was a good thing, too, because the next thing she said was, "We're not here to argue." The leaders told us we should take care not to drag personal politics into our discussions over the next two days.

Next, we learned to channel discord into a standard format in an exercise entitled "Constructive Feedback." We divided into pairs and were given a hypothethical situation to act out: one worker leaves early without telling the other, who must take over, clean up, and close up the Center by herself. The confrontation takes place the following morning. The disgruntled employee was to compress her sentiments into the formula: " When you _____ I feel _____ because I _____." She then would allow time for the early leaver to respond and, next, request a change in behavior and courteously invite the early leaver to respond: "I would like _____ because _____. What do you think?" I played the role of the disgruntled employee; Tanya was the early leaver. I said to Tanya, "When you left early yesterday without telling me, I felt angry because I was left with all the work." If I followed the formula properly, it was difficult for me to call her irresponsible; the focus had to be on *my feelings*. Then she could legitimately shift the focus to *her* feelings: "When you tell me you're angry, I feel defensive because . . . " The formula worked neatly, but Tanya and I agreed that it felt unwieldy, awkward, and contrived to use it. Tanya told me she felt uncomfortable during the exercise because she did not deal well with confrontation. Even this pretend brand made her want to just apologize and have it over with. (She agreed immediately to my request, "I would like you to inform me in future if you need to leave early because . . . ")

How would this innocuous exchange alter if racism were the contested topic of "Constructive Feedback"? Notwithstanding the discomfort of those who have problems with confrontation, my sense is that it would dilute accusations into feelings, making interactions easier for whites. Maybe I am overreacting against the scriptedness of the exchange, but this mode of discourse seems too simple. It also seems tempting to disregard the formula's repression of hard-to-hear accusations. I think about the firing of Allison. Would black women's complaints work effectively in this form: "When you fired Allison we felt angry because we believe the grounds for her dismissal were unfounded"? Or "We felt angry because we thought you were racists"? The second formulation seems precisely the sort of expression the script proscribes. How the complainants feel becomes the crucial information to be conveyed, not what they think about the person they confront nor what they think about the person's erroneous behavior. In the exercise, judgments cannot be expressed unless "owned" and rescripted into emotional responses.

After lunch, the neatness slowly began to break down as we moved into various exercises designed to examine racism explicitly. The diversity-training consultants gave us special language to use, perhaps to strip our conversation of the tension involved in invoking contested words (like racism!). For instance, they used the terms "target group" and "nontarget group." They had designed one exercise to teach that "nontargets" are the targetters of the "targets," though this was never explicitly said. In other words, the trainers cast racism as structurally enacted by individuals (nontargets), presenting a schema in which it was difficult to lay blame.

The diversity-training seminar did include some radical (as contrasted with liberal) elements; it was not designed wholly on the premise that racism could be eradicated through adopting appropriate communication skills. (This liberal-radical mix is not new; nor do Katz's exercises present racism as solely psychological and, thus, correctable through individual action or therapeutic interaction; they also portray it as a structural monolith.) The leaders of the Center's diversity-training workshop interspersed such "practical" interactive exercises like "Constructive Feedback" with minilectures and exercises designed to illuminate the structural roots of racism. For example, some time after the "target/nontarget" exercise, they lectured on the differences between racism and prejudice. They stressed that privilege must be the dividing factor and that whites, by virtue of being born white, enjoyed privileges that people of color were denied in U.S. society. Thus, blacks who hated or disliked whites were "prejudiced" rather than racist. There could be no such thing as "reverse racism" in a system where blacks were systematically disempowered. Whites had rational reasons for maintaining racist systems since they benefited from them in many ways; black prejudice was a rational response to white racism. But both racism and prejudice were morally wrong.

We spent about half the second day in groups segregated by "race" engaged in an exercise entitled "Earliest Racial Encounters," where we shared stories about the first memories we had of learning about "race." After lunch, we reconvened for an exercise entitled "Cultural Style Differences," in which we watched a filmstrip that illustrated several (alleged) black-white differences. The film may as well have been entitled "There's Truth in Stereotypes." Blacks and whites clashed in each scene because the characters made assumptions based on their mutually exclusive "cultures"—for example, a black woman felt ill at ease because she perceived her white employer's inquiries about her personal life as intrusive (while he thought he was making casual conversation); whites were taken aback by the enthusiastic greetings of blacks.

The exercise corresponded with a handout in our notebooks entitled "Differences between Black Community Culture and White Middle-Class Culture." The examples here reinforced the message of the film: whites and blacks were essentially culturally opposed. Under the heading "Emotions," the handout states, "A common goal of Black Cultural activities and events is the revitalization of energy through emotional and spiritual release. Black presentations are emotionally intense, dynamic and demonstrative." In contrast, whites "repress emotions and are frequently inexperienced in managing intense emotions and fear loss of control." In other words, blacks are loud, impetuous, and creative; whites are cautious and calculating. Blacks have strong communities; whites are linked merely by a sort of bland, middle-class identity.

For the day's penultimate exercise, we subdivided into groups of about five and wrote notes to each person in our group telling her something we admired about her, something she uniquely contributed to the Center. This exercise symmetrically echoed the way we started off the day before, when we introduced ourselves and talked of our own uniqueness. Here, we confirmed the uniqueness of each other. For me, it felt partly sweet, partly nauseatingly touchy-feely, and partly dangerously false. I knew people had a difficult time with the workshop itself because of specific tensions among staff and administrators, and this kind of patting-each-other-on-the-back closure seemed, on one level, a joke. No one resisted, but I could see several people looked rankled by the intimacy the exercise assumed. We all complied, nonetheless, and then reconvened in a larger circle to talk about the workshop as a whole. In this last go-round, we talked about what steps we were willing to take to make a difference in the "racial" politics at the Center or in our lives more generally. The mood seemed much more relaxed than it had the day before, but by this time I felt incapable of judging who was faking what when. Maybe everyone was feeling all warm and united. (I sort of did.) Maybe everyone was just happy it was over. (I definitely was.) The diversity consultants had carefully crafted the exercises to build in intensity as the first day of the workshop wore on, to pick up the second morning where we left off, and then gradually to reduce in intensity over the course of the second day. People went home angry or upset the first day, and relieved and at least somewhat pleased when the workshop ended.

Center workers seemed to agree that the workshop resulted in at least a short-term sense of closeness among staff members and agreed that people got along better for several weeks afterward. After a while, though, that camaraderie dissipated. It was as if the group experience produced a little high that could only fade as Center workers plunged once again into too much work. From this point onward, I heard fewer complaints about racism from black staff members while I was at the Center. There were no major "racial" incidents like Allison's firing. But black women remained cynical about whether white co-workers and administrators really cared about eradicating institutional racism.

White staff members tended to speak more approvingly about the workshop's effects on them and on staff in general. Trudy, an administrator, saw it as a positive move on the part of the Center, one that raised consciousness and solidified her own personal commitment to "trying to create an organization where women of different races can work and feel supported." And Mimi, an administrative worker who had not wanted to attend the workshop, called it an inspirational learning experience:

I thought it was great. . . . One of the problems I was having is that I believed women could be sexist. I also believed blacks could be racist.

And I just learned a lot. . . . I realized that I was very close-minded because when people would tell me how they felt and tell me why . . . blacks can't be racist, I'd be like "no, no, no, no." And I wouldn't listen. And I really tried to listen, and I really tried to learn. And I realized that I was wrong in my way of thinking. . . . I realized that blacks can't be racist and that women can't be sexist . . . because white men—well, men in general, basically white men—run the country so women really can't be sexist towards them, and because white people really run the country. . . . I still think that blacks can say racist things, but because I'm white, I'll always have that . . . white privilege.

Mimi said she learned to reconsider racism by stepping outside herself to consider the structural position of others. She congratulated herself for her raised consciousness by criticizing the insincerity or resistance of many of her white co-workers, saying, "I think a lot of people went in there close-minded. They didn't really care. They didn't want to be there. And they didn't really give it a chance, so they didn't learn anything. A lot of white people think that there's not a racism problem here, and don't want to deal with it. . . . A lot of people wanted to deal with other problems besides race. . . . But that's not what it was for." Mimi first referred to "racism" as the problem, then shifted to "race." This unconscious linguistic maneuver provides evidence for a critique of diversity-training seminars as essentializing racialization into concrete categories (blackness and whiteness). Difference is portrayed as an inevitable consequence of "race." If these categories are considered problematic, in and of themselves, then Mimi—and others—might see racism as a natural development (or at least an understandable one) in environments that are "diverse." (See Frankenberg 1993 on the construction of whiteness.)

A focus on "diversity" or "difference" ultimately raises the question, Different from what? This approach can be read as reifying white as the norm, and all else—once seen as differently wrong—becomes simply "other," with special attention paid to relativism. This strategy questions the centrality of whiteness but does not interrogate whiteness, blackness, Asianness, or whatever. The categories themselves are reified as separated from each other by cultural divides. Each is, above all, acceptable—or, in more enthusiastic moments, wonderful or special. In workshops like this one, participants may wonder how these representations of difference may be distinguished from stereotypes. This question crops up in various training programs reported on in the mass media and management literature, and it indicates, I think, how problematic these new simplifications of difference are, how unpracticed and sloppy we are at examining the complexities of racialized identity. During part of the workshop, I sat thinking about how my parents had taught me people were "no different" under their skins and how that liberal strategy has been deemed inappropriate by the new focus on "diversity," "recognizing differences." We pay a different kind of lip service. We have moved to the other end of the spectrum: now we are so different we need workshops like this one to help us bridge the abysses between us.

As with much of the management literature that exhorts diversity consultants to tread carefully on white toes, the Center's diversity-training workshop taught that white guilt must be seen as counterproductive to fighting racism. For instance, one of the handouts in our notebook stated, "The acquisition of the [negative] conditioning information is involuntary and 'in the air,' in the institutions and the culture of society. . . . It is a painful, harmful process which is involuntary." Racism, we learned—and many diversity trainers teach—occurs not by accident but nevertheless without our volition. Whites are first indoctrinated as children who have no choice in the matter. With newly raised, postworkshop consciousnesses, whites have the power to combat the influences of the past; but diversity trainers insist white racism ought not be considered to be the fault of anyone present. "BLAMING," the handout continues, "is not helpful. . . . TAKING RESPONSIBILITY is helpful." If we purge guilt, do we not also disallow accusations? It sounds appealing to say that guilt is not the route to change; but as I read the management literature and think back on the workshop, I also wonder why diversity trainers go to such lengths to ensure that white people never feel uneasy.

The implication behind the efforts taken to protect the comfort of whites is that we are *made* to feel blamed, uneasy, guilty by talk of "race," racialization, and racism. This rhetoric sounds far less benign when one asks, Who blames? Who takes responsibility? The rhetoric insists that whites must take some sort of action against racism and thus holds whites accountable; but what are whites accountable for if no accusations can be made? Whites are accountable only to the degree that whites decide to be accountable. The recommended language refuses claims of racism made by people of color, casts them as blamers. In the Center's diversity-training seminar, for example, it would have been appropriate for a white woman to "own" her own racism but not for a black woman to point it out to her. Can whites really be accurate arbiters of racism? Can whites make progress at overcoming conflicts at an interpersonal level without discomfort?

Tellingly, diversity trainers—and evaluators of the diversity-training trend—take the discomfort of whites as a sign that seminars need revision. They rarely acknowledge that people of color may have problems with diversity training. This focus on whites' responses suggests that, underneath all the talk of mutual understanding that goes on in these corporate exercises, diversity training continues to operate *for* whites. In my view, diversity-training lingo and boundary setting tend to inform participants that power differentials can be leveled without a straightforward acknowledgment of power dynamics. The seminars eschew guilt and ultimately let white participants off the hook: oddly, we are to claim responsibility for something for which (we are told) we are not responsible. Need guilt mean we are incapacitated to act? What is guilt, after all, beyond a sense of regretful responsibility? Guilt may be an appropriate response for whites to feel in addressing racism. Guilt turned inward becomes pitiful perhaps, but I believe guilt might be turned productively outward as well.

For white women at the Center, the belief that an open-communication system was crucial to effecting change coexisted with the fear that they could unintentionally say "something wrong." Again, they expressed the notion that racism could mysteriously emerge out of white women's mouths unbidden, without the knowledge that it was there or that it was racist. Thus, black women must keep white women posted. At the same time that white workers insisted on being told when they said or did something racist, though, the sanctioned rhetorical framework for examining racism disallowed black women's voices. Here was a Catch-22: white workers wanted to "know" about racism but permitted no unobstructed way for black workers to tell them.

Rae illustrated this dilemma when she talked about how she felt both more tolerant of and angrier at her white co-workers after the workshop:

> I think the first racism meeting was very informative, very informative. . . . It opened my eyes to a lot, . . . how white women view black women, for instance, body language, acceptable things to ask versus the unacceptable. Whereas what I would consider being nosy and disrespectful, they're not thinking of it like that. So it puts a whole 'nother dimension on the situation because you can't get perturbed or an attitude with somebody if they don't understand that they're being disrespectful to you. So, it's like my tolerance level became greater. But, on the same token, it made me very angry because I had to deal with a lot of pain to be able to talk about the things that had been done to me because of my color. That comes up a lot of pain and anger. And a lot of anger that's kind of like you have anger when you watch a movie like *Roots* or *Mississippi Burning*. You have all this anger, and then what do you do with that anger? That's the reason why I don't go see the typical "Boyz 'n the 'Hood" type of movies. I can't personally handle that. Because after all that anger, what do I with it? . . . That's just too close to reality for me. . . . And I had a real problem with how these white women wanted *me* to heal their guilt and their pain. It really made me angry. Just like "*Hello!* Can I deal with my own stuff?"

Rae gained insight into white women's ignorance, as she described it, and also found herself frustrated by both being on display for white co-workers and then being expected to commend these women for their efforts. Her narrative demonstrates the no-win position into which diversity-training seminars typically place people of color: they are made into "racial" representatives whose experiences are appropriated as examples of the evils of racism. Then they are given the role of arbitrating absolution for whites.

Center women were both stymied and enlightened by the formal exercises in which they participated in the hopes of eradicating racism at the Center. Despite their doubts about others or hesitations about themselves, most Center women nurtured some hope about moving toward sisterhood and away from discord (without imposing assimilation), regardless of "racial" divisions. They believed that some mutual ground might be found amid the antagonism of "racial" polarization and the murky rhetoric of "diversity." And most felt this ideological battle was of the utmost importance for feminists to fight, even as they expressed a great deal of confusion or cynicism about proceeding with it. It is essential to consider the rifts among Center women (and among all feminist women) against a broader political landscape. Though this chapter (along with Chapter Four) chronicles discord among Center women, they stood united—despite the discord—against those who challenged their most cherished feminist ideals (as previous chapters demonstrate). They struggled to preserve and build on the unity they did feel.

Feminism and (F)utility

Assessing the Future of Procreative Freedom

When I began interviewing Womancare Center staff members in 1990, many said they believed the Supreme Court might reverse *Roe v Wade* and make abortion illegal within the next couple of years. They took the *Webster* decision to allow states to limit abortion as evidence that the Court was not committed to protecting *Roe*. Between 1990 and 1992, Center women's work lives were less embattled, in a sense, because their encounters with antis had gradually diminished since Operation Rescue's intense onslaught in 1988.[1] Most staff members worried about impending legislative action; some of those interviewed in 1990 and 1991 said they felt as though they were waiting for the axe to fall. Many of the women carefully evaluated each abortion-related court decision or relevant election, trying to discern what it would mean for the future of procreative freedom. They watched Clarence Thomas's confirmation with dismay; many were convinced that his appointment augured the reversal of *Roe*. When the Court agreed to hear *Casey* (which put various proposed restrictions on abortion to the test and provided an opportunity for the Court to undo *Roe* if it chose), most staff members apprehensively awaited the verdict.

But the *Casey* decision did not turn out to be the final defeat that many Center women feared it might be (no thanks to Thomas, of course). Because

Casey stopped short of overturning *Roe*—upholding all of Pennsylvania's restrictions except for spousal notification—the Center women I interviewed in 1992 and after were less fearful of complete illegalization than those I spoke with earlier. Staff members agreed, though, that while the *Casey* decision saved *Roe*, it also paved the way for the continued dismantling of abortion rights at the state level because it upheld the constitutionality of most state-imposed restrictions on abortion. Indeed, many staff members believed that access to abortion had already been curtailed, especially for poor women. Sarina said the *Casey* decision cemented the obstacle that *Webster* had implemented. "I am more optimistic than I was two months ago . . . [before the decision]. But the fact that there are restrictions and more restrictions than we had a year ago is of great concern to me because it's already very difficult for some women to obtain this procedure, even if they can come up with the money. . . . And I think by putting other roadblocks in their way, once again it's being made more difficult."

Though they felt relieved by the salvaging of *Roe*, Center women refused to celebrate as if a pro-choice victory had been won when only the bare bones of *Roe* remained. As Lois described the *Casey* decision, "I think they're just trying to gut *Roe v Wade*. . . . It's the court saying, 'Okay, you're not mature enough to decide if you want an abortion, so you *are* mature enough to have a child.' That doesn't seem really logical."

As the 1992 presidential election approached, most staff members refused to speculate hopefully, not wanting to be disappointed if Clinton lost. Janice was one exception; she was the most optimistic among those interviewed in the months preceding the presidential election:

Before the Supreme Court decision, I was very nervous. Even when the decision came out, I was very disappointed and bummed out. . . . It was like, "What the fuck's going on?" . . . In one way, it's sort of a relief, but you're not going to get happy about a decision that lots of women are not going to be able to get abortions now. . . . But if we can get just one more Justice who's pro-choice . . . and a Democrat in the White House, which it looks like we can do—and I really felt that during the convention, I felt like he [Clinton] was electable, and this was definitely a potential thing that could happen. That was very encouraging for me.

I interviewed Sarina, Lois, and Janice within weeks of each other during the summer of 1992 (after *Casey* but before Clinton). Janice felt encouraged; Lois, angry; and Sarina, guardedly optimistic. In this chapter, I explore the range in staff members' attitudes about the politics of abortion in general, both as they varied among the group and as they shifted over the course of my association with the women. I return to questions about maintaining feminist commitment that have interested me throughout my study: How are activists able to sustain a vision of a better world in discouraging times, and how do such visions emerge from and shape collective experience?

The interview excerpts in this chapter are taken mostly from the ends of interviews, when I would say something like, "The final thing I want to talk about is the future of abortion." In 1990 and 1991, interviewees would often remark, "Oh God, let's not! It's too depressing!" Considering the concluding comments together, I rediscover a set of ambivalences that form the basis for Center women's feminist theorizing. They talked about how their desire to be at the forefront of an underground feminist movement (that would keep abortion available) was tempered by reservations they felt about risking themselves for anonymous, possibly undeserving, women. Staff members expressed both faith in American legal and political processes and disgust at "the system"; while they mistrusted politicians and legislative and political processes, most of them also held that positive change was possible and that it could come about as a result of democratic action. Center women expressed belief in the goodness or righteousness of people along with the conviction that this potential would triumph eventually, that people would one day recognize the utility of feminism. Yet, at the same time, they also felt the efforts of feminists like themselves might eventually prove futile. The women who avidly followed every development were angry at the events themselves and at people in general for letting these things happen. At the same time, they understood feelings of helplessness and apathy because their own daily experience of the politics of abortion threatened to wear them out. A few staff members claimed to have little interest in following the news or keeping track of legal developments or political battles surrounding abortion. They said they found these activities too frustrating and professed a deliberate lack of involvement.

A thorough exploration of the range of activists' perceptions—their ambivalence, anger, hope, and frustration—may facilitate the development of feminist politics and praxis for the future. Center women struggled to achieve a sense of equilibrium in the middle of what they saw as an intense battle; they sought to advance political aims, as well as to protect themselves from the burn-out of difficult work and the fallout from the war over abortion (and other heated political debates in which feminist positions were fervently contested by the Right).

Imagining Illegality

Would five robed men dare to abolish legal abortion? For many Center staff members, considering this possibility meant reconceptualizing their notion of historical movement as necessarily progressive. In 1990 and 1991, many of the women I interviewed said they had come to believe the criminalization of abortion was possible, and some even called it probable. Ilene said, for example, "I'm a pessimist. I think of course that *Roe v Wade* will be overturned soon . . . because I have no faith in the government at all; I have no faith in the structure of this society." Most Center women were less vehemently pessimistic, but they all agreed that the antis had created an ideological climate in which most Americans considered abortion to be at best a regrettable course of action for a woman to take (and at worst an unconscionable, sinful act). Thus, it struck them as inevitable that the Court, stacked with conservatives by Reagan and Bush, would drift toward the right in its opinions on abortion.

In 1992 interviews, Center women focused on all the damage that had been done—the "chipping away" of abortion rights. They no longer feared imminent de jure criminalization. Rather, they talked about the ways in which antis had achieved de facto criminalization by successfully interjecting their rhetoric into the public consciousness and further stigmatizing (and thus restricting) abortion. When I interviewed her in 1992, Carrie said she felt that abortion would in all likelihood remain legal, but she sounded as pessimistic about the public cultural climate as Ilene did about political trends in 1990:

> I can't imagine it getting better, and that . . . really shocks me because I feel that it's so obvious that abortion isn't something that women should have to seek in back alleys, and something they shouldn't have to fight for, and something they shouldn't have to pay a thousand dollars for. . . . It's something they shouldn't have to apologize for. But I feel that way about a lot of things in the country. And I'm more shocked by the way the government is treating the AIDS epidemic and HIV, and scapegoating certain groups instead of taking responsibility for protecting everyone and helping people already infected. I just feel I don't trust this government. I don't trust society. And I especially don't trust whatever it is that has made most of the population pretty apathetic. It's a lot easier to have prejudices instead of politics. . . . I feel like anti-politics, they spread quicker. . . . I don't think [abortion is] going to become illegal, you know, any time soon, . . . but the restrictions are bad enough for me.

So while staff members' predictions of illegality diminished from the first set of interviews (1990–1991) to the second (1992 and onward), Center women remained consistently distressed about the overall political picture. They felt that progress had fallen by the wayside. Feminists were left clinging to the bits and pieces that were left of legal abortion, unable to guess what would happen next. Especially in the earlier interviews, staff members described the future of abortion as completely unpredictable.

ELISE: As far as where *Roe v Wade* is going to go, I mean I just think that can go any way at all. And as far as state to state is going to go, I think that can go any way at all. And as far as women banding together as a group, I don't think we're there yet. But I do know one thing. . . . If *Roe v Wade* is overturned and we're back to illegal abortions, that fewer women will die with illegal abortions because there are a whole lot of us who have a lot of information that we didn't have before.

GRETA: It's like a big tree where they chip and chip and chip on both sides and there's just a toothpick fiber holding the tree up. It scares me. I don't know what's going to happen. What do I think is going to happen? I *hope* that we all get together and do something about it. I hope we do. . . . I don't think it's just abortion that's at stake. It's everything.

CELIA: I'd like to say that people out there are really going to wake up. And I think, you know, in some places they have, but . . . I really see things going backward before they go forward. They've already started to go backward. . . . All this Reagan and Bush era, it's going to leave a very long legacy. . . . It's not that OR [Operation Rescue] threat anymore, you know. It's not that they're going to come and circle our building. That's not my fear anymore. . . . The fear is just all these laws that they keep throwing up there. . . . It's people who see themselves as pro-choice too. People who think that parental notification is a good thing. You know, my brother thinks that parental notification isn't—you know, "Why get upset about that?" You know. "Why get upset about people not being able to have abortions in the second trimester?" . . . He's what you would call a liberal man. . . . It's like parental notification going into effect here . . . or [taking away] Medicaid funding. . . . They're just whittling things away.

As Celia described, the antis had created an atmosphere in which self-pronounced pro-choice people felt comfortable denouncing certain abortions. Staff members believed that qualifying a commitment to procreative freedom essentially negated it. The whole value in pro-choice rhetoric was that it asserted women had the right to make procreative decisions for our-selves—period. Now, clearly, attacks on women's decision making had be-come acceptable even among "liberal" thinkers. Center women saw willingness to compromise as dangerous, supporting the "chipping away" of abortion.

Center women blamed the antis for enabling lawmakers and politicians to disregard women in their discourse on abortion, but they also denounced government as a "male institution" that worked to further the interests of white men. The majority of governing, legislating men, they felt, would per-petuate women's oppression because it sustained their own power; as Anne said, "I really, personally, don't think that they will ever just totally end abor-tion. And I don't think that that's what they want to do politically. I think they just want to—just chop away at it slowly. . . . I really don't think that they want to see time switched back to the clothes-hanger days. . . . They want to control who can and who cannot have an abortion. It's not that they want to stop abortion." Even staff members most optimistic about democracy's capa-bility to protect the interests of American women—like Anne, who felt the situation would inevitably improve in the long run—described the political and legislative systems as cold-hearted and misogynistic.

Yvette was unique in her excitement about the radical potential of in-creased repression, envisioning a complete collapse of the U.S. political econ-omy:

> One good way that I look at it is . . . I have lots of heroes as far as civil rights activists and women's rights activists . . . that had really hard times to work in, and so . . . if I want to be committed, I won't have to look far to find a place to stand. And so I don't think the future is dim at all. I think, realistically, it's different. . . . I think that abortion will be made illegal, and, you know, it's kind of interesting. It's going to be a real period of change. . . . My optimistic idea is that . . . the economy will just collapse and all of this superficial industrial consumerism stuff will just *go*. You know, people will have to grow their own food because Kroger will just go bankrupt. Or . . . only a very small percentage of the popula-tion will be able to afford to shop there. This is kind of lunacy advanced thinking . . . . The world is just so large and impersonal that I think it's interesting to see it breaking apart.

Yvette relished the notion that the structure of American culture might crumble. She fantasized that such dramatic upheavals in everyday life would give rise to a situation in which progressive politics would appeal because people would see old ways as obviously corrupt. Unlike Yvette, most staff members interviewed in 1990–1991 imagined that conditions would slowly worsen, but they did not propose revolution, except wistfully or jokingly.

Center women learned to live with uncertainty about the future as time passed; ironically, instability became consistent and their responses to it routinized. By 1992 (after *Webster*), many believed a legislative stalemate had been at least temporarily achieved, though no one suggested even limited access to abortion would ever be assured. When I interviewed Mira and Lee during the summer of 1992, they expressed their apprehensions about the upcoming election:

> MIRA: I'm really depressed. . . . If George Bush wins another election, I'm moving to Canada or Israel. . . . I can't believe this country is electing these people. . . . Everybody keeps saying, "Oh, it's all right. *Now* people are going to get really pissed. Now people are really going to go vote." I'm like, "Yeah, sure. Right. Mm hmm. I'll believe it when I see the election results."

> LEE: I think my basic intuition was clearer two years ago than it is now because, on a good day, I feel like things are pretty secure; but on a bad day, I feel like . . . everything *is* just going to be swept away next week.

Some Center women (in both the early and later interviews) called the prospect of illegality incredible, even when they believed it was possible. One might expect that younger women would consider legal abortion to be more secure than older women would because they could not remember when abortion had not been legally available. However, younger staff members imagined illegality vividly, even though they had not experienced it firsthand. Young Center women had learned all about back-alley abortions. They spoke angrily about women who died aborting themselves or at the hands of untrained or uncaring underground practitioners. They talked proudly about the Chicago-based Jane collective's provision of clandestine hygienic and affordable abortions, invoking this history as their own heritage. (Baehr 1990 was one of their favorite sources.) So when these younger women said they could not imagine that lawmakers would reinstate illegality, they did not mean that they could not envision illegality but that they could not fathom that legislators and politicians would deny the relevance of the lethal history of criminalized abortion. As Julia said, "Part of me just can't imagine that they will do that, given the fact of what has happened and given . . . how many women's lives were lost."

Staff members who did remember the time before *Roe* were just as likely as their younger co-workers to profess disbelief that abortion could be made illegal again—precisely because of their memories. Nancy told me in 1991 that she thought a ban on abortion was possible, but she said, "I can't imagine living in a world where it is totally illegal. . . . It would be really hard to live, you know, knowing how it could be. . . . I was in college before it was legalized, so I remember all the fear." None of the Center women who would have been fifteen or older when abortion was illegal (Trudy, Emma, Nancy, Meryl, Deborah, and Elise) said they had had illegal abortions, but they described the secrecy and shame surrounding unwanted pregnancy during this period as a crucial fearful memory.

Imagining Underground Activism

Center staff members agreed that if abortion were to be outlawed, women would be much better off than they had been in the decades before *Roe* because so many more people would have access to the knowledge (and equipment) necessary to perform abortions. As Mira said, "You know how many criminals there'd be—between people providing and people getting illegal abortions? Jails would be full. I mean, we've had abortion technology available for, you know, for how long? . . . What exactly do they think? It's just going to disappear?" Many staff members noted the simplicity of performing menstrual extraction, an abortion technique done (ideally) during the first eight weeks after a missed period, in which the contents of the uterus are removed with an easy-to-make device consisting of a cannula, a jar, a syringe, and tubing (Boonstra 1993).[2] Though a handful of staff members met sporadically (outside of work) to practice menstrual extraction on each other during 1991 and 1992, the group eventually disbanded.

Center women contemplating illegalization found cold comfort thinking about a new, improved underground, but it was the only consolation when they imagined a ban on abortions. They feared that if abortion were outlawed, many women would continue unwanted pregnancies and bear unwanted children; indeed, they thought this was already happening as a result of diminishing access to abortion. They believed that some women would undoubtedly resort to dangerous, unhygienic, and life-threatening measures as they do whenever and wherever abortion is illegal.

I asked staff members what they thought they would do if abortion were outlawed in the United States. None of the women interpreted this question to mean that I was asking what they would do for alternate employment: they all focused on their potential participation in an underground movement. Every woman who had given the matter some thought said that she would be likely to, at the very least, help women to obtain abortions. Many had

214

thought about whether they would be willing to perform abortions themselves, and they discussed the risk of engaging in illegal actions.

Only a few Center women said outright that they would do abortions illegally. When they did, they tended to speak of menstrual extraction:

> LOIS: I'd go underground and offer M.E.s. I don't have the skill to
> do it; I'd need to get in a group and learn.

> GRETA: We already know how to do it now—M.E.—you know,
> and I've had one of those done on myself. . . . And it was like one of
> the most empowering things I've ever done, to have all these
> women around that I was friends with and that knew me and cared
> about me and were there just being supportive. . . . So, I already
> know how to do that. Yeah, if it was illegal I would do abortion.

> HANNAH: I'd like to do . . . menstrual extraction—in a heartbeat.
> . . . I think that that's real empowering, to have that knowledge. It's
> not going to help, unfortunately, the majority of the women though.

> MERYL: I would be real careful about who I would do [menstrual
> extraction] for, but I would do it. . . . I don't *want* to have to do it
> though! . . . I don't know if I could do D&E's; they take an awful
> amount of skill. . . . But I'm sure I could learn.

Some staff members liked to imagine they would deliberately subvert laws
against abortion but felt unsure about whether they actually would. Several
said the context of illegality would mean they would have to judge potential
clients in an entirely new manner: each woman would have to be assessed as
deserving an abortion. She would have to be deemed truly pro-choice, honest, and trustworthy. Thus, the provision of feminist health care would be
greatly circumscribed by illegality; it would no longer be seen as a service
offered to all women. As Yvette said, "I feel in a way very angry at women,
that women are letting this happen to themselves. And so I don't think I
would risk going to prison for first-degree murder to do an illegal abortion
for someone . . . unless it was a woman I knew and cared about."

Other Center women did not see themselves as practitioners. They felt
more comfortable imagining that they would assist others performing abortions rather than becoming illegal abortionists. Actual provision would be a
greater risk, would carry greater penalties, and would be more emotionally
difficult. These women said they would continue to engage in feminist health
care activism by providing information to women (about gaining access to
abortion) and by facilitating the work of underground abortionists.

215

AUDREY: I would definitely try to get in some way with a safe, illegal clinic of some sort. I mean, I've already talked to another woman that works with me who says, you know, the day that it looks like it's going to happen, she's going to hoard up all the instruments that she can get and do 'em herself. . . . I don't think that you need to have an M.D. to do a safe abortion. I think you need to know a lot about what you're doing. . . . I wouldn't go out and do 'em, but I'd certainly support someone else who knew what she was doing.

RISA: I don't think I could perform an abortion for somebody, but I know I could assist. . . . And I'd be willing to. . . . I don't worry about it [illegalization]. I just make sure that I just suck up every bit of information that I can get. . . . If it becomes illegal, hell, we can do it ourselves!

MIRA: You certainly have to weigh putting yourself and your family and everybody else at risk for being found out. There's the responsibility of a complication and not being able to admit a woman to a hospital. You know, it's a lot of responsibility. . . . I think probably what I would do is help women get that information. Do you know what I mean? I mean, I've certainly thought about how I would help make it more accessible to women. I don't know that I've thought about being an actual provider. . . . Maybe it's just because I'm not a medical kind of person. . . . But I do see that it would be vitally important for me to make menstrual-extraction technology available to women. The information, and where to go, and how to get it—yes, that I could do.

The medical workers I interviewed—Sarina and Ellen—and Nancy, one of the original founders of the Center, contemplated the danger involved in illegal activity most explicitly. When I interviewed her in 1992, Sarina described her life as already quite constrained by working as a legal abortionist because of the security measures she had to take to protect herself from antis (see Chapter Three). She said the effort necessary to maintain clandestine activity might become too overwhelming. She also framed her response in terms of professional risk taking, saying that she did not know whether she would jeopardize her right to practice medicine by performing illegal abortions. Ultimately, she refused the question, saying she would address it only if the situation demanded:

I had thought about it, but I don't know that I had really made a decision in my mind. The idea of basically being on the run, going from place to place to place, having to do things underground or closeted in some form, didn't really appeal to me. However my sense of commitment is overwhelmingly strong. And I don't know what I would do. . . . I do have other things that I want to do besides just provide abortion services, and it would depend upon which way the balance was tipped at the particular time. . . . I do feel hopeful that it's not going to get to that stage.

Ellen, like Sarina, weighed the potential professional risks involved with illegal activity against her commitment to keeping abortion available. She invoked her family life as the primary factor in her speculations. She and Nancy both described how motherhood mitigated against undertaking the most risky underground activities. They evaluated illegal activity in terms of how it would affect them as mothers (both as nurturers and as financial caretakers):

ELLEN: The issue for me as any health care provider is, Would you lose your license forever and not be able to practice? And I think if I didn't have a child, I'd be more willing to take that risk. But now that I have a child, I would never want to lose my license forever. Or if I had a child and a husband who could support me, which I do right now, that wouldn't be so much an issue either if I only lost my license for like a few years. If I had to go to jail, that's another issue altogether because—it's not so much spending time in jail, yeah, that would be terrible—but spending time in jail and having to be away from my child would be overwhelming. I just, I can't deal with that thought.

NANCY: I think that I would still be involved in the women's health movement in some kind of way which would probably be providing information to women about where they could go. You know, I don't know what I, personally, would choose to do. I've got two children. . . . I don't know that I would want to, you know, do any-thing that would jeopardize them. . . . I very much admire the women who were in Jane. . . . The technique isn't that complicated to learn, but it's just, you know, more [a question of] what risks are people, you know, willing to take at different times of their life. And the other thing is . . . would it make sense for me or Emma to do that when we're the more obvious people that they would be looking at? You know, probably not.

Emma, the executive director, was much more vague about her role in an imagined future where abortion would be prohibited; she seemed deliberately to refrain from mentioning the actual doing of abortions. Like Nancy, Emma saw her current stance as a public activist as an impediment to future underground work. She said:

> I would be involved in some level of helping women get an abortion. I don't think that I'm going to put my convictions and my knowledge and my skills aside and just crawl up and die out of pure depression and cynicism—which is how I might feel sometimes, but I don't think I could do that. So there's various things [like] . . . helping women go to other states where they might have better laws. It might be . . . having illegal abortion services—organizing that or being connected up in some way.

Whether reticent or bold in their speculations, Center women all pictured themselves as continuing the battle for procreative freedom somehow, even if they had to work against the law.

Imagining Grass-Roots Politicization

Center women repeatedly stressed that the right to abortion would certainly be lost if people did not recognize abortion as a symbol of women's liberty and autonomy rather than—in the antis' terms—a matter of fetal life or death. And because they viewed abortion as one element in a battle for control over women's bodies, they believed losing abortion would mean opening the door to rampant oppression and the negation of civil liberties of all kinds.

> EMMA: I don't know that this society will buy illegal abortion, but I think [people] will accept a lot of restrictions, so that you have to beg for an abortion, and it's individual by individual, begging. . . . Restrictions on abortion are, in general, sexual oppression and then broader political oppression. It's not isolated. So I don't think it bodes too well for what women have to look forward to.

> TANYA: I have a lot of friends who get tired of hearing me talk about this, but I think it's so integral to being—to being a *human being*. I mean, you're talking about people's sexuality. . . . Everything seems to relate to it. And especially when you see . . . through feminist-colored eyeglasses, you know, like I do.

> MIRA: Some days I'm really optimistic, you know, the pro-choice forces have mobilized, we're out there. . . . I feel like we're getting on the stick; we're starting to realize how serious this is. We're all right, and they're not going to do this to us. On the other hand, . . .

I just get really nervous. . . . There are days I just can't sleep, and it's not just abortion, it's not just reproductive rights that divide us. If they start touching laws, you know, regarding my body and what I can and cannot do with it, what's next? You know, they're going to tell me who I can and cannot sleep with, you know? . . . Who's going to decide that I *can* have a baby—is the law going to do that? I mean, you know, what—where does it stop?

Center women considered access to abortion one among many basic liberties that were collectively endangered because those working to constrain or eliminate it had other repressive goals in mind as well: banning or limiting birth control and sex-education programs; legislating against premarital, extramarital, "interracial," lesbian, and gay sex; eliminating government funding for the Aid to Families with Dependent Children program (AFDC), battered women's shelters, and other social welfare programs. Staff members considered anti-abortionists to be sexist, heterosexist, and racist; so fighting against them meant challenging their entire political agenda.

Though they often spoke about clients who seemed politically apathetic and unable to move beyond the antis' framework for evaluating abortion (that is, clients who felt sinful, guilty, or just plain bad for having abortions), some staff members also believed abortion experiences at the Center could motivate clients to take political action. Mira said:

A lot of women have said, "You know, I never really paid much attention to any of this stuff before it happened to me, but I'm telling you *what*: they are not going to get away with this! You know, I haven't been registered to vote, but I'm going out tomorrow and I'm registering." . . . Or they say, you know, "What can I do?" And we say, you know, "Volunteer to be an escort somewhere. Call your Congresspeople. . . . Register to vote and vote for pro-choice candidates only." You know, so, yeah, they do. Women have called, saying . . . "I saw y'all on the news. I am furious! What do I do?" "Vote. Get out there and vote."

Many staff members told me about similar political advice they commonly incorporated into their counseling scripts. They tried to impress upon clients the view that each abortion was inherently an endangered political act and that, in exercising their right to private decision making, clients were demonstrating an unstated public connection with other women making procreative judgments. A threat to *any* woman's abortion, they tried to convey, must be understood as a threat to *every* woman's sexual freedom.

Staff members tended to invoke various "we's" and "they's" when they offered their interpretations of how the future of abortion rights came to hang by a slender thread and when they contemplated how this situation might develop. They speculated about what reactionary legislators and politicians (the bad guys, together constituting a capital-T "They") had done and would do and about how people in general (a less powerful, yet potentially revolutionary "they") reacted. (Rank-and-file anti-abortionists were a troublesome part of "them"; anti-abortion leaders were considered a component of "Them.") Center women wondered what, if anything, those among "them" unaffiliated with the antis could or would do to stop "Them." Sometimes staff members included themselves as part of this little "they" and shared in "their" helplessness or even accepted some of the blame for what "they" had done wrong or not done right to advance a feminist agenda. More often, staff members counterposed themselves and other like-minded, politically aware people as a "we" working against "Them" to convert "them" to the cause.

Center women also believed "they" (and "we") might construct and utilize their (and "our") own agency. Many of their narratives explore the interplay between individual agency and social control. For example, Anne explained her belief that people would take action when an issue hit home, and Lee described the forces working against personalizing the issue of abortion.

ANNE: A lot of people out there say, "Oh, I believe in abortion," and "Abortion is great," but you can't make them go out and vote for candidates who believe in abortion. You can't make them go out there and escort and stand and do those things. But the moment it hits home, when it's their sister, . . . their wife, their daughter, their niece, or whoever, then that's when they want to get out there and do something about it.

LEE: If we can convince people that abortion is a single little isolated thing—when in fact it's not—then I think if . . . men and women—but more particularly women—if women don't understand what's at stake, then they won't be as upset by legal restrictions because they can live with the . . . misunderstanding . . . [that abortion] is just something that applies to somebody else. . . . You can even pretend that that somebody else isn't your daughter, your sister, your best friend's daughter, or whatever. You know, you can remove it—"It's certainly not *me*. And it's nobody I know. Nobody *I* know has had an abortion." And then . . . you can just keep pushing the rings farther and farther away till you can pretend that it means nothing to anybody.

Just as Center women described women's decision making about abortion as enmeshed in individual life circumstances as well as limited by socio-economic and political structures (see Chapter Two), they saw each individual's political action as likewise constrained. Abortion became politically relevant to people when it entered their lives in some tangible way and when they were also somehow enabled to view it as a political event. Staff members agreed that the cultural climate of the 1980s and early 1990s conspired against the politicization of abortion and against feminist identification. At best, Center women depicted people in general (the little "they") as misguided but capable of enlightenment. Lee believed the anti-abortionists had more power than Anne allowed; she saw the scale tipped in the direction of social control and away from individual agency and altruistic action. Like Lee, Yvette explained how aborting women might disavow the political potency of abortion. "It's not that people are apathetic and assume abortion will always be legal, it's that they think abortion is wrong and they won't need it— until they do. And then they experience such guilt that they think, 'We'll never need it again.'" If people accepted the antis' stigmatization of abortion, they could cordon off their own (their sister's, mother's, lover's, or wife's) abortions as aberrant apolitical acts. Several health workers reiterated this view, telling me of clients' (unsolicited) descriptions of their particular situations as unique and uniquely justifiable. "I'm not like all those other women out there" and "I would never do this ordinarily" were the kinds of claims some clients made, implying that abortion was simply an idiosyncratic and usually morally indefensible course of action. When pregnancy is viewed as an embarrassing mistake, it makes sense to consider abortion another (albeit corrective) error.

Since people in general tended to lack a political perspective on abortion as well as knowledge of the history of criminalized abortion, Center women believed "they" were incapable of perceiving what would be lost if *Roe* were reversed or if restrictions continued to proliferate. As Meryl said, "I think that a large portion of the population thinks that abortion really will always be there because it has been [since *Roe*]. . . . I mean, 'You can't go back!' But you can. And I can see how it can happen. It *can* happen." She went on to talk, as many Center women did, about narrowing access to abortion, the dearth of abortion training in medical schools, and doctors' reluctance to perform abortions because of the danger, stigma, and resulting drop in status within the profession associated with abortion work. With the murderous attacks on abortionists and abortion supporters beginning in 1993, staff members believed that involvement in abortion necessitated confronting the possibility of one's own death and no doubt such involvement became far more frightening for physicians already performing abortions.[3] Interestingly, Roger Alton told me in 1995 that the murders did *not* frighten him; rather, they strengthened his commitment to go on providing abortions. "It's not a matter of denial," he said. He knew he could possibly be killed. He just was not afraid of dying. His father had brought him up not to fear death, he told me.

Most Center women believed the general public had the power to impede the reactionary legislative action "They" were taking against abortion if "they" could be made to properly understand abortion and if "they" were then motivated enough to organize and work toward achieving change. Center women also depicted this little "they," though, as comprised of apathetic, selfish, and self-centered people. Staff members attributed self-involvement and the lack of felt connections with others to American consumer culture. People were not encouraged to think beyond themselves or beyond the present. (And if seduced by the antis, they were encouraged not to think beyond what they were told.)

Elise told me that she asked clients whether they had registered to vote, saying, "You know, the reason for this is the people we voted in. You know, if you don't vote and you don't read, you can blame yourself." Elise spoke of herself as part of an errant voting "we" though she never voted for Reagan or Bush; she talked this way in order to invite clients to join in the process she recommended, to draw them in courteously before frankly indicting them for inaction ("you can blame yourself"). Elise—and many of her co-workers—made voting sound like potential salvation, describing it as the most promising road to the achievement of progressive policies on abortion (and across the board). Mira said, "I really do think that if we elect people who are pro-choice and tell them that their jobs are on the line next term if they don't vote pro-choice during that term, what could be wrong? . . . How can it not work? But people just don't do it." Mira linked apathy about voting to a lack of knowledge, ignorance, self-centeredness.

The other problem, of course, was the people among the little "they" who voted wrong; Center women found people's support for reactionary politicians more disturbing than apathy because they envisioned apathy as potentially transformable into a feminist stance. (But they saw people who voted for anti-choice or otherwise reactionary politicians as a lost cause.) They understood why people might feel overwhelmed or powerless to make a difference, and so "they" would distance themselves from political processes.

Lee, who was exceedingly articulate about her sense of herself as feminist told me that she "protected" herself by not following political developments. "Everybody's supposed to do something, and I'm certainly doing my part. And I'm really glad that somebody *else* is going into the courtroom because— I don't know—I don't read the paper, I don't really—you know, every now and then I'll turn on NPR [National Public Radio], but, in some ways, I'm real kind of apolitical. But not in an apathetic kind of way." When I suggested that her work was political, she replied, "Right, and you know that thing that feminists were saying when I was born about 'the personal is political'—my, the way I live my life is very political—and everybody's is. But political in the sense of courtrooms and elections and that kind of thing, I think that that's a responsibility that I am willing to let somebody else take care of." Similarly, Ilene said she was "not a political person" and that she did not vote, watch television news, or read newspapers to keep up with current events because she found these activities too distressing.

Their challenge (the challenge for feminists), as Center women described it, lay in maintaining their commitment productively and striving to rally the disaffected yet potentially progressive people to counteract the conservatives. Though many were familiar with radical feminist writings from the 1970s, they rarely spoke of revolution. Center women expressed both doubts and hopefulness about a burgeoning feminist movement.

> DEVA: I think that one issue [abortion] has brought feminists [with different agendas] together. . . . If that results in any larger agenda beyond abortion, I don't know. . . . I think this is so personal that a lot of women do get involved. And if not coming out in the streets, they do it with their vote and their money. . . . So I do think it has the power to organize people, and I don't think people are going to get tired or give up.

> DEBORAH: Well, a year ago [1991] I would have said that I felt like it was going to be over a lot sooner than I think it's going to be at this point. . . . I think actually that there is more willingness to have abortion in this country than sometimes the media projects. . . . People really have to find a way to get out of themselves and to express their ideas to others in whatever way works for people, and hopefully all of it together will make a difference.

So while staff members sometimes disparaged the obstacles to abortion and the apathy they saw as producing them—or described their own feelings of helplessness regarding the achievement of systemic change—they also hoped people would wake up, "get out of themselves," and dedicate themselves to the establishment of feminist ideals.[4]

Though some staff members interpreted Clinton's election as a sign that Americans were fed up with the Reagan-Bush era and its attendant reactionary policies, they also knew that procreative freedom was not a central issue for voters in the 1992 election. And while they were heartened by Clinton's election, they agreed that the tide could easily turn against him (especially as he had never enjoyed a majority of voters' support anyway). Several Center women said they thought the conservatism of the 1980s resulted in part from a complacent inactivity on the part of progressives in the 1970s; thus, feminists should learn from the past and maintain vigilance. When I interviewed her in 1993, Rae said she thought feminists were already relaxing too much. "Once Clinton got in office, everyone did a big *sigh*, and when they sighed, they got lazy. . . . That's why the crime is able to go on the way that it is, the anti activity is able to flourish the way that it has." Center women argued for a historically informed politics: the past cannot ever be considered over and done with. The battle against anti-abortionists will not ever be irrevocably won.

Looking Back: Changes at the Center

When I completed this book, nearly five years had passed since I first began escorting at the Womancare Center and interviewing the women who worked there. Of the seventeen staff members I interviewed between October 1990 and July 1991, only two, Elise and Hallie, were still working at the Center in October 1995. (Elise moved from health-working to bookkeeping in 1991; Hallie quit as a full-time worker in 1992 but continued part-time doing phone counseling and sonography.)

Among this first group, many left to pursue educational goals or completed degrees while working at the Center. Nancy completed a master's degree in management before she left the Center; Deva entered medical school; Greta began a physician's assistant program; Audrey began a graduate program in social work; Lee began a college nursing program; Tanya finished a college degree in nursing while working at the Center and got a job working as a pediatric nurse; and Mira entered rabbinical school.

Drastic changes in management shook the organization beginning in late 1992 and affected morale for years thereafter. According to staff members who were critical of these changes, Emma talked increasingly about the Center as a business and during 1992 worked to establish this focus firmly and to supplant whatever she felt stood in its way. In late 1992, Emma gave negative evaluations to both Nancy and Trudy. Both were taken by surprise and deeply offended. When Emma showed she was not amenable to negotiation, Nancy and Trudy felt they had no choice but to resign. Not wanting to disrupt the Center, both pretended (to the staff) that they were leaving willingly. Nancy feared if health workers and supervisors knew what really happened between the administrators, many would resign in protest (in support of Nancy and

Trudy). Nancy likened the situation to having a child, raising it until adolescence, and then losing custody. She did not want the Center to fall apart as the management "team" came apart (she wanted to protect her "baby"), yet she felt bitter about her loss, and because of what had happened, she lacked faith in Emma's ability to run the Center fairly.

Earlier that year (1992), Sarina had told me she found Emma impossible to bargain with and mistrustful of the people around her. As Sarina told it, she had approached administrators after she'd been working as the staff physician for about a year because she wanted to have more of a say in how the Center was run. Since she was so deeply involved in daily events, she felt she should have a voice in policymaking; she resented it when administrators made medical decisions without consulting her. She discovered, she said, that Emma simply would not share power with anyone. Sarina resigned in February 1993. (She left Anyville and is currently not working as an abortionist.)

Emma never discussed what had happened with Nancy and Trudy or Sarina when I talked to her in 1993. At the time, I knew only that Nancy and Trudy had resigned (I thought voluntarily). About Sarina, Emma said only that things "did not work out" and that Sarina had been unhappy for a long time before she left. When people appeared reluctant to discuss interpersonal matters at the Center, I did not probe much; I did not want to push them to reveal what they felt uncomfortable telling. As a result, though, Emma's view of these issues remains a mystery to me.

Staff members feared the Center would have a difficult time replacing Sarina, based on Emma and Nancy's two-year search preceding her hiring. This time though, administrators were fortunate in finding several physicians to work on a per diem basis (covering all scheduled clinics) beginning immediately after Sarina left. The staff's fear when Sarina quit that physicians would become increasingly scarce dissipated at first and then was revived by the 1994 murders. By early 1995, the executive director had collected a waiting list of available physicians, but by April she bagan having difficulty hiring enough doctors to staff all the abortion clinics. At this time, the Center began running night clinics to accommodate the schedules of the physicians who were willing to work there. Staff members sometimes worked until midnight, only to return to the Center early the next morning. This erratic schedule caused morale to plummet once again. Susan Gilbert writes in the *New York Times* that the killings in 1994 and 1995 sparked a wave of training programs in abortion and inspired growing numbers of physicians and medical students to learn how to perform abortions (1995), so perhaps the situation at the Center, and at clinics nationwide, will improve with time.

Two interim directors served and resigned between September 1993, when Emma resigned, and June 1994, when Claire was hired. Many staff members left during this transition period and the tumultuous year preceding it. According to many Center women, these two years were an especially difficult time. Of the fourteen staff members I (newly) interviewed after 1991 (between July 1992 and June 1994), four remained by the summer of 1995. Janice continued as a health worker; Julia became a clinic coordinator in 1994; Hannah was promoted to clinic manager in 1994; Mimi had become a health worker in 1993 and then was promoted to manager of support services in 1994.

Claire's predecessor had initiated a restructuring scheme that, in a sense, simplified the hierarchy. Only the executive director, director of health services, clinic manager, and manager of support services constituted the management. The role of supervisors had been scaled back to coordinating clinics, and there were only two such positions (instead of four). Claire told me it "wasn't that different" from how the Center was run before. What had changed drastically was the board's role in managing the Center. When Emma and Nancy established the board in the late 1970s, it served as an advisory rather than a policymaking body and was made up of staff members, former staff members, and people the founders knew who were sympathetic to their vision. Before Emma left in 1993, the board had (with her cooperation) begun to take a much more active role. Staff members could no longer serve on the board, and Emma sought members with fund-raising and business expertise. The board increasingly oversaw clinic operations. Emma's successors could no longer expect their decisions to be rubber-stamped. Instead, they functioned as agents of the board and had to clear everything they did with the board, according to Nancy, who told me about these developments as she observed Center workings from an estranged distance.

Often in ethnographic projects, the best informants have a peculiar outsider-within status. (Myerhoff writes compellingly about marginals as informants in *Number Our Days* [1978].) Two of my best informants and closest friends at the Center, Lee and Rae, came to occupy positions on the fringe. I do not mean they were loners or unliked; rather, both women were articulate critics of management and felt administrators came to perceive them as troublemakers. Both had been quite forthcoming at the Center about their dissatisfactions with how it was run, and both felt resentment toward Center management for its unresponsiveness. Eventually, they were both fired: Lee for alleged insubordination in 1993, and Rae for allegedly not showing up to work one day in 1994 (she told me she had asked Julia to work in her place). In retrospect, both women said that the time had certainly come for them to leave the Center, but, like Nancy, they regretted being forced out of a workplace they had once cared about deeply.

Both of these dismissals made me feel funny about going back to visit the

Center. Because it had been a while since I had spent a lot of time there (especially by the time Rae got fired in 1994), I was out of the loop and kept up with what happened there only sporadically through the few people I talked with on the phone. Because I felt badly about my friends losing their jobs, yet also felt a conflicting sense of loyalty to the Center, I visited less frequently than I might have otherwise. I was reminded anew of the comparative ease with which social scientists can travel in and out of other people's worlds. I had felt part of this place, yet because my work was done, I could safely avoid the Center when I felt ill at ease; staff members could not. Even when I did visit, I could distance myself from the everyday dramas and traumas; Center staff members did not have this option. I could hang out on both sides of an issue without taking sides, with little personal risk; Center staff members had too much at stake to take a disinterested stance. I began this project because of my commitment to abortion rights; this political motivation remained, when it was over, but meanwhile I also came to care for particular women working in a particular place to maintain this commitment. It had become difficult for me to separate one from the other as Center women increasingly embodied, in my mind, the theoretical struggles of feminism.

Reading the Past, Writing toward the Future

In this book I develop two different, yet intertwined, sets of stories. All the stories are about how feminists deal with conservatism as it trickles into—or, in the case of anti-abortion forces, surrounds—their workplace. The first set of stories tells how Center women crafted feminist identities through their work: how they learned to be abortion providers, how they battled anti-abortion forces outside, how their conceptions of feminism affected their view of abortion, and how the "reality" of abortion, in turn, worked on their ideas about feminism. The other set of stories concerns conflicts among feminists. These conflicts, too, are driven by the sociocultural forces at work outside the Center. The politics of feminist health care provision that Center workers used as a guide in their work were grounded in the convictions that, as consumers of health care, women were entitled to self-knowledge unobscured by medical authority and that we deserved fair and nurturing treatment. Center operations, according to many staff members, extended this feminist treatment to clients while neglecting workers. In addition, many of the women depicted racism as a dangerous, perhaps incurable virus infecting even the most innocuous interactions between white and black women. All the stories, I believe, are relevant to feminists working to define and advance feminist goals—serving as both inspirational and cautionary tales.

The first stories—about doing abortion work, contending with anti-abortionists, and conceptualizing feminism—seem to have a happier resolution than the second set of stories. The services Center women offered were, for the most part, in keeping with the rhetoric of 1970s health care activism. And Center women's experiences on the job generally led to their reworking of a standard feminist line on abortion. They acknowledged that abortion work challenged pro-choice rhetoric, revealing it as an inadequate framework for evaluating abortion. Though watching abortions made many of the women ambivalent, their ambivalence was ultimately contained by their belief that their clients' need for abortions outweighed the doubts or disgust they felt at handling fetal parts. They learned that "choice" was a weak expression of what aborting women exercised; many clients were painfully trapped in situations in which their own agency seemed impossible. Abortion could be seen as an act of protest against an unhappy biological consequence of sexual expression (though for many women, sexual expression might have had little to do with the act that led to unwanted pregnancy). Abortion could be seen as an "only choice" some women made in order to gain a modicum of control in circumstances that allowed for little freedom in the first place.

The right to abortion, in the context in which Center women came to view it, was paramount to assuring women's survival in an often hostile environment. Indeed, the sheer hostility of the anti-abortionists confirmed staff members' sense of their work as righteous, as part of a quest to realize the ultimate truths that women's bodies are our "own"; that the fetuses that grow within us are parts of our bodies and that they grow there subject to our will. Center women worked toward an ideal world in which everyone could feel collectively bound to supporting individual expression and eschewing domination and oppression—even as their day-to-day activities confirmed the sense that the realization of such ideals was unlikely.

When I first interviewed Mira in 1990, she mused about whether she would one day be a "handmaid," referring to Margaret Atwood's dystopian novel about a fundamentalist state (forged by terrorists) in which women are defined solely by their procreative capacities and abortion is punishable by death (1985). In 1992, Sarina told me I had to read *The Amendment*, a science-fiction novel set in a time when abortion has been made illegal by the passage of a Human Life Amendment to the Constitution, which extends personhood to fetuses (Robinson 1990). In the novel, the mother of a woman murdered in a police raid on an illegal abortion clinic orchestrates a plan, which revolves around kidnapping the avidly anti-abortionist First Lady in order to finance a free abortion clinic for U.S. women in Stockholm. In *The Handmaid's Tale*, an underground movement may overcome the forces of evil (depending on how one reads Atwood's ending). Both novels demonstrate the subversive capabilities of ordinary people and also the power of the state to suppress resistant impulses. Unlikely alliances are formed in reaction to the fictional regimes. Center women hoped that in real life women and men would join forces across dividing lines that larger dangers eventually would render of little significance. They wanted desperately to prevent the realization of frightening fictional worlds (whether in novels or in their own imaginary projections). They hoped triumph was possible but feared for the worst.

In 1990, Louisiana state legislators sought to restrict abortion to women who had been raped or who were victims of incest. (Ultimately, they were unsuccessful.) They proposed that in order to be granted abortions women would have to report these crimes to the police within two weeks of their alleged occurrence. At the time, I suggested to several Center health workers that we needed to design new creative—and dramatic—protest techniques. In this case, I thought it would be a good idea for masses of women to clog Louisiana police stations claiming they had been raped and giving the names of the legislators who drafted the bill as their rapists. This sort of activism would show men who feared that women would lie in order to obtain abortions that, yes, we *would* dissemble en masse to protect ourselves and our lives. We would overwhelm the system in order to subvert it.

A couple of staff members responded negatively to my idea, saying they thought it might trivialize rape. But I maintain that to "offer" rape as the only way out of pregnancy, in a society where women's charges of rape are consistently called into question anyway, simply reifies the misogyny undergirding the patriarchal and paternalistic "justice" system. The system decides whether we have been raped and imposes a two-week statute of limitation. The system decides whether we are entitled to end pregnancies. The system decides whether we are worthy mothers, legitimate mothers, and so forth. Denying women access to safe abortion (whether we have been raped or not) is itself a form of figurative, if not literal, violation—akin to sexual violence. Rape denies us bodily integrity; so does restricting abortion. Both are strategies designed to subjugate women. To have drawn attention to this ludicrous rape loophole would have been a creative protest against the proposed law and against the system that generated it. We need forms of political protest that aggressively confront the opposition.[5]

Meanwhile, it has become increasingly difficult for clinics to protect themselves and the people who enter them. A segment of the opposition has developed a deadly form of terrorism, making Operation Rescue's blockades, lock tampering, and stink bombs seem innocuous. During the weeks I was completing this manuscript, John Salvi 3d murdered Shannon Lowney and Leanne Nichols. In the *New York Times* coverage of the killings, Salvi was profiled—like his predecessors (and, no doubt, his heroes) Michael Griffin and Paul Hill—as a lone-wolf lunatic who had been attracted to anti-abortionist organizations and who, acting on his own, had slipped over the edge of sanity into dangerous fanaticism. His mental illness, rather than contact with anti-abortionist organizations, is seen as the precipitating factor. (See, for example, Rimer's "Suspect: Quiet Loner and Odd Man Out" [1995].) I believe, along with many pro-choice activists, that the actions of all three murderers resulted from anti-abortionist rhetoric and aggressive (though weaponless) practices. These killers may be out of their minds, but they do not pervert the anti-abortionist message; they take it to its logical conclusion. They each had contact with anti-abortion organizations before they killed in the name of the anti-abortion cause; that movement's rhetoric served as their inspiration. I have no doubt that "nonviolent" anti-abortionists applauded the killers behind closed doors, even as they issued public statements condemning their acts. Consider, for example, the remark made by Don Treshman, the director of Rescue America, after Salvi killed Lowney and Nichols: "We're in a war. . . . The only thing is that until recently the casualties have only been on one side. There are 30 million dead babies and only five people on the other side, so it's really nothing to get all excited about" (Manegold 1995: A8).

In a *New York Times* op-ed piece, David Garrow argues that these killings are the last gasps of a dying movement (1995). He compares the anti-abortionist killings to the Klan-sponsored murders that occurred after the civil rights gains in the 1960s. The assassins were spurred to action upon realizing "that they and their more genteel segregationist allies had indisputably lost the legal and political war against fundamental black equality," Garrow writes (A17). James Chaney, Michael Schwerner, and Andrew Goodman were killed in Mississippi just weeks after it became obvious that Congress would pass the 1964 Civil Rights Act, for example. It seems sensible to argue—as Garrow does—that the deeds of anti-abortionist terrorists make it more difficult for the not(-yet)-murderous anti-abortionists to gain converts to their cause. At the same time, it seems difficult to imagine there is a shortage of lunatics in whom exposure to or involvement in the anti-abortionist movement can initiate fits of devastating violence.

Because of the ways in which abortion has been contested and endangered over the years, Center workers felt forced to devote most of their time and energy to defending (and maintaining) abortion services. Abortion took center stage because people misunderstood abortion, because politicians and lawmakers worked throughout the 1980s against abortion, and because the anti-abortion movement became aggressive and began spawning killers. Many staff members lamented this focus, telling me of their ideas for diversification: special programs for teens, more attention paid to their AIDS hotline for women and their donor-insemination program, prenatal care, special services tailored to menopausal and postmenopausal women. But everything else took a backseat to abortion. In an ideal clinic where all these services were available, they felt, abortion would be seen as one path clients could take, one service workers provided. They hoped for the normalization of abortion, though they also clearly understood that abortion had gained a reputation as anything but a regular medical procedure.

Louise Osborn, a counselor at the Planned Parenthood clinic where Lowney was killed, writes about her clinic in a way that resonates with Center workers' comments. "Over and over, the news media and protesters call this place an abortion clinic. I hate that term. We do much more than provide abortions. . . . We help [women] plan when and whether they will become parents" (1995: A17). The focus on abortion, Center workers wanted to make clear, was not something they chose or considered ideal for feminist health care practice. They cared about women's lives holistically, but their motivating framework was ignored or obscured because of the way abortion had been culturally constructed. Women were rendered either immoral or invisible: either way, we lost. So sometimes Center women disparaged all the energy they felt forced to put into abortion; more often, though, they depicted abortion as a potentially profound organizing force, a representative symbol in the struggle to advance women's agency to protect sexual and procreative freedom and to ensure women's very survival. As Lee eloquently stated, "Part of what abortion is about is a woman's *wholeness*. . . . *That's* what's at stake. It's not just having a cannula put in your uterus. It's whether the world has enough room for you."

The second set of stories I tell here—about organizational discord—seems to end much less satisfactorily in terms of feminist idealism because the stories chart both the intransigence of racism and the demise of collectivism within a feminist "community." Viewed in light of these developments at the Center, feminism in practice seems flawed by the ideological inconsistencies of its practitioners. For some staff members, feminism itself became suspect because its proponents seemed to reproduce the same sorts of power imbalances they allegedly sought to render untenable.

Before I was admitted entry as a participant-observer, I romanticized the Center as an idyllic environment because the workers I interviewed early on told me about their love for the place and their respect for each other. Celia's interview during the summer of 1991 marked a turning point for me; I first began to consider the organization as having a character different from that of its workforce. "Hanging out" there, I found a rapport that I had never experienced in a workplace, except perhaps when I worked as an arts and crafts specialist at a summer camp as a teenager. But as workers showed me, the Center was no summer camp. The work was exhausting, even at its most exhilarating. And the rapport waxed and waned.

How can I resolve the issue of a collective structure gradually replaced by a hierarchy that felt oppressive to many workers? If one ignores administrators' assertions that the collective simply could not get the work done, this transformation looks like a cop-out, a betrayal of feminist egalitarian principles. If, however, one sets aside the dissident claims of workers, the defense offered by administrators—of stratification as necessary for growth—seems sensible. Both sides, seemingly at an impasse during the time I spent at the Center, were "right." But neither side would substantially compromise or recognize the other side's "rightness."

The health workers and medical workers who complained were right to resent a power structure that was relatively inflexible when confronted with criticism. They were right to want more say in how their work got done. To them, questioning Center administrators' authority exemplified feminist method: everyone should be held accountable for her actions; status ought not divide women. Wasn't that an organizing principle of the Center, crucial to the organizationally sanctioned conceptualization of ideal health care practice? Yet to the administrators (and the supervisors who sympathized with them), workers' resistance seemed to convey a lack of respect, seemed to indicate a lack of recognition of the tremendous effort necessary to sustain the Center as a viable business. Many younger women saw the administrators as straying from the in-your-face feminism they (the administrators before they were officially administrators) had espoused in the Center's early days, as they fought to demystify medical knowledge and to make women feel truly at home in our bodies. Now administrators cared more, several dissidents said, about a financial bottom line—or, more crudely put, they cared more about money than women. These critics felt the administrators had abandoned the ideological tenets crucial to the feminist health care movement, which had enabled the Center's founding.

Administrators (and some supervisors who defended them) countered that, as management, they were ultimately responsible for the Center's survival, and since they had been there from the outset, they were most qualified to ensure its survival. Everything they did was geared to keep an always shaky organization afloat in an increasingly hostile world. Administrators were right to assert that the Center probably would not have survived had it remained a collective, that the volume of the work done at the Center would not be manageable unless the labor was systematically divided. They were also right in their proclamations that staff members varied in their commitment to the organization, even though they had, in part, contributed to this differential response with their style of governance.

Creating or sustaining solidarity based on a culturally denigrated ideologi-cal commitment is, at best, a risky business. And the Center was not a polit-ical organization in the sense that its primary function was political action; it provided a politically charged service. The reasons why some events led to closeness among staff members and others produced seemingly irreparable discord are bound up in the women's perceptions of the problem at hand. An external enemy contributes to solidarity, while internal stresses deplete it. If the problem can be seen as a distinct enemy that is radically different from the collective self and also as completely morally repugnant, then the experi-ence of fighting this enemy will, in all likelihood, lead to the sort of reassur-ing (yet tenuous, temporally) sisterhood Center women recall from the 1988 Operation Rescue blockades. This solidarity was crafted, after all, at a time when hierarchy structured Center workings; it dissipated in a wave of resig-nations after the blockades ended (according to Emma and Nancy—see Chapter Three). As the Center's battles over hierarchy and racism show, the confrontation of internal enemies is a messier, more difficult process than joining forces against definite and easily definable hostilities outside. These struggles were fraught with the hazards of introspection, marked by the ten-sions of a family argument that threatens to undo connective bonds or, worse, to show that they are baseless.

I am reluctant to conclude that this second set of stories serves as evidence that feminism failed at the Center as an organizational force; rather, I hold that feminism has to be modified as political sensibilities and realities change, and that such modifications ought not be seen as an erasure of feminist sensi-bility. The period when I observed the Center is one segment of its lifetime, a time of both development and devolution. The shift from collective to hier-archy at the Center highlights the ways in which the struggle to advance feminist goals is circumscribed by a sociopolitical environment that under-cuts these very goals. The Center compromised with the world around it. I can envision compromises that I feel would make the imbalance of power less deleterious to morale. Indeed, so could Nancy; when I spoke to her in 1995, she was working as a consultant to Claire, the current executive director, to implement TQM (Total Quality Management) plans that she felt would al-low everyone to feel responsible for and involved in decision making on a broader scale. Of course, TQM, like diversity training, seeks to defuse work-ers' dissatisfactions and to strengthen morale without abolishing hierarchy. One could argue, as Kathy Ferguson (1984) does (see Chapter Four), that feminist ideals simply cannot be achieved with programs that abet hierarchy and that attempts to ameliorate workers' discontents do not truly give work-ers power as long as the hierarchy remains. Once again I return to a contest between a beckoning, seemingly unattainable, ideal and a practical, seemingly necessary, adoption of conventional arrangements. Asking the Center to live up to ideals that are antithetical to the corporate-capitalist and predominantly anti-feminist culture in which it operates may well be insisting it do the impossible. I would, thus, merely like to see it do better.

I was disquieted by what appeared to be the seamy underside of a rosy sisterhood. Did the backbiting, the petty disputes, the unpleasant disagreements, and the charges of racism preclude solidarity? Wasn't feminism supposed to take women beyond ugly stereotypes (that women are "bitches" who can't get along with each other or that we are incompetent at large-scale management)? I admit I was also plagued by the naive hope that women equipped with feminist ideology would never behave "like men"; we would be fair, noncompetitive, solicitous of each other's needs—sort of magically ideal mother-sisters. I longed to discover this stereotype at the Center, which made the animosity I observed all the more troubling. The disparity between what I hoped for and the worst of what I encountered made me wonder what I could have been thinking when I entertained platitudinous notions of feminism as a unifying force. But, at times, the Center had been exactly that sort of refuge for workers. (Sisterhood is sometimes possible!) That feminism could not conquer all, that feminism was subject to all that it held most reprehensible, ought to have come as no surprise. As Toby and Hannah described (in Chapter Four), I, too, had been privy to the pitfalls of collectivist feminism: in a college feminist organization, in which the conflicts between the "process oriented" and the "action oriented" often turned acrimonious and caused us to accomplish little; and in a feminist professional organization (with elected officials who generally sought consensus), in which discussions over seemingly minor issues could blaze into unresolvable, tedious discord. So I report the obvious: feminists are complicated people, operating from a variety of ideological standpoints that do not necessarily cohere—that may indeed conflict in unappealing ways.

I BEGAN this book by detailing how public events and public consciousness shape "private" life. *Roe v Wade* had no impact on my ten-year-old self, but it certainly played an influential part in my coming of age. I am a member of the first generation of Americans in well over a century to grow up at a time when abortion was legal (albeit stigmatized). My own feminist awakening was spurred by reading about the work of feminist health care activists and those who exposed and deplored violence against women—that is, by learning about feminists dedicated to promoting women's bodily autonomy. I discovered academic feminism as it discovered its own exclusionism, as it began to deconstruct its own "whiteness" and privilege and sought to address subjectivity within the feminist tradition. The feminism I discovered in my college reading grew out of (and itself critiqued) the rebellion of disempowered housewives (as presented by Friedan 1963 and Greer 1970); it began linking itself with denser critical theories (like psychoanalysis and postmodernism). And yet it seems clear to me in retrospect that this intellectual awakening was enmeshed in my own lived (as opposed to read) experience. My mother was my first feminist mentor; she taught me to question authority and to value myself.

Some twenty-five years have passed since she gave me my first reading assignment, *How Babies Are Made.* The "public" and "private" circumstances of my life gradually produced the activist/scholarly self who found herself simultaneously pregnant and at work on an ethnography of an abortion clinic. I was surprised when people I knew outside the Center considered these two facts to be at odds with each other, yet, at the same time, I sometimes fell into this line of thinking myself. Inside my pregnant body, I sometimes felt distanced from the abortions going on around me. The time I spent at the Center enabled me to envision a truly connective, holistic procreative sensibility.

One day, when I was well into my second trimester, a client on her way out of the aftercare room after a second-trimester abortion patted me on the belly. "I guess you decided to keep yours," she said amicably. I chuckled nervously. I had heard from other pregnant women that many people consider pregnant bellies public property: I had been fully intent on dispelling this notion in the mind of anyone who tried to touch me without asking. But this woman had just ended her own pregnancy and was—perhaps unintentionally—linking us together with her gesture. We all travel the sea of procreative experience in different boats. We face opposition to our liberty that varies by degree, depending on our own privilege or lack of it. The anti-abortion opposition highlights our similarities by reducing our bodies to procreative vessels. Advancing a liberatory procreative philosophy and uniting against those who seek to deny us "room" in the world has the potential, I believe, to enable feminists to bridge at least some of the gaps that make us feel separate.

For me as a researcher, pregnancy served well as a topic of conversation that allowed me to interact easily with the staff and often with the clients at the Center. Staff members celebrated my pregnancy with me. They knew a lot about pregnancy, of course, and liked to talk about it, liked to offer their expertise. They felt my ever-enlarging belly proprietarily, checked my hematocrit, offered to do "sonos" for me, marveled at my purple cervix in a self-exam group. They inquired and advised about nausea, asked about my birth plans, and discussed with me what life would be like with a baby. What had seemed to me at first potentially strange—this pregnancy in the context of pregnancies ending—felt, eventually, part of a larger whole.

But many people I knew outside the Center considered the combination of my work and my "condition" odd, ironic, or even incompatible. Several women have told me that the experience of wanted pregnancy (especially the sensation of fetal movement) had made them rethink the "rightness" of abortion. For me, the experience of pregnancy while engaged in work on abortion deepened my sense of a commitment to procreative freedom. Having a baby and not wanting to would be unthinkable, whether I could feel it moving in me or not. I consider the feat my body performed to be truly amazing: but no one should have to let this happen to her if she is unhappy about the prospect of the outcome. Because my baby grew in me and felt, during this time, so much *of* me, I see with reinforced clarity that a woman's desire to have a baby ought to be essential to continuing her pregnancy. My conviction has been strengthened by my connections with Center women, by my experience of pregnancy, and by my new life as a mother.

CENTER PERSONNEL TABLE

Name	Position	Age	"Race"	Interview Dates	Left
Emma	Executive Director	38	White	10/90, 9/93	1993
Lee	Health Worker	25	White	10/90, 7/92	1993
Deva	Health Worker	28	Iranian	10/90	1991
Elise	Health Worker	52	White	10/90	
Nell	Health Worker	19	White	10/90	1993
Ilene	Health Worker	35	White	10/90, 12/92	1993
Audrey	Health Worker	22	White	10/90	1992
Karen	Intern	18	White	10/90	1990
Mira	Supervisor	25	White	10/90, 7/92	1992
Greta	Health Worker	24	White	11/90	1993
Meryl	Donor Insemination Director	32	White	12/90	1991
Hallie	Health Worker	27	White	2/91	
Nancy	Clinic Administrator	39	White	2/91, 3/94	1993
Anne	Supervisor	28	Black	6/91	1992
Celia	Supervisor	23	White	7/91	1993
Tanya	Health Educator	30	White	7/91	1992
Yvette	Health Worker	28	White	7/91	1993
Janice	Health Worker	23	White	7/92	
Lois	Health Worker	30	White	7/92	1993
Risa	Health Worker	26	Black	8/92	1992
Julia	Health Worker	26	Black	8/92	
Carrie	Health Worker	24	White	8/92	1994
Toby	Health Worker	23	Black	8/92	1992
Deborah	Health Worker	48	White	8/92	1993
Sarina	Staff Physician	33	White	8/92, 12/92	1993
Rae	Health Worker	28	Black	9/92, 9/93	1994
Hannah	Supervisor	32	White	9/92	
Mimi	Administrative Worker	24	White	10/92	
Trudy	Director of Administrative Services	42	White	11/92	1993
Ellen	Nurse-Practitioner	35	White	7/93	1993
Diana	Health Worker	23	Black	6/94	1995

NOTES

Introduction: Abortion Work and Feminist Ideology

1. Faludi gives evidence of this trend: "In 1988, United Way stopped funding Planned Parenthood, and in 1990, under pressure from the Christian Action Council, AT&T cut off its contributions, too (after twenty-five years), claiming that shareholders had objected to the agency's association with abortion—even though 94 percent of its shareholders had voted in favor of funding Planned Parenthood" (1991: 418).

2. All poll data discussed here, unless attributed otherwise, were provided by Planned Parenthood and the National Abortion Federation. Support for abortion is correlated with education (the more schooling, the more likely a person is to support legal abortion); with political orientation (people who define themselves as "liberals" and "moderates" are more likely to support legal abortion than "conservatives"); with knowing someone—or being someone—who has had an abortion; with age (younger people are more likely to support abortion); and with marital status (unmarried people are more likely to support abortion). One of the biggest predictors of opposition to abortion is religiousness; people to whom religion is "very important" are much more likely to oppose abortion than those to whom religion is "not so important." A small gender gap in support for abortion appears because older women and women who do not work outside the home are less likely to support abortion rights; poll data also show a racial gap (of about 10 percent) between whites and blacks because "African-Americans are more likely than whites to have been raised in rural areas or in the South, and to have lower levels of education"—all predictors of conservative views on abortion. African Americans are also more likely than whites to "hold orthodox religious beliefs, to attend doctrinally conservative churches, to attend church regularly, and to pray frequently" (Cook et al. 1992: 46).

3. Hallie requested that I not use my tape recorder because she said she thought it was "creepy" to have her voice taped. All interviews took place in private except for Diana's, at which Rae was present and during which she occasionally participated. The two women had come to visit me, and both said they thought it would be "fun" to take part in Diana's interview together.

4. Teenagers need a parent's written or oral indication that the parent has been notified of—but has not necessarily consented to—the abortion.

5. *Casey* was preceded by *Hodgson v Minnesota*, in which the Court ruled that the state could require the notification of both parents of teenagers before they could have abortions (along with providing the alternative of a judicial hearing), and *Ohio v Akron Center for Reproductive Health*, in which the Court upheld the state law requiring notification of one parent (and also specified the provision of judicial hearings). Since *Casey*, state legislators have passed, introduced, or are expected to introduce bills limiting abortion in the following ways: requiring parental consent or parental notification; restricting abortion to women whose lives are endangered by their pregnancies, or who have been the victims of rape or incest, or whose fetuses are "deformed/handicapped"; reformulating clinic licensing to make providing abortion much more difficult or impossible; instituting "viability tests" on fetuses aborted during the second trimester; and stipulating waiting periods between pregnancy tests and abortions. In the *Casey* decision, spousal notification or consent clauses were the only restrictions deemed unconstitutional.

6. The approximate dates when staff members left (quit or were fired) are included in the Center Personnel Table.

Chapter One: Feminist Work

1. Gestational age is calculated using the first date of a woman's last menstrual period as a starting point; it is confirmed with a sonographic measurement of the biparetal diameter (width of the fetal head). Because of the risks involved with general anesthesia and because of the Center's commitment to treat women as active health care recipients, the Center opted to perform abortion using local anesthesia, sedatives, or both. Most second-trimester abortions in the United States are induction abortions, in which labor is induced with a saline-solution injection and the woman then delivers the fetus. Some clinics offer second-trimester abortions under general anesthesia. Because late-term abortions are often painful procedures, many practitioners prefer that a woman be unconscious, so they do not have to deal with the possibility that she might move, as movement can result in various injuries to the cervix or uterus.

2. During the years of my involvement with the Womancare Center, many changes occurred. For the sake of convenience, I freeze the Center in time and, unless I specify otherwise, discuss procedures and staff composition as they were during the midpoint of my fieldwork, the fall of 1992.

3. Large-scale changes in board governance procedures began to occur in 1993; I discuss these changes briefly in the Conclusion.

4. Downer and Coleen Wilson were arrested in 1972 for practicing medicine without a license at their clinic, the Feminist Women's Health Center in Los Angeles. "Wilson, charged with 11 counts, pleaded guilty to the charge of fitting a diaphragm and was fined $250 and placed on two years' probation" (Ruzek 1978: 57). Downer went to trial and was finally aquitted.

5. Unlike Hannah, most health workers find sterile-room work (for second-trimester abortions) emotionally stressful and prefer contact with clients. This issue is discussed in detail in Chapter Two.

6. I present the reasons why various staff members left the Center in the Conclusion.

7. I discuss the ways in which African American staff members challenged racist behavior, along with white workers' responses to these challenges, in Chapter Five.

8. In Chapters Four and Five, I return to the issue of establishing and maintaining feminist community.

Chapter Two: Feminist Abortion Practice

1. During the period of my fieldwork, I never heard any other prices quoted to women on the phone. Health workers always asked whether women had insurance that might cover the abortion; sometimes, before stating the prices, they said, "If your income is $50,000 or under . . ." or they asked, "Is your income less than $50,000?"

2. Diana and Rae told me that only Roger would negotiate fees, in which case the Center kept its share and Roger cut or forfeited his.

3. Depending on the number of clients scheduled during a clinic, one or several groups of approximately six to eight women might run consecutively; at very busy times, two groups met simultaneously.

4. The list of risks on the consent form included: uterine infection; reaction to medication; hemorrhaging, laceration, or tearing of the cervix; perforation of the uterus; need for surgery (including hysterectomy); inability to get pregnant or carry to term as a result of complications; shock; cardiac arrest; and death. Health workers reassured clients that no one, in the history of the Center, had "ever had to have a hysterectomy as a result of an abortion. But it could happen if you had bleeding that we could not get under control."

They also stated that shock, cardiac arrest, and death could happen as a result of an allergic reaction to medication, uncontrolled hemorrhaging, or a "pre-existing medical condition."

5. For instance, teenagers having late abortions might be allowed to have their mothers with them. Men could not accompany clients to the groups or into the aftercare room.

6. The Center required that clients from out of town stay in Anyville overnight in case of an emergency (in rare cases, an abortion may begin as a result of the dilation). A nearby hotel offered a discount to Center clients.

7. The BPD during the first trimester is less than 2.0 centimeters; at sixteen weeks it ranges between 3.1 and 3.4 centimeters; at twenty-six weeks, it ranges between 6.3 and 6.4 centimeters.

8. Over the course of my fieldwork—one year—I knew of only two perforations.

9. Rothman (1989: 115) elaborates on Janet Gallagher's analogy between the "cultural fascination with the fetus" and whale watching: "The fetus, like the whale, symbolizes something pure, something of the world and innocent of the world. Both, fetuses and whales, have been made 'real' for us by science, by an invasion of their watery worlds with recording equipment. People who live hundreds of miles from the sea can picture the sounding whale, see its smooth back, its spouting blowhole. And people who have never been pregnant, never shared anyone's pregnancy intimately, can visualize the fetal head shape, fetal hands, fetal movements in utero."

10. The form is used so that the state can collect statistical information. It asks for the facility name and location, the type of abortion procedure performed along with any complications that resulted, procedures performed after the induction, the name of the attending physician, the aborting woman's date of birth, her marital status, her state and county of residence, her "origin or descent," her education history (in years), her history of alcohol or drug abuse, the date of LMP and the clinic's estimation of length of gestation, the date of pregnancy termination, the woman's procreative history—that is, number of live births and of spontaneous and induced abortions. Under the boxes requesting information on "all other pregnancy terminations which did not result in a live birth" the words "date of last fetal death" appear; this item is the only literal reminder that the form itself used to be a "certificate of fetal death."

11. Several health workers told me of rare cases when everything—the LMP, the doctor's estimation, and the sonogram—was "wrong" and what had appeared to be a twenty-six-week fetus turned out to be "bigger."

12. I present Center women's discussions of apathy and the politics of abortion in the Conclusion.

Chapter Three: Anti-Feminism Personified

1. Blanchard writes that some scholars believe that Joseph Scheidler, leader of a far-right antiabortion group, helped Terry organize Operation Rescue as a front after Scheidler had been charged in several civil suits (1994: 64). Blanchard writes that Terry "served on the board of Scheidler's Pro-Life Action League when he conceived of Operation Rescue and first proposed that type of action to the league before forming Operation Rescue" (64–65).

2. I discuss Center women's epistemology of abortion in depth in Chapter Two.

3. Antis, interestingly, get a lot of mileage out of portraying themselves as underdogs who aren't treated fairly. See, for example, Terry's (1989) and Nathanson's (1989) prettified portraits of Operation Rescue's tactics; Leo's collection of Operation Rescue member's accounts of police brutality against them (1990); Joseph Foreman's defense of Operation Rescue groups as law-abiding (in Frame 1988); and Frame's descriptions of police who "dragged demonstrators along the pavement," "bent fingers and arms, and applied pressure to the soft spot under the ear" (1988: 34).

4. Blanchard and Prewitt (1993) compare anti-abortionist arsonists and bombers to rapists. Men who commit arson or bomb clinics attempt to justify these violent acts by asserting that abortionists or clinic owners deserve them; likewise, many rapists say that women deserve to be raped. See the chapters of Scully's *Understanding Sexual Violence* entitled, tellingly, "Nothing Is Rape" and "No One Is a Rapist" (1990: 97–136). Anti-abortionists have now extended such victim blaming to justify the murder of physicians.

Chapter Four: Feminist Workplace?

1. I discuss developments since 1992 in the Conclusion.

2. In the summer of 1993, shortly before she resigned, Emma drafted a description of "transitions" the Center was going through, in which she promoted a businesslike orientation and budget cuts designed to streamline the organization. Ironically (in light of Rae's comments), these cuts included the elimination of "achievement awards" for staff "anniversaries," reimbursement for transportation and most conference expenses, Christmas bonuses and parties, going away presents, and employee-of-the-month cash bonuses.

3. I also discuss this situation in Chapter Five because Rae and Diana saw it as a way of singling out black women as inappropriate dressers.

4. In the first chapter of *Humanizing the Workplace* Berg (1974) skeptically assesses this wave of reorganization that Zager and Rosow herald; Berg concludes, "The fact is that we are not likely to see the new concern with

worker stratification move much beyond the 'fad' state . . . we find . . . in the United States in 1974" (15).

Chapter Five: Purging the Enemy Within

1. I use quotation marks to frame the word *race* to highlight the fuzziness of the term, which is erroneous in its official dictionary definition and in common usage as a physical or genetic demarcation of differences among groups of people. Bonnett (1993) and Gould (1981) both discuss early racial classification systems as political endeavors, often sanctioned as science, designed to justify the subjugation of various groups (inferior "races") by whites ("*the* race"). "'Racial reasoning,'" writes Gates, "is reasoning from causes to effects without reference to experience, in terms of a fixed essence" (1985: 402). A social process of differentiation creates "race"; *racialization* would be a more precise name for what we mean when we talk of "race." But as Donald and Rattansi write in the Introduction to *"Race," Culture and Difference* (1992), "Reiterating that 'there's no such thing as "race"'' offers only the frail reassurance that there *shouldn't* be a problem"; instead of asking "whether 'race' exists," scholars should "ask how the category operates in practice" (1). I share the view that the term should be problematized—thus, the quotation marks.

2. Cohen, too, may overgeneralize. I have noticed a tendency against simplistic interpretations, even in analyses of public-opinion polls about "race" and racism. (See, for example, Schuman, Steeh, and Bobo 1985, and Sniderman and Piazza 1993.)

3. The Center's clients were racially diverse. (My informal estimate is that a slight majority of the abortion clients were black, that a majority of well-woman-clinic clients were white, and that almost all donor-insemination clients were white.) Black staff members rarely talked about "race" relations between clients and workers however. I recall only one instance during my involvement at the Center. Rae told me one of the nurses was more likely to refer black teenagers than others "out" (to places where general anesthesia was available) when they displayed nervousness about second-trimester abortions. Rae complained, and the Center began keeping track of who got referred out and who was responsible for the referrals. The disparate treatment disappeared.

4. The Civil Rights Act of 1964 prohibited discrimination based on "race," color, religion, or nationality in employment, commerce (as in hotels and restaurants), and the use of public facilities.

5. Criticism of Katz's technique coheres with the work of Gilroy and Cohen; the model is seen as reductive, antisociological in its psychological focus, and, ultimately, essentializing. See Wetherell and Potter (1992: 216),

for instance. Critics of Katz are, in my view, too harsh. She does acknowledge the historical and political roots of racism. For example, she writes, "From the time of formalized slavery to the present Whites have oppressed Third World people through the perpetuation of racism at every level of life. It is present in our institutions, our culture, and our individual actions" (1978: 9). She does call racism a disease, "a critical and pervasive form of mental illness" (12); taken figuratively, though, such a condemnation of racism as pathological need not render Katz's entire program useless. Though she does not design a strategy capable of revolutionizing the status quo, she certainly ought not be accused of causing any harm.

Conclusion: Feminism and (F)utility

1. During the 1988 Operation Rescue blockades, the local chapter of NARAL began providing volunteer escorts to the Center and other city abortion clinics. The organization continues to coordinate a citywide escort system as necessary.

2. Menstrual extraction may also be used to empty the uterus just prior to menstruation; American feminist health care activists began the practice "in 1971 as a way women could have active control of their periods and reproduction. The technique . . . was developed in self help groups that sought to empower women by demystifying simple body functions such as menstruation and early abortion" (Boonstra 1993: 244).

3. I summarize the gist of staff members' response to the murders here based on the few interviews I conducted after the killing began and on short social visits I made to the Center, and informal phone conversations I had with a few staff members (and former staff members) after I finished formal interviewing.

4. One exception to this optimism was Ilene's pronounced pessimism; another was Yvette's talk of everything falling apart as a result of American selfishness, reactionary politics, and consumerism.

5. In California, several clinics have begun a fund-raising campaign called "Adopt a Protester" in which people agree to give a certain amount of money per anti-abortionist protester or per day of protest. The clinics then send letters of thanks to the antis for the money they've helped to raise to fund abortions.

SOURCES

ATWOOD, MARGARET. 1985. *The Handmaid's Tale*. New York: Fawcett Crest.

BAEHR, NINIA. 1990. *Abortion without Apology: A Radical History for the 1990s*. Pamphlet 8. Boston: South End Press.

BAILEY, ROY D. 1985. *Coping with Stress in Caring*. Oxford: Blackwell Scientific Publications.

BALL, DONALD WHITE. 1967. "An Abortion Clinic Ethnography." *Social Problems* 14 (winter): 293–301.

BARRINGER, FELICITY. 1993. "Abortion Clinics Preparing for More Violence." *New York Times*, March 12.

BELENKY, MARY FIELD, BLYTHE MCVICKER CLINCHY, NANCY RULE GOLDBERGER, AND JILL MATTUCK TARULE. 1986. *Women's Ways of Knowing: The Development of Self, Voice, and Mind*. New York: Basic Books.

BELKIN, LISA. 1993. "Planned Parenthood Starting to Train Doctors in Abortion." *New York Times*, June 19.

———. 1994. "Kill for Life?" *New York Times Magazine*, October 30.

BERG, IVAR. 1974. "Worker Discontent, Humanistic Management, and Repetitious History." In *Humanizing the Workplace*, edited by Roy P. Fairfield. Buffalo, N.Y.: Prometheus Books.

BLANCHARD, DALLAS A. 1994. *The Anti-Abortion Movement and the Rise of the Religious Right: From Polite to Fiery Protest*. New York: Twayne.

BLANCHARD, DALLAS A., AND TERRY J. PREWITT. 1993. *Religious Violence and Abortion: The Gideon Project*. Gainesville: University of Florida Press.

BONNETT, ALASTAIR. 1993. *Radicalism, Anti-Racism and Representation*. London: Routledge.

BOONSTRA, HEATHER D. 1993. "Menstrual Extraction." In *The Encyclopedia of Childbearing*, edited by Barbara Katz Rothman. New York: Henry Holt.

BRENTON, PAUL. 1992. "Casualties of the Abortion Wars." *Christianity Today* 36, no. 12 (October 26): 22–24.

BUECHLER, STEVEN M. 1990. *Women's Movements in the United States: Woman Suffrage, Equal Rights, and Beyond.* New Brunswick, N.J.: Rutgers University Press.

CAUDRON, SHARI. 1990. "Monsanto Responds to Diversity." *Personnel Journal* 69, no. 11 (November) 72–80.

———. 1993. "Training Can Damage Diversity Efforts." *Personnel Journal* 72, no. 4 (April): 51–62.

CHERNISS, CARY. 1980. *Staff Burnout: Job Stress in the Human Services.* London: Sage.

CHIRA, SUSAN. 1994. "When Hope Died." *New York Times Magazine*, June 26.

COFFEY, JOHN F. 1987. "Race Training in the United States: An Overview." In *Strategies for Improving Race Relations: The Anglo-American Experience*, edited by John W. Shaw, Peter G. Nordlie, and Richard M. Shapiro. Manchester: Manchester University Press.

COHEN, PHILIP. 1992. "'It's Racism What Dunnit': Hidden Narratives in Theories of Racism." In *"Race", Culture and Difference*, edited by James Donald and Ali Rattansi. London: Sage.

COLEMAN, BRENDA C. 1995. "Abortion Training a Must in Obstetrics." *Philadelphia Inquirer*, February 15.

CONDIT, CELESTE MICHELLE. 1990. *Decoding Abortion Rhetoric: Communicating Social Change.* Urbana: University of Illinois Press.

COOK, ELIZABETH ADELL, TED G. JELEN, AND CLYDE WILCOX. 1992. *Between Two Absolutes: Public Opinion and the Politics of Abortion.* Boulder, Colo.: Westview Press.

COX, TAYLOR H., AND STACY BLAKE. 1991. "Managing Cultural Diversity: Implications for Organizational Competitiveness." *Academy of Management Executive* 5, no. 3: 45–56.

CRYDERMAN, LYN. 1988. "A Movement Divided." *Christianity Today* 32, no. 11 (August 12): 48–49.

DAVIS, NANNETTE J. 1985. *From Crime to Choice: The Transformation of Abortion in America.* Contributions in Women's Studies 60. Westport, Conn.: Greenwood Press.

DETLEFS, MALINDA. 1984. "Abortion Counseling: A Description of the Current Status of the Occupation Reported by Seventeen Abortion Counselors in Metropolitan New York." Master's thesis, Graduate Center, City University of New York.

DONALD, JAMES, AND ALI RATTANSI. 1992. "Introduction." In *"Race", Culture and Difference*, edited by James Donald and Ali Rattansi. London: Sage.

ECHOLS, ALICE. 1989. *Daring to Be Bad: Radical Feminism in America 1967–1975*. Minneapolis: University of Minnesota Press.

EISENSTEIN, HESTER. 1991. *Gender Shock: Practicing Feminism on Two Continents*. Boston: Beacon Press.

ELLIS, CATHERINE, AND JEFFREY A. SONNENFELD. 1994. "Diverse Approaches to Managing Diversity." *Human Resources Management* 33, no. 1 (spring): 79–109.

ESSED, PHILOMENA. 1991. *Understanding Everyday Racism: An Interdisciplinary Theory*. Newbury Park, Calif.: Sage.

EVANS, SARA. 1979. *Personal Politics: The Roots of Women's Liberation in the Civil Rights Movement and the New Left*. New York: Knopf.

FADERMAN, LILLIAN. 1991. *Odd Girls and Twilight Lovers: A History of Lesbian Life in Twentieth-Century America*. New York: Penguin.

FAIRFIELD, ROY P. 1981. "Introduction" and "Epilogue." In *Humanizing the Workplace*, edited by Roy P. Fairfield. Buffalo, N.Y.: Prometheus Books.

FALUDI, SUSAN. 1991. *Backlash: The Undeclared War against American Women*. New York: Crown.

FAUX, MARIAN. 1990. *Crusaders: Voices from the Abortion Front*. New York: Birch Lane Press.

FERGUSON, KATHY E. 1984. *The Feminist Case against Bureaucracy*. Philadelphia: Temple University Press.

FINKELSTEIN, PETER. 1986. "Studies in the Anatomy Laboratory: A Portrait of Individual and Collective Defense." In *Inside Doctoring*, edited by Robert H. Coombs, D. Scott May, and Gary White Small. New York: Praeger.

FISHER, SUE. 1993. "Gender, Power, Resistance: Is Care the Remedy?" In *Negotiating at the Margins: The Gendered Discourses of Power and Resistance*, edited by Sue Fisher and Kathy Davis. New Brunswick, N.J.: Rutgers University Press.

FODERARO, LISA W. 1990. "Suburban Journal: Shellshocked in the War on Abortion." *New York Times*, November 20.

FRAME, RANDY. 1988. "Atlanta Gets Tough." *Christianity Today* 32, no. 16 (November 4): 34–36.

FRANKENBERG, RUTH. 1993. *White Women, Race Matters: The Social Construction of Whiteness*. Minneapolis: University of Minnesota Press.

FREEMAN, JO. 1972–1973. "The Tyranny of Structurelessness." *Berkeley Journal of Sociology* 17: 151–164.

———. 1975. *The Politics of Women's Liberation: A Case Study of an Emerging Social Movement and Its Relation to the Policy Process*. New York: David McKay.

———. 1992. Discussant presentation, Feminist Organizations Conference (February).

FREUDENBERGER, HERBERT. 1975. "The Staff Burn-Out Syndrome in Alternative Institutions." *Theory, Research and Practice* 12: 73–82.

FRIEDAN, BETTY. 1963. *The Feminine Mystique*. New York: Norton.

GARROW, DAVID J. 1995. "A Deadly, Dying Fringe." *New York Times*, January 6.

GATES, HENRY LOUIS. 1985. "'Talkin' That Talk." In *"Race," Writing and Difference*, edited by Henry Louis Gates. Chicago: University of Chicago Press.

GIDDENS, SALLY. 1990. "The Abortionist's Tale." *D Magazine* (August).

GILLIGAN, CAROL. 1982. *In a Different Voice: Psychological Theory and Women's Development*. Cambridge, Mass.: Harvard University Press.

GILROY, PAUL. 1990. "One Nation under a Groove: The Cultural Politics of 'Race' and Racism in Britain." In *Anatomy of Racism*, edited by David Theo Goldberg. Minneapolis: University of Minnesota Press.

———. 1992. "The End of Antiracism." In *"Race," Culture and Difference*, edited by James Donald and Ali Rattansi. London: Sage.

GINSBURG, FAYE D. 1989. *Contested Lives: The Abortion Debate in an American Community*. Berkeley: University of California Press.

GITLIN, TODD. 1987. *The Sixties: Years of Hope, Days of Rage*. New York: Bantam Books.

GOLDMAN, ARI L. 1990. "Catholic Bishops Hire Firms to Market Abortion Attack." *New York Times*, April 6.

GORDON, LINDA. 1974. *Woman's Body, Woman's Right: A Social History of Birth Control in America*. New York: Penguin.

GOULD, STEPHEN JAY. 1981. *The Mismeasure of Man*. New York: Norton.

GREER, GERMAINE. 1970. *The Female Eunuch*. New York: Bantam Books.

HAFFERTY, FREDERIC W. 1991. *Into the Valley: Death and the Socialization of Medical Students*. New Haven, Conn.: Yale University Press.

HISKEY, MICHELLE. 1988. "Thousands Join 'Rescue Movement' around Nation." *Christianity Today* 32, no. 18 (December 19): 52.

HOCHSCHILD, ARLIE RUSSELL. 1983. *The Managed Heart: Commercialization of Human Feeling*. Berkeley: University of California Press.

HOLE, JUDITH, AND ELLEN LEVINE. 1971. *Rebirth of Feminism*. New York: Quadrangle Books.

HUGHES, EVERETT C. 1971. *The Sociological Eye*. Chicago: Aldine.

HUNT, RAYMOND G. 1987. "Coping with Racism: Lessons from Institutional Change in Police Departments." In *Strategies for Improving Race Relations: The Anglo-American Experience*, edited by John W. Shaw, Peter G. Nordlie, and Richard M. Shapiro. Manchester: Manchester University Press.

JAGGAR, ALISON M. 1983. *Feminist Politics and Human Nature*. Totowa, N.J.: Rowman and Allanheld.

JOFFE, CAROLE. 1986. *The Regulation of Sexuality: Experiences of Family Planning Workers.* Philadelphia: Temple University Press.

JOHNSON, DIRK. 1993. "An Abortionist Returns to Work after Shooting." *New York Times*, August 21.

KANTER, ROSABETH MOSS. 1990. "The New Work Force Meets the Changing Workplace." In *The Nature of Work: Sociological Perspectives*, edited by Kai Erikson and Steven Peter Vallas. New Haven, Conn.: American Sociological Association Presidential Series and Yale University Press.

KATZ, JUDITH H. 1978. *White Awareness: Handbook for Anti-Racism Training.* Norman: University of Oklahoma Press.

KLINKENBORG, VERLYN. 1995. "Violent Certainties: A Report from a Milwaukee Abortion Clinic, Where the Crowd Outside Brandishes the Weapons of Righteousness and the Women Inside Bear the Weight of Their Choice." *Harper's* 289, no. 1736 (January): 37–53.

LANDEN, D. L., AND HOWARD C. CARLSON. 1982. "Strategies for Diffusing, Evolving, and Institutionalizing Quality of Work Life at General Motors." In *The Innovative Organization: Productivity Programs in Action*, edited by Robert Zager and Michael P. Rosow. New York: Pergamon Press.

LEBER, GARY. 1989. "We Must Rescue Them." *Hastings Center Report* 19, no. 6 (November/December): 26–27.

LEE, MELISSA. 1993. "Diversity Training Brings Unity to Small Companies." *Wall Street Journal*, September 2.

LEE, NANCY HOWELL. 1969. *The Search for an Abortionist.* Chicago: University of Chicago Press.

LEIDNER, ROBIN. 1993. *Fast Food, Fast Talk: Service Work and the Routinization of Everyday Life.* Berkeley: University of California Press.

LEO, JOHN. 1990. "The Abortion Protesters and the Police." *U.S. News and World Report*, August 6: 13–15.

LEWIN, TAMAR. 1992a. "Hurdles Increase for Many Women Seeking Abortions." *New York Times*, March 15.

———. 1992b. "In Bitter Abortion Debate, Opponents Learn to Reach for Common Ground." *New York Times*, February 17.

———. 1994. "Abortions in U.S. Hit 13-Year Low, a Study Reports." *New York Times*, June 16.

LIPSKY, MICHAEL. 1980. *Street-Level Bureaucracy: Dilemmas of the Individual in Public Services.* New York: Russell Sage Foundation.

LORBER, JUDITH. 1984. *Women Physicians: Careers, Status and Power.* New York: Tavistock.

LUKER, KRISTIN. 1984. *Abortion and the Politics of Motherhood.* Berkeley: University of California Press.

MacDonald, Heather. 1993. "The Diversity Industry." *New Republic* 209 (July 5): 22–25.

McDonnell, Kathleen. 1984. *Not an Easy Choice: A Feminist Reexamines Abortion.* Boston: South End Press.

McKeegan, Michele. 1992. *Abortion Politics: Mutiny in the Ranks of the Right.* New York: Free Press.

MacKinnon, Catharine. 1983. "The Male Ideology of Privacy: A Feminist Perspective on the Right to Abortion." *Radical America* 17, no. 4.

Manegold, Catherine S. 1995. "Anti-Abortion Groups Disavow New Killings: Some Leaders Continue Radical Talk." *New York Times,* January 1.

Mansbridge, Jane J. 1980. *Beyond Adversary Democracy.* New York: Basic Books.

Manuel, Marion. 1994. "Abortion-Training Programs Decline." *Atlanta Constitution,* November 1.

Marshall, Nancy L., Rosalind C. Barnett, Grace K. Baruch, and Joseph H. Pleck. 1991. "More Than a Job: Women and Stress in Caregiving Occupations." In *Current Research on Occupations and Professions,* vol. 6, edited by Helena Z. Lopata and Judith Levy. Greenwich, Conn.: JAI Press.

Martin, Patricia Yancey. 1989. "The Moral Politics of Organizations: Reflections of an Unlikely Feminist." *Journal of Applied Behavioral Science* 25, no. 4: 451–470.

———. 1990. "Rethinking Feminist Organizations." *Gender & Society* 4: 182–206.

Melosh, Barbara. 1982. *"The Physician's Hand": Work Culture and Conflict in American Nursing.* Philadelphia: Temple University Press.

Messer, Ellen, and Kathryn E. May. 1988. *Back Rooms: Voices from the Illegal Abortion Era.* New York: St. Martin's Press.

Mishler, Eliot G. 1984. *The Discourse of Medicine: Dialectics of Medical Interviews.* Norwood, N.J.: Ablex.

Mobley, Michael, and Tamara Payne. 1992. "Backlash! The Challenge to Diversity Training." *Training & Development* 46, no. 12: 45–52.

Mohr, James C. 1978. *Abortion in America: The Origins and Evolution of National Policy, 1800–1900.* New York: Oxford University Press.

Morgen, Sandra. 1983. "Towards a Politics of 'Feelings': Beyond the Dialectic of Thought and Action." *Women's Studies* 10: 203–223.

Muldoon, Maureen. 1991. *The Abortion Debate in the United States and Canada: A Source Book.* New York: Garland.

Mullard, Chris. 1985. *Race, Power and Resistance.* London: Routledge & Kegan Paul.

MURRAY, KATHLEEN. 1993. "The Unfortunate Side Effects of 'Diversity Training.'" *New York Times*, August 1.

MYERHOFF, BARBARA. 1978. *Number Our Days*. New York: Dutton.

NATHANSON, BERNARD. 1989. "Operation Rescue: Domestic Terrorism or Legitimate Civil Rights Protest?" *Hastings Center Report* 19, no. 6 (November/December): 28–31.

NORDLIE, PETER G. 1987. "The Evolution of Race Relations Training in the U.S. Army." In *Strategies for Improving Race Relations: The Anglo-American Experience*, edited by John W. Shaw, Peter G. Nordlie, and Richard M. Shapiro. Manchester: Manchester University Press.

OAKLEY, ANNE. 1981. "Interviewing Women: A Contradiction in Terms." In *Doing Feminist Research*, edited by Helen Roberts. London: Routledge & Kegan Paul.

OSBORN, LOUISE A. 1995. "The Killer and the Healers." *New York Times*, January 6.

PAIGE, CONNIE. 1983. *The Right to Lifers: Who They Are, How They Operate, Where They Get Their Money*. New York: Summit.

PAYNE, ROY, AND JENNY FIRTH-COZENS, eds. 1987. *Stress in Health Professionals*. Chichester: Wiley.

PETCHESKY, ROSALIND POLLACK. 1984. *Abortion and Woman's Choice: The State, Sexuality, and Reproductive Freedom*. New York: Longman.

———. 1987. "Fetal Images: The Power of Visual Culture in the Politics of Reproduction." *Feminist Studies* 13, no. 2 (summer): 263–292.

REINHARZ, SHULAMIT. 1983. "Experiential Analysis: A Contribution to Feminist Research." In *Theories of Women's Studies*, edited by Gloria Bowles and Renate Duelli Klein. London: Routledge & Kegan Paul.

———. 1992. *Feminist Methods in Social Research*. New York: Oxford University Press.

REVERBY, SUSAN M. 1987. *Ordered to Care: The Dilemma of American Nursing, 1850–1945*. Cambridge: Cambridge University Press.

REYNOLDS, AMY L., AND RAECHELE L. POPE. 1991. "The Complexities of Diversity: Exploring Multiple Oppressions." *Journal of Counseling and Development*, 70 (September/October): 174–180.

RIMER, SARA. 1993. "Abortion Foes in Boot Camp Mull Doctor's Killing." *New York Times*, March 19.

———. 1995. "Suspect: Quiet Loner and Odd Man Out." *New York Times*, January 1.

ROBINSON, SUE. 1990. *The Amendment*. New York: Birch Lane Press.

RODRIGUEZ, NOELIE MARIA. 1988. "Transcending Bureaucracy: Feminist

Politics at a Shelter for Battered Women." *Gender & Society* 2, no. 2 (June): 214–227.

ROE, KATHLEEN M. 1989. "Private Troubles and Public Issues: Providing Abortion amid Competing Definitions." *Social Science and Medicine* 29, no. 10: 1191–1198.

ROHTER, LARRY. 1993. "Doctor Is Slain during Protest over Abortion." *New York Times*, March 11.

ROTHMAN, BARBARA KATZ. 1982. *In Labor: Women and Power in the Birthplace.* New York: Norton.

———. 1986. *The Tentative Pregnancy: Prenatal Diagnosis and the Future of Motherhood.* New York: Viking Press.

———. 1989. *Recreating Motherhood: Ideology and Technology in a Patriarchal Society.* New York: Norton.

ROTHSCHILD, JOYCE, AND J. ALLEN WHITT. 1986. *The Cooperative Workplace: Potentials and Dilemmas of Organizational Democracy and Participation.* Cambridge: Cambridge University Press.

ROTHSCHILD-WHITT, JOYCE. 1982. "The Collectivist Organization: An Alternative to Bureaucratic Models." In *Workplace Democracy and Social Change*, edited by D. Lindenfield and Joyce Rothschild-Whitt. Boston: Porter Sargent.

RUDDICK, SARA. 1989. *Maternal Thinking: Toward a Politics of Peace.* New York: Ballantine.

RUZEK, SHERYL BURT. 1978. *The Women's Health Movement: Feminist Alternatives to Medical Control.* New York: Praeger.

SCHUMAN, HOWARD, CHARLOTTE STEEH, AND LAWRENCE BOBO. 1985. *Racial Attitudes in America: Trends and Interpretations.* Boston: Harvard University Press.

SCULLY, DIANA. 1990. *Understanding Sexual Violence: A Study of Convicted Rapists.* Boston: Unwin Hyman.

SILVERMAN, D. 1987. *Communication and Medical Practice: Social Relations in the Clinic.* London: Sage.

SIMONDS, WENDY. 1991. "At an Impasse: Inside an Abortion Clinic." In *Current Research on Occupations and Professions*, vol. 6, edited by Helena Z. Lopata and Judith Levy. Greenwich, Conn.: JAI Press.

———. 1995. "Feminism on the Job: Confronting Opposition in Abortion Work." In *Feminist Organizations: Harvest of the New Women's Movement*, edited by Myra Marx Ferree and Patricia Yancey Martin. Philadelphia: Temple University Press.

SIVANANDAN, A. 1990. *Communities of Resistance: Writings on Black Struggles for Socialism.* London: Verso.

SMITH, PETER B. 1987. "Group Process Methods of Intervention in Race

Relations." In *Strategies for Improving Race Relations: The Anglo-American Experience*, edited by John W. Shaw, Peter G. Nordlie, and Richard M. Shapiro. Manchester: Manchester University Press.

SNIDERMAN, PAUL M., AND THOMAS PIAZZA. 1993. *The Scar of Race*. Cambridge, Mass.: Belknap Press.

SPITZER, ROBERT J. 1987. *The Right to Life Movement and Third Party Politics*. New York: Greenwood.

STACEY, JUDITH. 1988. "Can There Be a Feminist Ethnography?" *Women's Studies International Forum* 11, no. 1: 21–27.

STAGGENBORG, SUZANNE. 1991. *The Pro-Choice Movement: Organization and Activism in the Abortion Conflict*. New York: Oxford University Press.

STEINBERG, STEPHEN. 1981. *The Ethnic Myth: Race, Ethnicity, and Class in America*. Boston: Beacon Press.

STEINFELS, PETER. 1990. "New Voice, Same Words on Abortion." *New York Times*, November 20.

SUH, MARY, AND LYDIA DENWORTH. 1989. "The Gathering Storm: Operation Rescue." *Ms.* 17, no. 10 (April): 92–94.

SZYKOWNY, RICK. 1992. "Life during Wartime: The Battle of Buffalo." *Humanist* 52, no. 4 (July/August).

TANNEN, DEBORAH. 1990. *You Just Don't Understand: Women and Men in Conversation*. New York: Ballantine.

TATALOVICH, RAYMOND, AND BYRON W. DAYNES. 1981. *The Politics of Abortion: A Study of Community Conflict in Public Policy Making*. New York: Praeger.

TAYLOR, WENDY. 1987. "Race Relations Interventions within a Probation Service." In *Strategies for Improving Race Relations: The Anglo-American Experience*, edited by John W. Shaw, Peter G. Nordlie, and Richard M. Shapiro. Manchester: Manchester University Press.

TERRY, RANDALL. 1989. "Operation Rescue: The Civil Rights Movement of the Nineties." *Policy Review*, no. 47 (winter): 82–83.

TONER, ROBIN. 1990. "Washington Talk: A City of Compromises Founders on Abortion." *New York Times*, May 1.

TORRY, SAUNDRA. 1992. "Tackling Race and Gender Bias through Diversity Training." *Washington Post*, April 27.

WALSH, EDWARD. 1974. "Garbage Collecting: Stigmatized Work and Self-Esteem." In *Humanizing the Workplace*, edited by Roy P. Fairfield. Buffalo, N.Y.: Prometheus Books.

WEBB, CHRISTINE, ed. 1986. *Feminist Practice in Women's Health Care*. Chichester: Wiley.

WETHERELL, MARGARET, AND JONATHAN POTTER. 1992. *Mapping the Language of Racism: Discourse and the Legitimation of Exploitation*. New York: Harvester Wheatsheaf.

YOUNG, IRIS MARION. 1990. "The Ideal of Community and the Politics of Difference." In *Feminism/Postmodernism*, edited by Linda J. Nicholson. New York: Routledge.

ZAGER, ROBERT, AND MICHAEL P. ROSOW, eds. 1982. *The Innovative Organization: Productivity Programs in Action*. New York: Pergamon Press.